HARD
ON
HOLLYWOOD

A memoir by
Robert Darwin

ISBN: 978-0-941421-00-3

This book is a memoir. It reflects the author's present recollections of experiences that occurred over the past sixty to seventy years. Some names, traits and characteristics may have been changed, some events compressed and some dialogue recreated.

Reasonable efforts were made to obtain permission to reproduce the photographs included in this book. If any acknowledgments have been omitted or any rights overlooked, it is purely unintentional. Please notify the publisher of any omissions or corrections and they will promptly be rectified in future editions.

Cover Design by Estella Vokovic at 99designs
Graphic Design by Patrice Taylor
Copy Editing by Darcy Kendall

Published by Express Press Ltd.
Post Office Box 1133,
Carmel Valley, CA 93924
www.expresspressltd.com

Printed in the United States of America

"We are each only as good as our last picture,
but if we haven't had a picture in a couple of years,
then we aren't even in the same league anymore."

– George Cukor –

CONTENTS

CONTENTS

HARD ON HOLLYWOOD

A memoir by Robert Darwin

Introduction

Since my early teen years I became aware of the fact that I possessed many inherently useful attributes most of my contemporaries simply lacked. I was blessed with an observant eye and a fertile imagination, enjoyed an insatiable appetite for information, and possessed a sponge-like curiosity that absorbed everything new, innovative or different that was thrust upon me. Early experiences were rarely forgotten and oftentimes many became useful in my writings. I was particularly adept at creating short outlines or treatments of a basic story line. Generally referred to as synopses, these concepts often served as starting points for a short story, screenplay or full-blown book.

My eyes were also the instrument that accessed my soul as an art enthusiast, a serious photographer and, ultimately, a cinematographer – all useful attributes for a career in film – and when it came to my ears, playing jazz piano, singing a Bach cantata or torching the blues all came as naturally to me as brushing my teeth. As a teenager I developed basic useful skills in mechanics, carpentry, plumbing and electricity, and these ordinary forms of labor often saved my day. Most important, however, was the fact that I was infused with wonderful health and an incredible longevity, which even at my present age – in the early nineties – is far superior to that of most humans thirty or more years my junior. Throughout my life I often wondered how lucky I could have ever been to be bestowed with so many positive traits at birth and then go on with the ability, means and desire to utilize and enjoy them all.

As far back as I can remember, even if my days consisted of forty-eight hours instead of twenty-four, I would still have never had enough time to accomplish all the things I set out to do that day.

I am loath to waste even an hour of my time on frivolous matters or on things that do not add to my overall sense of accomplishment. It is the driving force within my personality that propels me forward, fuels my imagination and instills the positive desire within me to do more and better things today than I might have done the day before.

I was born to loving immigrant parents from Austria and the Ukraine who quickly carved out a winning American lifestyle in their adopted homeland that was due primarily to my father's uncommonly successful business acumen and investment expertise. The family, therefore, survived the 1929 depression in far better financial condition than most, leading my dad to foster the idea that the pursuit of business and finance in the United States would be the best way for his son to access the winning lifestyle, as well. According to him, study, determination and an inherently sharp mind were the only requirements, so after pounding the books for three years in the U.S. Navy and four more in college, I was deemed ready to make a go of it. In the interim, however, I needed to earn a living, so with impromptu jazz and the love of swing as my only playbook, I took a job as the lowly piano player at the humblest watering hole in town, the Hawaiian Palms, playing and singing my life away with little satisfaction and no reward. After college, however, when I was thrust out into the real world for the first time, I felt that a serious stab at writing had to come first – just to get it out of my system – and after much soul searching, my dad reluctantly agreed. Writing, after all, was what I had been doing since I was a teen, and I loved it.

Thus, with my dad's blessing, I became one of the multitudes of newcomers who arrive in Hollywood each year to seek fame and fortune in the film industry, which in my case would be as a screenwriter and, ultimately, a film director. In spite of those hopes, however, it soon became clear that screenwriting and film directing would not be the first of my budding talents to be recognized. It seems I was also attractive enough to be tapped as an actor for the silver screen. It was not that I deliberately went out on casting calls or otherwise had the explicit intent of getting acting jobs on my own, but agents, casting people and others in the position to recommend individuals for specific roles all seemed to like what they saw in me. I had a good, clean-cut masculine visage, a great smile and a rich baritone voice. Apparently, this was exactly what was needed to get me in front of the cameras, so bit parts and supporting roles simply came along at regular intervals whether I wanted them or not.

Acting, however, was not my chosen profession, and I was eminently aware that I was getting acting jobs strictly on my looks and not as the result of any seriously demonstrated talent. I did not study acting and never considered that I was very good at it. Although I found acting to be the conduit that allowed me to commingle with all the professionals in the business, I quickly determined that my primary objection to acting in movies was the terrible waste of time between shots and, ultimately, between the individual acting jobs themselves. Generally referred to in Hollywood as being "between pictures," this waste of time appeared to be accepted as a necessary evil, not only affecting most actors, but many full-fledged movie stars and the biggest and brightest writers and directors in the business, as well.

I've had several pivotal moments in my life, the earliest one having occurred when I was only five. I was enrolled in kindergarten at a local Catholic school where I was summarily discriminated against, strapped into a straightjacket of sorts and verbally degraded in front of my classmates simply because I was left-handed, then forced to kneel in the corner for hours on end until I repented. It was a senseless, depraved act by a devious-minded nun that left me in a mindless stupor for months. At the tender age of ten, however, Providence made up for the evil nun by allowing me the pleasure of enjoying my first sexual experience. I was seduced by an older woman – a beautiful, blond, high school freshman – and I loved it. At the time, however, sex was not taught in our schools and the subject had never been broached in our home, so I knew nothing about it other than the extreme pleasure that the event had bestowed upon me. Nevertheless, it proved one of the wonders of life to me and the reason we had been given all those incredible feelings, so intense, when we touched ourselves in certain places.

Even so, when it came to my own sex life, it was clear that I was destined to be a late bloomer as more important things like school, sports and simply growing up took precedence. It wasn't until I completed my education and came to Hollywood that things really took a turn for the better, allowing me the luxury of as much sex as I could handle. It seemed that so many of the girls – and a hell of a lot of the boys – all wanted a piece of me, and once I got used to all the adulation, I availed myself of the opportunity whenever, wherever and however I wanted it. From brief, furtive encounters to full-blown extended affairs, I soon found I was allowing myself to proceed unabated from one surreptitious episode to the next. It was a recurring happenstance that overwhelmed the senses and became that irresistible part of life that had eluded me for the better part of my youth, yet I soon made up for that loss with a vigor, enthusiasm and satisfaction previously unknown to me.

Therein, however, also rests the furtive, uncontrolled appetite of Hollywood, the abyss that few on the outside ever think of or know about. I soon learned that sex was the driving force in the movie capital, and especially with those in charge of making movies – the producers, studio bosses and financiers – who all seemed to use sex as their bargaining tool when casting their films, and otherwise. The casting couch, in fact, was invented for no other reason than to ease the process of seducing the next unsuspecting starlet who dared venture into the producer's dreaded chamber. Men, however, were just as easily duped as their female counterparts – it all depended upon the sexual orientation of the aggressor – and apparently this had been going on in Hollywood since its very beginnings. Woe to all those pretty young hopefuls that dared come to Hollywood to attain stardom yet wished to retain their virginity. That wish clearly represents the undeniable oxymoron that Tinseltown presents to all its newcomers. Perhaps one can achieve immediate success with the loss of self-respect on the one hand, or else be saddled with years of drudgery on the other hand, with little or no chance of achieving anything. It seems that one's future simply boiled down to one of those extremes or the other.

Am I being hard on Hollywood to present the problem so bluntly? Not at all, because that's the way it was, always has been and most likely always will be. Now, with the alleged devious revelations concerning the likes of Harvey Weinstein and other Hollywood luminaries having finally been made public, victims of other predators at least have hope for some final vindication. Nevertheless, Weinstein alone represents only the tip of the iceberg, with dozens if not hundreds of others who will surely be outed in the future. The current #MeToo movement clearly represents a growing power most victims could have only dreamed about in previous years. Yet, with the crack in the dam seemingly growing by the day, hopefully, the tide of ugliness, degradation and despair so many victims have experienced over the years will ebb as women and men worldwide finally join in strength with enough will to unite and fight back.

The overriding problem as we now know it, however, is that it is not confined to Hollywood itself, but is clearly one of national import. Alleged lecherous predators like Roger Ailes, Charlie Rose and Bill O'Reilly prove that the practice of seducing young hopefuls with a promise of success extends far beyond Hollywood's borders. In fact, it prevails in politics, religion and every business wherever predators with power exist.

The difference with Hollywood, however, is that Hollywood itself has been permeated with sex since its very beginnings, and sex is still present in every fiber of its being. Sexually imbued posters and advertising layouts featuring well-endowed, half-naked young women are routinely distributed by every major Hollywood studio, thereby empowering every red-blooded American male to believe that to respond to such enticement is normal; to abuse that enticement, however, is obviously criminal and patently wrong. On a personal level, yes, I too was accosted on more than one occasion by persons of power who might have contributed something to my career. You can call it blackmail, coercion or simply a favor with a possible reward, but it was not in my psyche to submit to it.

In the end, I achieved what I went to Hollywood to do, and I did so on my own accord and without sacrificing my body to get there.

I did, however, receive the honest, unimpeachable help of the few dedicated professionals who believed I possessed a great inner talent and had only my best interests at heart.

Thus, when considering the most important people in my life besides my loving parents, it should be obvious there are also those most worthy of my eternal gratitude. In that regard I must first mention Jack Benny, the greatest of all television comedians, who overheard me tell a raunchy joke one day, believed I could become a great stand-up comic like him and gave me my first meaningful work in television. Second, I never could have achieved anything in Hollywood without the gracious help of George Cukor, the great director, who mentored and encouraged me and then introduced me to so many of the right people. For those heady days in Paris, I can only thank Dorothy Marchini, that wonderful woman who became my secretary, Girl Friday and social affairs manager extraordinaire and then continued on to remain as one of the best of my life-long friends. Most important to me, however, was John Hernstadt, who brought me down to earth after Hollywood, became my trusted business partner, and allowed me to embark on the greatest and most rewarding period of my life. Last, my good friend David Korda, who after years of coaxing and suggesting the idea to my deaf ears, convinced me – and finally inspired me – to write the book you now hold in your hands.

But why Hollywood? Why Hollywood, at all? Because Hollywood is where all the beautiful people are – and especially the most beautiful ones of all, the movie stars, those captivating, neurotic, narcissistic creatures we all adore and dote upon. What better subjects could there be to work with and write about than these overly self-obsessed mortal beings who are eminently known to us all? That at least was one of my missions in coming to Hollywood. But Hollywood itself is the main subject of this writing, and that includes not only the worst negative aspects of the place, but the good and the best of it, as well. Why Hollywood? Because the same could not be said about any place else on earth. My role, therefore, is that of the messenger, nothing more or less.

Overall, my road through life has been an immensely exciting, interesting and fruitful journey that, in the end, has been as rewarding for me as I trust the various accounts I cite in this book will aptly demonstrate. I ask only that you read on with an open mind and be aware that I bare my soul exactly as I remember each event having occurred. Nothing has been embellished and very little has been left out. That's the way it was in Hollywood but a brief few years ago; I ask only that you savor it, digest it and enjoy it to the fullest.

CHAPTER 1:

Welcome to Hollywood

Since my days in the U.S. Navy I had fallen in love with California, and I knew in my heart that the Golden State was where I wanted to live, seek my fortune and spend the rest of my life. Thus, when I graduated from Rutgers University in June 1952, with diploma in hand and a great anticipation for the new life ahead of me, I wasted no time in making my move. In preparation for that event, I purchased a new Oldsmobile 98 convertible. It was custom-painted a beautiful two-tone, light gray and dark royal blue color combination that made this car sharp, unique and unlike any other vehicle on the road. As previously planned, I would set out on this long-anticipated trip the day after my graduation. Naturally, I had discussed my plans with my parents beforehand, explaining that I just wanted to kick back and relax in Los Angeles for a couple of months in order to orient myself to my new surroundings. While there, I could investigate a number of different career possibilities before settling down and deciding on exactly which path I might finally wish to follow. Obviously, they were aware of my interest in writing and ultimately in film directing. My dad was willing to accept that aspiration as long as I assured him I would abandon it after a respectable period of time if nothing worthwhile had materialized for me, and I agreed.

As the day for my departure arrived, I arose early to check out the car, then dropped the top and made certain I had packed all the appropriate tools I might need in the event of an emergency en route. After breakfast, my mom brought out a large package of fruits, cookies and other goodies for me to enjoy along the way. We kissed and hugged each other many times and at the appropriate moment I started the engine, gave my folks a broad wave, threw them a final kiss and was gone.

1

It was just before 7:00 a.m. when I rolled out of our driveway in Linden, New Jersey, for my initial trek through central New Jersey to Trenton, where I crossed the Delaware River to join the Pennsylvania Turnpike. This major stretch of concrete roadway was the first superhighway in the United States, and it sported the most prolific abundance of Burma Shave signs in the country; best of all, they were fun to watch as I passed each one, all the while anticipating the next line in the slogan before it appeared. By dusk I was off the turnpike, diverting to the southwest to bypass Chicago on a direct heading for St. Louis, and this is where I joined Route 66, the world-famous gateway-path to my destination in Southern California.

By 6:00 p.m. on the third day, I passed the towering city hall in downtown Los Angeles and was proceeding westbound on Sunset Boulevard to the eastern outskirts of Hollywood. Suddenly, the huge "Hollywood" sign high above the upper Beachwood area came into view. At first it could be seen only in short flashes between the buildings and tall palm trees before making its formal debut when it emerged in full view from behind the cityscape now spreading out all around me. From all indications at this point in time – an hour or so from the coast – it appeared as though I had "made it" to my destination, but that is not exactly the way the fates decided the event would occur for me.

As I approached North Western Avenue, I felt the engine cough a couple of times and then sputter, and when I looked at the fuel gauge I noticed the needle hovering just above the empty mark. In my excitement to get to the coast I totally forgot to check my fuel. It was clear that I was running out of gasoline, but of all the times I could have done so, why now?

Sputtering along for the next couple of blocks and looking for a service station along the way, I decided to get out of the traffic on Sunset Boulevard and park the car on the next available side street. As destiny planned it for me, that street was Van Ness Avenue, and as I turned the corner the engine sputtered along for another block or two until it simply refused to go any farther. Finally, I pulled over to the curb, the engine gave one last gasp, coughed and quit. Pondering my predicament, all I could think of saying to myself was,

"Shit!"

But that, miraculously, was not the end of the story. To my surprise – appearing like an apparition out of the blue or as scripted for some cheap Hollywood thriller – I looked up the street to see a large Richfield gas station sign only a couple of blocks ahead.

"Damn," I mused to myself, "how lucky could I be?" As I walked up to the station I noticed an attendant just finishing up with another customer. Then when he spotted me out of the corner of his eye he greeted me with a cheerful,

"Be with you in a minute."

And as it turned out, he was a man of his word. In thirty seconds or less he came over with a big smile on his face, thrust out his hand and welcomed me with a hearty,

"Hi, I'm Scotty. You're new in town, aren't you?"

When I told him, "Yes I am," his immediate response was an enthusiastic, "Well, welcome to Hollywood," which he followed almost immediately with, "So, who referred you?" Surprised and a little miffed by his question, I emphasized the fact that no one referred me and that I had just run out of gas. Strangely, he seemed surprised at my excuse, but when he looked me in the eye he saw something in my expression that put him completely at ease. A flippant shrug of my shoulders was the only positive response he required, because a moment later I was greeted by a broad smile from ear to ear and a poke of his index finger before he delivered his apology.

"Hey, don't get me wrong – I'm just the curious type."

Sometime later, when thinking back at this moment, I came to the conclusion that this guy could have simply given me some gasoline, I would have continued on my way and we would have probably never seen each other again – but that is not the way our meeting went. With the ice apparently broken between us, this very inquisitive guy simply proceeded to question me some more, and he did so in such a positive manner that it was totally unforgettable.

"So tell me, where'd you come from? How long'd it take you? Wow, that's pretty good. Know anybody in town? Are you stickin' around for a while or just passin' through?"

As the question-and-answer session was going along full-bore, he filled an empty container with gasoline, walked me to my car and emptied the fuel into my tank.

"Wow, I like your wheels…nice paint job…just bring it in when you need a grease job or an oil change…I'll give you a good deal."

This guy had the gift of gab like no one I had ever met, but he was upbeat about it and I immediately fell for his style. He was a fast talker and I gave him fast answers, and by the time we got back to the station I was convinced he knew everything he wanted to know about me. I found him to be uncommonly friendly when compared to what I was used to on the East Coast, but I fell for his style and found that I enjoyed being with him, sharing in his space and learning firsthand what he was all about. Our conversation segued into sports, hobbies and mutual interests of all kinds. Interestingly, our discussion never got around to sex or what I soon learned was the major preoccupation of almost everyone I would meet in Los Angeles. Nevertheless, we got along very well, we obviously enjoyed each other's company and I quickly felt that somehow we would soon become close friends.

What a welcome! Before I even arrived at my destination, Providence had clearly determined that I was to meet and be befriended by one of the nicest and most likable people I would ever meet in my life. What I did not know at the time, however, was that he was also one of the most famous, highly respected and popular people in town – a real superstar in his own right. Unfortunately, however, all that would need to wait for a different time. When Scotty and I finished talking, that special first sunset at the beach I had anticipated witnessing upon my arrival was long gone. It was approaching 11:00 p.m., but I was still intent on getting to the beach and at least falling asleep on the sand. Scotty said he understood, handed me a business card from the station and scribbled a phone number across the back of it.

"That's private, OK? But if you need anything like a job, money or a place to stay – anything – just give me a call."

I assured him I would, he gave me a quick wave and I was on my way, arriving at the foot of Sunset Boulevard just before midnight. This is where Route 66 terminated at the Pacific Coast Highway. I made a left turn proceeding southbound on the Coast Highway a short distance and then made a right turn into the first available parking area. It was a dark, moonless night. The ocean was directly in front of me and although I could smell the sea and hear the sound of the surf pounding onto the shore, there was nothing for me to see. As a cool breeze from the west lapped around my ears, I decided it best to postpone my first dip into the ocean until morning when I could really appreciate it. In its stead I spread out a warm jacket, took off my shoes and socks and walked down the beach for awhile just to see what was going on.

Although it was now long past midnight, there were still many people scattered about. Most were in blankets, some single and others obviously not, an occasional stroller here or there, and one or two stray dogs rummaging around for handouts. There were also a few campfires in view with small groups huddled around them. It seemed as though life on the beach simply continued all through the night, and here I was right in the middle of it. I made it to the coast all right, but then I suddenly felt very cold, very tired and very alone. Thus, I walked back to my car, put the top up, raised all the windows and curled up in the back seat to get some sleep. I promised myself that the morning would dawn clear and warm for me; it would be the first day of the rest of my life and I wanted to wake up early to take it all in.

And what a glorious day it was. I awoke at first light, but since it was still quite chilly outside, I waited for the sun to warm the air before braving the boiling surf. Then, finally, when I felt the time was right, I took a deep breath and jumped in. As the first waves roiled up over my head I actually touched bottom before the next wave thrust me back up to the surface. I could see the Santa Monica Pier a short distance to the south and the many surfside cottages in the opposite direction that pointed the way to Malibu. I swam around for a short while just to take in the changing topography and then noticed that both the parking lot and the beach were rapidly beginning to fill up. Gone were the campfires and the people nestled in blankets from the night before. This was a whole new crowd. When I returned to my car, I dried off, put on a clean T-shirt and jeans and decided to head toward the pier for something to eat.

The first place I came upon was a small open-air eatery with a half-dozen seats at the counter that looked clean and inviting. A hand-painted sign over the counter promised "Good Food and Drink," and the fact that most of the seats were taken quickly convinced me it must be true. As I sat down I noticed that the two young guys on my left sported tans that would have made any white-skinned camp follower envious – including me – but before I could even pick up a menu to order my meal, the one seated next to me leaned over and made me an offer I couldn't refuse.

"Man, you gotta get a bowl of this chili…it's great. Here, try it."

With that, the guy slid his bowl over to me, even offered a package of his crackers to go with it. Well, I was hungry, I took a whiff and with the aroma of sautéed onions and baked beans wafting through my nose, I couldn't say no. I picked up a spoon, took a taste, loved it and ordered a bowl for myself. And that, in a nutshell, is how I met my first new friends on Santa Monica Beach.

"Hi, I'm Bobby," I offered,

"Hey, I'm Kenny and this is Dan."

After all the usual questions and answers about where we were from and what we were doing here, I learned that Kenny and Dan were college students from the Midwest. They came to Santa Monica each summer for the same reason I did, to hang out at the beach and have a good time. Kenny and Dan and a couple of other guys shared a small apartment just a couple of blocks from the beach and this is where they spent their days. The weather in Southern California was justifiably ideal during the early summer months, and with the prevailing winds coming in from the west, the ocean air was always fresh, clean and inviting. What a way to live!

Santa Monica, as I soon learned, was the "Body Beautiful" capital of the world, the home of a myriad of self-worshipping activities all designed for adoration of the human form. The physique was "in" and no one could prove otherwise. It was a microcosm of beings, male and female, all hell-bent on being as beautiful as nature could make them – and then some. Modesty be damned! Youth and skin were in! I was just 25 years of age, so I liked what I saw and was pleased to become a part of it.

All kinds of physical activities were available in Santa Monica to pique a young man's interest, but I soon learned that most of my contemporaries preferred surfing, body building or scuba diving. Kenny and Dan then offered that they had taken up scuba diving and loved it. Since I knew nothing about the sport but swam well and enjoyed water sports of all kinds, I decided to tag along with them for the day just to see what it was all about. There was a place that offered scuba diving courses down near the pier, and after meeting some of Kenny and Dan's other friends who were also into the sport, I decided to have a go at it myself.

The most interesting aspect of my new life on Santa Monica Beach was how friendly everyone seemed to be, but I soon learned that the friendliness was really all about sex. Boys and girls, young men and women alike, were all on the make, and I soon learned how to take it all in and make the most of it. Before my first week in Santa Monica was out, I met a whole cadre of new friends and partook in more sex than I had ever had in my life. It was all oral sex at first – I guessed it was because the girls didn't want to risk a pregnancy – but then what better way could one devise for two people to get to know one another? A good blow job was all it took, and I quickly decided it was the only way to live.

To more routine matters, however, during my first week in town I enrolled in a scuba diving course and even found a nice place to live. It was a small motel on Sepulveda Boulevard just a mile or so from the beach. My rent for the rest of June was $200 – a lot of money at the time – but I was told that because of a prior booking I had to move out by July 15 which was fine with me. The place was clean and comfortable and I could come and go as I pleased.

My first month on the beach turned out to be more satisfying than anything I could have ever dreamed of. We had wonderful weather that allowed me to spend most of every day out in the sun. I soon acquired a deep tan, the girls all seemed to like what they saw and the combination turned every evening into a new sexual adventure for me. The boys all seemed to hang around me as well, but I didn't really know how to handle that one as yet. I found there was a fine line between recognizing a guy who was on the make as opposed to one who was just being friendly, and it took me some time before I thought I could tell the difference. Finally I just accepted the fact that this was the way it was here in paradise, and I was not going to be the one to change it.

But as new and interesting as my time at the beach had become, the month only seemed to come and go and was now gone. Then, before I even realized it, we were approaching the middle of July. The Independence Day weekend was now past history and I was due to move out of my motel room by the fifteenth. I had completed my scuba diving course and had even flown out to Catalina Island with a small group of divers just to practice our new skills in the wild. As luck would have it, movie star Lloyd Bridges, who was also a skilled scuba diver, was out on the island scouting locations for a new project he was working on. Upon meeting our group, he encouraged us to continue pursuing the sport ourselves, suggesting matter-of-factly that it could even lead to some work in the movie business if we stuck with it.

Unfortunately, Kenny and Dan both indicated they had to return home to resume their studies, and it looked more and more like I would soon be making a change in my daily ritual as well. As much as I hated to think so, I had grown restless and bored with the entire routine at the beach and determined that it was time for me to get on with my life.

Thus, after another glorious day in the sun, I came back to my room, cleaned up and put on a fresh shirt and slacks. My landlady commented on how neat I looked and that I should go out and find myself a nice girl. How naive, I thought, that my landlady didn't know how much sex I had accumulated during the brief six weeks I had been living under her roof. OK, so they were all just overnight dalliances on the beach or a quick blow job on the broad back bench seat of my Olds – but at least I got my cookies off on a daily basis and after all, isn't that really what it was all about? Apparently not, because once I got in my car and drove all the way back to Hollywood, I determined that sex was not what I wanted that evening. On the contrary, I needed to talk to someone about life, my future and the best way for me to terminate my stint at the beach and get on with it.

Scotty Bowers

It had been almost six weeks since I last set foot in the Richfield gas station at the corner of Hollywood and Van Ness, but here I was and there was Scotty just waiting for the next customer to come along. He recognized me instantly and called me out by name before coming over and giving me a big friendly bear hug.

"Hey Bobby, I'm glad you came back," then adding roguishly, "I was wondering how long it would take you."

I couldn't help but laugh at his remark before realizing he was absolutely right. The question wasn't "if" I would ever come back but "when," and it was only then that I knew for certain that my return to the Richfield gas station was inevitable. Then, as he checked out my tan, envying how good I looked, Scotty invited me in to share a Coke with him.

"Wow, you look great. It's wonderful what a little sun will do. I bet you drove all the girls crazy down there. Any good ones I should know about?"

Scotty hadn't lost his penchant for inquiry and I was pleased to give him all the answers he was looking for. He wasn't a bit surprised when I told him about all the sex I had experienced during those six short weeks I resided at the beach, and when I was finished he asked for all the details.

Twenty minutes later we were still talking about sex and its obvious connection with Hollywood, but it was only then that Scotty presented the connection to me in a simple manner I never considered. In his mind the drawing power was nothing more than all the half-naked, strikingly beautiful girls that grace every magazine cover, poster and billboard in the country – all advertising sex as the major product coming out of Hollywood.

"With an incentive like that, why would any newcomer want to find employment elsewhere? Obviously, they wouldn't, and that's what has kept it going all these years."

Eventually, it was clear that Scotty felt well enough to open his heart and confide his overall philosophy to me – and he did so with all the wit and aplomb of a learned college professor. According to Scotty, a career and a sincere loving relationship were more important than anything else in our lives and they necessarily needed to come first, but he then emphasized that our need for sexual release comes next, with no single activity being more important to fulfill our daily bodily requirement than a totally satisfying orgasm.

"That is the plain and simple truth of it, Bobby. We are all sexual creatures, but like mom's apple pie, each one of us prefers it in a slightly different manner."

Although I didn't quite understand where Scotty's conversation was headed at this point, from the tone of his rhetoric I was certain he would soon get right to it. One thing leading to the next, he finally acknowledged the fact that, yes, he knew hundreds of people of all persuasions – straight or not straight and those who were ready to try anything that came along – but most of them, as he explained, were just plain sexual with no hang-ups about sex in any manner. He then concluded, matter-of-factly,

"As long as sex is consensual and between adults, and if everyone is satisfied with the result and goes home happy, then there is nothing wrong with that. Right?"

Obviously, there was no way I could disagree with him. It was also clear that Scotty had purloined all of the necessary information out of me that he needed to place me in the proper cubbyhole of his book – and as I soon learned, what a book it was! His was the biggest date book in town and, amazingly, it was all in his head. He had an incredible memory for names, numbers, dates and facts. He was a virtual walking encyclopedia of information about people in town – and especially what each one was like in bed. This Scotty, as it turned out, was none other than Scotty Bowers, the one and only person acknowledged to be everyone's best friend in Hollywood and the number one procurer in town. Scotty had a roster of diverse tricks in his head unlike anyone you could ever meet, male or female, and what quickly became apparent to me was that if you were a friend of Scotty's, you were allowed access to the entire lot. Within the next few months, I saw Scotty often; he introduced me to some of his closest acquaintances and I became friends with a number of them. As he put it to me soon afterward,

"Bobby, you're a young, good-looking, obviously well-endowed guy in every respect and you are exactly what everyone in town is interested in. That's why you got so much sex out at the beach, and I can guarantee you that if you hang around here long enough, you will get all the sex you want and can handle."

Over the years I met many Hollywood celebrities who knew Scotty, used his services regularly and revered him. They all loved Scotty and availed themselves of his generosity whenever they required it. But the reader will learn after reading Scotty's memoir, *Full Service*, which was finally published in 2012, that Scotty was not a pimp. He never got paid for procuring. He only arranged meetings for his friends with other friends because he enjoyed fulfilling their needs and making them happy. Although I realize that some readers might consider this statement to be unbelievable, I can assure them it is absolutely true. If Scotty had been inclined to do so, he could have easily become a millionaire from all the meetings he had arranged – but he never did. Scotty only made certain that those who supplied the services were properly compensated. He never expected a cut for his own services unless, of course, he was asked to perform in the deal himself. Scotty, as it turned out, was a proverbial sex machine himself and unlike any human being I had ever met. He could literally go at it all day long without tiring. Were he only able to patent his secret and market it in pill form, I believe everyone would be making love instead of war and the world would be a better place for all of us.

When considering the overall body of our discussion, it was clear that Scotty had delivered his entire epistle on sex to me, and he did so clearly with no sense of intimidating me in any way. For my part, I was pleased that he allowed me the privilege of sharing in his space and I told him so. I also mentioned that I did not come out to see him that evening just to talk about sex, but to inquire about what he might suggest about my life, work and possible future in the Los Angeles area.

"Bobby, our little discussion today was just the beginning; your life and future in Los Angeles comes next."

CHAPTER 2:

Betty A and Yvette Duguay

A couple of days later, with my July 15 vacate date looming before me, I realized I hadn't made plans for where to go or what to do next, so I decided to call Scotty and take him up on his offer to help me find a place to stay. "No problem," was his immediate reply. He asked only what I wanted to get and how much I was willing to pay, then told me he would check around and see what he could find. It was less than an hour later that he called back to ask me to meet him at a certain address on Gramercy Place, just a couple of blocks from the Richfield gas station. He mentioned that there was a nice apartment on the second floor of one of the apartment houses he thought I would like, adding it was small but fully furnished and very comfortable. We checked the place out, I liked it and I took it on the spot. Everything I had in the world was in my car, so it didn't take me long to move in.

My new apartment was managed by an older gentleman who also managed two or three other apartment houses on the same block. These buildings were all in a row and all built to the same standard 1930s-era Southern California–style lathe and plaster stucco construction. They were not very elegant and certainly not something to write home about, but I decided to call my folks anyway just to let them know I had found a nice place to live. The furniture was old and tacky, but I decided I could live with it. The kitchen was equipped only with an old aluminum coffee pot and a cast iron pan – both of which had seen better days – but I figured I could buy some new ones in the morning. Later that day, I went down to the local Bank of America office on Sunset Boulevard and opened a checking account, then gave my apartment manager my rent check for the rest of the month. He said he was very pleased I liked the place and was going to stay for a while.

On July 21, less than a week after I moved in at Gramercy Place, I was startled out of my sleep by a huge 7.3 magnitude earthquake. The Tehachapi earthquake struck the region with a vengeance; it was the strongest temblor in California since the San Francisco quake in 1906. It was just before five o'clock in the morning when the first shaking occurred. Luckily, it did little damage to my apartment or its contents, but it did rattle my nerves. Later that morning, I learned that the epicenter was seventy or more miles north of Los Angeles near Tehachapi, which was severely damaged and suffered many casualties. Clearly, Los Angeles was lucky this time; had the epicenter been only a few miles farther to the south, it could have easily devastated a good portion of the Los Angeles basin.

The following day, my apartment manager assured me not to be concerned, suggesting that old-time Californians just take these events in stride. Then, as an extra added bonus to his plea, he advised me of a neighborhood pool party with beer and hot dogs that would occur the following Sunday at a house up the street a few blocks, which as a new tenant in the area, I was automatically invited to attend. As it turned out, the party was an early afternoon poolside brunch at one of the nicer town houses in the Beachwood area, one of the older but more upscale neighborhoods in Hollywood.

The moment I walked in through the open front door, I met Betty A and Yvette Duguay. Yvette was a strikingly beautiful, dark-haired young enchantress from Patterson, New Jersey. She was an actress in her early twenties who possessed a great charm, a clever wittiness and a hip way about her that immediately attracted me to her. Although she had been in town for some time and had amassed a number of minor roles in film, she had only recently been given her first real starring role as Minnehaha in a new low-budget film titled *Hiawatha*, which was scheduled for release later in the year. As Betty explained it to me later, the film offered Yvette her first real opportunity at stardom or, at the very least, the opportunity to broaden her career and achieve some sense of respectability – that elusive quality in an actor that had eluded her to this time.

Betty A was a diametrically different type of creature from Yvette.

She was attractive enough in her own right but did not possess the unbridled natural beauty generally considered essential for an acting career, and she knew it. In its stead – and to her credit – Betty developed a friendly, open charm and wittiness most young women simply lack. I soon discovered that Betty was a dedicated social climber with her entire life devoted to meeting new people. Despite that, we got along fine and I enjoyed her friendly banter. After all, she pursued her penchant openly, while poking fun at herself for doing so, and I felt there was nothing wrong with that.

As I expected I would, I found the instant gathering replete with some of the most beautiful people I had ever seen. Being early on a bright, sunny California afternoon, it gave all of those so inclined the opportunity to expose some skin – and many of them did so in grand style. Several guests were in the pool or posing adroitly around the perimeter. Actually it seemed like everyone in Hollywood was good at posing a good deal of the time. The idea, I thought, was to always be ready for that big break, because you never knew when it would come along. It was a long shot to be sure, but there wasn't a person at this poolside gathering who didn't think it would eventually happen for them. It was the one thought that kept them going, and for many it would permeate their entire lives. I had a really hard time taking my eyes off all the beautiful bodies – not to mention the gorgeous faces – but I soon became aware that Yvette had latched on to me and was leading me around the pool like I was a close personal acquaintance of hers, introducing me to a number of her friends along the way. Actually, I didn't mind what she was doing because I was new in town and was desirous of meeting as many new people as possible, so I was pleased that she thought well enough of me to do so and simply went along with it, but her friendly banter and open natural style immediately told me that this was a woman I could seriously fall in love with. Sometime later Yvette and I caught up with Betty and her boyfriend, whom she introduced to me as Gene, and before long they suggested that the four of us go to Lake Arrowhead later in the week to spend a day in the high country. Lake Arrowhead, they explained, was one of the great getaway destinations for Angelinos.

It was only a couple of hours from Hollywood by car and offered some of the best leisure activities available anywhere in California. Gene then explained that he went there often and always had a good time. Considering the fact that I had met a nice new group of fun people along with the chance for visiting Lake Arrowhead for the first time, I decided the day could be a grand success and accepted.

A few days later Gene picked me up at Gramercy Place around six o'clock in the morning, then collected the girls and had us on our way to Lake Arrowhead shortly thereafter. Lake Arrowhead is located at an elevation of more than five thousand feet, so it became progressively colder as we approached our destination. Yvette and I were cuddled in one corner of the back seat, thus allowing our joint body heat to keep ourselves warm. Naturally, I enjoyed the close proximity of Yvette's lovely body next to mine. It was a display of affection I did not expect from her – at least not this soon in our relationship. When we arrived at our preordained destination, we immediately sought out the first available beach area where we could take an early morning swim, click off a few snapshots and relax to enjoy such a beautiful place. Luckily, there was also a nearby rest area with dressing-room and shower facilities that we could all use. After breakfast at a small local eatery, we drove around the lake for some sightseeing, an extended tour of the area and another spat of picture-taking before finally calling it a day. Best of all, the trip gave Yvette and me our first chance to really check each other out and – more important – get to know one another, and in the end, I felt we were both very pleased with the way it turned out.

On our drive back to Los Angeles, while Betty and her beau were singing along to some old ditty on the radio up in front, Yvette had fallen asleep on my lap in the back seat with her hand firmly entrenched in mine. Yvette and I had held hands on several occasions throughout the day so I knew it was not something she simply decided to do on the spur of the moment. On the contrary, I felt that Yvette did so consciously and enjoyed it as much as I did. I definitely felt a pang in my heart that told me she wanted me to know that she liked me more than just being a casual friend, and simply holding my hand was her way of telling me so. What I feared next, however, was that if our friendship turned into anything more serious than what it was at that moment that we would soon find ourselves involved in a tumultuous liaison. Yvette, though, was not an ordinary pickup. She was absolutely gorgeous, intelligent, fun and the kind of woman I could love and cherish and bring home to introduce to my parents. Obviously, an unwanted pregnancy was not something either one of us would have been interested in at that time. We were both very young and had our entire lives ahead of us. At the same time, I didn't think it would have been prudent for us to consider marriage at a point in our lives when our careers hadn't even had the chance of getting started – and I told Yvette so. Of course, she agreed, and we tempered our emotions accordingly.

Back on Gramercy Place, I was content with my new digs as being the perfect place where I could get on with my career, except that a serious romance or marriage was strictly out of the question. It was only then that I came to the realization that I had already had more casual sex during the few short weeks I had been living in California than I had enjoyed during my entire life to that point. "Damn it," I thought, "I better temper my libido before I get myself into some real serious trouble." And in the end I did. Yvette and I became close friends and we remained as such throughout our short but very enjoyable relationship.

A week or two later, a large package arrived from my folks with enough new appliances to outfit an entire kitchen. Now I had too much new stuff to ever move back to New Jersey, so I concluded cheerfully, "It looks like I'm here in California to stay."

CHAPTER 3:

Sammy Davis Jr.

A few months later, Yvette informed me that her film *Hiawatha* was scheduled to premiere in New York City on Christmas Day, and that the studio required her to be present for the showing. As it turned out, I had made plans earlier to spend the Christmas holidays with my parents, so since Yvette's family lived in Patterson, just a half-hour drive from my family home, we decided to fly back on the same plane. As I recall, we arrived at Newark Airport on December 15, giving us a good ten days with our families. A week or so later, however, Yvette called to say that an old friend of hers, Sammy Davis Jr., was appearing in Atlantic City and that she wanted to go down to see him, then asked me whether I wanted to come along to meet him? I had heard good things about Sammy and was anxious to make his acquaintance, so I agreed.

Sammy was appearing at the 500 Club along with his father and uncle. At the time they were billed as "The Will Mastin Trio featuring Sammy Davis Jr." Sammy was beginning to make a name for himself and it was clear to many in the business that he would soon reach the realm of superstardom. Those were the heights Yvette had been seeking in Hollywood but which had eluded her – at least to this point in her career. Sammy was very gracious when we arrived, picking up our tab at the club and then taking us out for a late dinner. Back at his place, it seemed that all Yvette wanted to talk about was the upcoming premiere of her film *Hiawatha*, and if that wasn't enough, she openly postulated that it would make her a star, gesticulating wildly while prancing around in a euphoric state. It was a tempestuous outburst neither Sammy nor I were ready for. But it was Sammy who throttled her on that one. To my surprise, he looked over at me, rolled his eyes at her rant, grabbed her by the shoulders to spin her around and, glaring directly into her eyes, reminded her that nothing was that certain in show business.

"Sweetheart, I've been through that one a hundred times, and I can tell you that you never know when it's going to come home to roost. Stardom is a vaporous thing. Here today and gone tomorrow, and we never know when it will come, or inevitably go."

Finally, Yvette seemed to come down to earth, at least momentarily, giving Sammy the chance to speak directly with me. It was clear that Sammy was interested in learning who I was and hearing more about my relationship with Yvette, who had suddenly become very quiet. In retrospect I think she was jealous of Sammy's success and was trying to compensate for it by showing off with her overly descriptive pantomime. Sammy, however, caught on to it before it could go any further and adroitly directed the conversation elsewhere. I thanked him for reeling her in, he gave me a "thumbs up" and we left it at that. Eventually, however, our little visit just seemed to go downhill. When we said our goodbyes, Yvette was still parked on a different cloud, absorbed in her own little world, with Sammy and me incapable of snapping her out of it. A final wave from Sammy and we were gone.

Yvette's film, *Hiawatha*, was produced by Monogram Pictures Corporation, one of the smaller studios in town. The picture was not a potential blockbuster since it had no major stars to propel it, so the premiere had none of the trappings one would expect from a major studio event. *Hiawatha*, in fact, was simply another "B" movie. As a result, the premiere was not well publicized, the attendance was modest and the reviews were cool. Yvette and her co-star, Vince Edwards, fulfilled their contractual obligations by attending the event, and when it was over they were allowed to leave the theatre and go on with their lives.

This was not the result Yvette had hoped for, and it was soon apparent that she was terribly disappointed. She had already assumed the trappings of a star – you could see it in her walk, her smile and her demeanor – but now, with the premiere done and over with, it was clear that stardom for Yvette simply did not occur. *Hiawatha* went into general release on December 28, 1952, to poor box office and after a short run was withdrawn. The film never earned back its cost and, eventually, was deemed an artistic and financial failure. *Hiawatha*, in fact, was so bad it helped bankrupt the studio – something akin to the straw that helped break the camel's back. Thus, it became the last film ever released under the Monogram Pictures logo.

After we left the premiere, Yvette was emotionally and physically drained and she showed it. She once told me her favorite place to go in Manhattan was Sardi's – a popular show-biz hangout on West 44th Street – so I proposed we go there for a late-night snack, but she declined. On the ride back to Patterson, as we were driving through the Holland Tunnel, all I could hear her say under her breath was "Damn it," and I knew in that instant that all the verve and vitality she once possessed for a Hollywood film career had been drained from her body.

Later that week, I flew back to Los Angeles alone, leaving Yvette behind to spend a few more days with her family. I busied myself with my own career possibilities after my return and simply thought Yvette would get back to me in due time, but she never did. In retrospect, I believe the disastrous aftermath from her film somehow became the catalyst that drove us apart. I thought she would call one day and come over and we would have a little chat and perhaps make up and get back together again – but that was not in our script. It was the end of what I hoped might become my first real romance since coming to Hollywood and I was truly sorry it did not occur. It might seem silly to some, but I had even visualized what our children might look like, had we been given the chance to have any. All youthful speculation on my part – nothing more or less.

I went on to see Sammy often over the ensuing years, usually before or after one of his many incredibly successful gigs, and we actually became rather close friends. We shared many like interests outside show business, including photography and scale model railroading, and invariably we spoke of Yvette – if not glowingly then at least with some compassion. She went on to do a number of films after *Hiawatha*, but none of them were blockbusters or garnered the rave reviews she once yearned for. Disheartened over the status of her career that was definitely on the decline, Yvette finally abandoned it along with her quest for stardom and – luckily for her – she did so before allowing age to do it for her. Sammy, however, went on to become a superstar – the sphere of success that had eluded Yvette – and he remained as such for the rest of his life. His was one of the few truly "rags to riches" show-biz phenomenons of the 20th century – the sort of rare and unique success story that most other performers can only dream of replicating.

CHAPTER 4:

Lookout Mountain Drive

Soon after the Christmas holidays, I ran into one of my scuba diving buddies who had taken a job of repossessing cars for a finance company named Universal CIT. According to him, the job paid well and since he was still a student in college, he considered that the many boring hours spent tracking down wayward vehicles and their delinquent owners offered him lots of free time in which to study. The job sounded ideal for me as well since I also required a job that offered time for my writing. After an interview with the local branch manager, and a cursory background check for any police record, the job was mine. The only training required was a couple of dry runs with one of the seasoned professionals; a few days later, I was sent out on my own.

My first few repossessions were a piece of cake. All were parked on the street in front of the offender's home, so it was simply a matter of hooking them up and towing them away. For a few days the job seemed to go quite well – perhaps just a bit too well – until the spell was summarily broken by one overly aggressive cowboy-type who harbored no qualms about taking a few pop-shots at anyone who came too close to "his wheels." Of course, they weren't "his" wheels at all, but there was no way I could have convinced him of that. One bullet was all it took to help me see the light, drilling a perfect hole straight through the center of my windshield. No wonder this job was so easy to get – there were few guys out there willing to risk their lives for it, and I wasn't one of them. My next journey into the realm of instant employment went only marginally better than the first. It involved offering questionable "investment grade" annuities to older investors who should have known better than to get involved. Fortunately, I did know better and quit before getting mired in the fraudulent scheme.

Suddenly I realized that this work ethic was quite different from what I had been taught to expect while in college. The business acumen in the City of Angels seemed more like that of a pack of wolves, but there was little I could do to change that. Not that Los Angeles was any worse than New York, Chicago or any other big city, because it was me who was out of step, not the city. Interestingly, my first and only trip to the Hollywood Unemployment Office proved that I wasn't the only one looking for a job in this city. I found the place to be full of Hollywood hopefuls all looking for "interim" jobs to hold them over until their first big break came along. In fact, it soon became clear that waiting for that first big break had been the accepted way of life in Hollywood since its earliest beginnings, and I believe that it most certainly remains the same to this day.

Luckily for me, however, doing odd jobs like repairing old furniture, working on a friend's car or remodeling someone's kitchen all came as second nature to me. I soon found that these were all ways I could support myself without standing in the unemployment line or prostituting myself for some ruthless employer. Being one's own boss sure as hell beats working for someone else, and that axiom soon became ingrained in my soul.

By the summer of 1953 I had met many people in the film business, but most of them were still would-be writers like me, assistant directors or regular nondescript workers employed at one of the studios in one of the crafts. I also met a plethora of people who eagerly called themselves "actors." So what, I thought, was an actor? Well, it seemed to me that everyone I met, male or female, young or old, tall or short, fat or thin, black or white, handsome or not, was an actor. Unlike in other professions, however, all these actors had second jobs, like waiter, gas station attendant, short-order cook, etc., and most, it seemed, had never studied acting or acted in any professional venue. Most of them lived in or around Hollywood and its immediate environs. My little apartment on Gramercy Place, in fact, was on the eastern edge of this milieu. It was on the periphery of the action, which was not where I really wanted to live. Thus, in order to get closer to where I considered the real action to be, I decided to abandon Gramercy Place and look for something more appropriate to my needs. It was only then that I remembered Betty once mentioning this large house she knew of up in Laurel Canyon where the owner, who was a friend of hers, rented out single rooms to young people who were just getting started in the business. It sounded ideal to me, so I called Betty, she came over for coffee, we had a little discussion about it and before long we were on our way to check the place out.

The house was located on Lookout Mountain Drive just off Laurel Canyon. It was owned by a charming older lady, Violet Darling, who was a sweet, charismatic leftover from a previous Hollywood era. Violet, I guessed, had been in films during the '30s and had obviously married well as her career waned. She had clearly been "a dish" in her day, with high cheekbones, a charming smile, glorious flowing blond hair and a body that still had most of the curves in the right places. Most fading Hollywood beauties never made out as well as Violet did, even though the Lookout Mountain house undoubtedly represented the principal remaining vestige of her estate. My first look told me the house had seen better days and that Violet did not possess the means or the ability to keep the place up. Nevertheless, with a wink of the eye to Betty, I could tell Violet was pleased with me. I liked Violet as well, so there was little more that had to be said. I was impressed with the overall look of the place, struck it off well with my new landlady and decided to make the move.

As you might have guessed, the house was inhabited primarily by would-be actors, studying actors and fledgling actors, i.e., those having one or more screen credits and on the next rung of the Hollywood success ladder. Hangers-on included those hoping to get a bite out of the system in one way or another, or at least march along with it as best as they could. This group invariably included the inevitable party animals, social gadflies and those other creatures on the periphery of the business who always seemed to show up at every preview, premiere and other event where movie stars could be found. They were, in fact, the ones who made Hollywood the dream capital of the world, and this is where Betty seemed to have found her niche.

Betty and I both loved the new house, its location just off Laurel Canyon and the fact it had a great built-in ambiance. She thanked me for deciding to move in, casually mentioning that she might need a place to flop once in a while, as well. But when I questioned her intentions, she made it clear that she did not wish to be tied down to any formal relationship. She just wanted the freedom to come and go as she pleased.

Betty did not hold a job nor own a car, and as far as I could tell had no visible means of support. She never asked me for money and I never offered her any, and after a few weeks it became clear our relationship ranked no higher than that of "occasional" roommates – and that being in name only. It was soon obvious that Betty actually preferred staying elsewhere, but she never mentioned where or with whom. After a few months, the overnight visits simply became "occasional" and finally she actually disappeared for several weeks at a time. I never questioned Betty about any of these excursions, nor did I consider it my right to do so. After all, she did come back eventually and she did crawl into bed again and, in the end, I was satisfied that she did.

One evening Betty dropped in on me unannounced. She seemed a little depressed and told me she just thought it would be nice if we went out for a quiet dinner somewhere. I had been working at my desk all day so I welcomed the respite. The place we decided to dine at was located down in Santa Monica Canyon, just a block or so from the ocean. It was a favorite of the beach crowd and one of the places I patronized when I was living at the beach. After dinner we drove back to town and had a late coffee at Tiny Naylor's. The place was always packed this time of night and Betty scanned the crowd like she was looking for someone, but when asked, she just quipped, nonchalantly,

"I saw John Garfield here once. Too bad he passed away. I thought he gave me the eye..."

Surprised by her remark, I responded, "He probably gave a lot of girls the eye. They say he died in the saddle with a hooker at some flea-bitten hotel down on Main Street. Aren't you glad it wasn't you he was in bed with when his ticker crapped out?"

"Oh, I just thought it would have been nice to have met him – to be friends – he just seemed like such a nice guy…"

One of the best things I can say about Betty's reappearances was the fact that we invariably had a good time together, laughing and swapping stories about what was going on in town or what we had done since our last meeting. After this particular reunion, I remember thinking to myself about how pleased I was that our relationship was not based on sex, because if it had been it probably would have been over by now.

When it came to my writing, I soon became aware that my move to Laurel Canyon was the best thing I could have done for myself. The place was quiet, peaceful and very primitive in its seclusion. It was exactly what the doctor ordered, offering me the perfect ambiance and environment in which to channel my thoughts back to the creative process – and they did so without any real effort on my part. Within weeks I had developed a variety of new story lines, putting the final touches on others. Even Violet seemed to relish the idea of having a real working writer in her midst, encouraging me to get back to work whenever I tired or otherwise appeared to flounder. For the first time since arriving in Hollywood, I really felt I was getting somewhere and I loved it.

CHAPTER 5:

New Business, New Name

By the fall of 1953, after my first full year in Los Angeles, I decided I really needed to rein in my libido and take a new look at things. It seemed I had become obsessed with achieving the ultimate sexual experience and was flippantly devoid of any serious thought about anything else. I had allowed myself to have more casual sex since coming to California than I had ever experienced before, but aside from some dubious bragging rights, it did little for my psychological well-being. Even Violet made note of it, encouraging me to forget about my transgressions and get back to my writing, but try as I might, I couldn't get sex out of my mind, failing miserably in the attempt.

Finally, however, it was Violet who came to my rescue. She realized my mind was in the doldrums and that I needed some external stimulus to get me back on track. She was aware of my background in electronics, and since the house was completely devoid of any music, she proposed that I build a small radio or record player to bring some life back into the place. Naturally, her idea piqued my interest, and the more I thought about it, the more I liked it. I told her I had an extensive record collection back home that I could have my folks send out and that I could build her anything she wanted. Violet quickly agreed, and by the time my records arrived, the new system was assembled, set up and ready to go. I had built the amplifier from scratch – a talent I had perfected while still in the Navy – and once we turned the system on, it soon became a staple for the whole neighborhood to enjoy.

It was during this period that I called an old acquaintance from my Navy days. His name was Don Honrath and he was the continuity director at NBC Studios. Just after the war he had arranged for a private tour of the studios for a group of electronic technicians from the Navy, and I happened to be one of them. I remained in contact with Don during my college years, and now that I was living in Los Angeles, I was anxious to let him know. A common thread between us was our love of classical music, so when I set up my first demonstration on Lookout Mountain, I invited Don to attend. At its conclusion, he was so impressed with the quality of the sound that he encouraged me to get into the new "High-Fidelity" sound installation business that was just beginning to evoke interest in Los Angeles. He explained that he had several friends in need of a technician with the specific expertise I possessed to build their systems for them, and if I agreed to do so, he would introduce me to the first one later in the week. Frankly, I was flattered. Working on electronics was a breeze for me and I enjoyed it, as well. Besides, I knew I could do it in my spare time, allowing me to bring in the extra money I needed to live on, so it was basically a no-brainer and I quickly agreed to do it.

Within the week, Don and I drove down to Palos Verdes Estates, where he introduced me to one of his closest friends, Dorothy Kirsten, the world-famous opera singer. Dorothy lived in a large and elegant home with handsome hand-crafted cabinetry, expensive antique furniture and off-white carpeting throughout the house. Incredibly, Dorothy possessed only a meager fifteen-year-old pre-war phonograph on which to play her recordings, so when Don told her about the incredible system I had constructed up on Lookout Mountain, she commissioned me on the spot. As she described it, she wanted speakers not only in her living room but also placed strategically throughout the house. Then, as an encouragement, she wrote me a check for $5,000 and told me to tell her when I needed more.

Admittedly, $5,000 was a lot of money back in 1953, but I promised Dorothy the best system available anywhere in the world, and that is what I constructed for her. Then, when word got out as to who built it for her, my new money-making sideline was born. Within the year, with some of my ex-Navy technician buddies hired to do all the grunt work for me, it had blossomed into a full-scale, successful business venture. Best of all, it was one I could pursue at my leisure, thus allowing me to continue with my writings without interference.

Until this time I had just been using my real family name, Horochowsky, for my writings along with the pseudonym, Bobby Wald, for my musical stints. Occasional gigs at local bars always brought in enough cash for me to live on. Most of these activities also kept me active in the social world and helped to hold me over until something concrete occurred with my writing. One day, however, my dad called to ask whether I had chosen a professional name as yet – his concern being that long, hard-to-pronounce, eastern European surnames, like ours, did not appear to be in vogue for authors in the United States. When I told Betty about the problem, she agreed, snapping her fingers in the process.

"Your dad is right. It's about time you changed your name anyway."

Since I was born in New Jersey and was writing primarily for English-speaking readers, Betty felt I needed a name that reflected that heritage.

"Bobby, it needs to be memorable, recognizable and easy to pronounce," and Violet quickly concurred.

"Betty is right. You need a new name that can be readily memorized. Look at Archie Leach, now Gary Grant, and Rita Hayworth, who was born Margarita Cansino. I know – I used to take dance lessons with her. Most of the people in the movie business use professional names, so why shouldn't you?"

Betty then admitted, sheepishly, that she had actually picked one out for me already.

"Bobby Wald is OK for a lounge act, but it's not strong enough for a serious writer like you. What do you think about the name Darin – Robert Darin? It's masculine, appropriate, easy to pronounce and very memorable."

There was a long pause while I contemplated the suggestion, but Betty just kept prodding.

"I always liked the name Darin. It's a name people will remember."

Betty then pumped her arms in a faux showing of strength while looking to me for approval. Then she wiggled her fingers at me in a further attempt to egg me on, but I wouldn't go for her shenanigans.

"Wait a minute, Betty, this is all going a little too fast for me. Can't we just relax a minute so I can think about it?"

"What's there to think about? It's a good name, a strong name – one you will be proud of one day."

Finally I realized Betty was right. I hadn't come up with a better one and had no valid reason to be upset about it. I looked over to Violet, who seemed to think it was satisfactory as well, so who was I to say no? The girls had me – it was two-to-one against me and there was no way I could let them down.

"OK, Betty, it's fine…just fine."

The following day I went down to the Department of Motor Vehicles and applied for my California Driver License with my new name. The Social Security office came next, then the post office and the telephone company and before long I had a whole pocket full of new IDs. Of course, all this was so easy to do during the '50s. It was also easy because this was Hollywood, where everyone seemed to have two or more names – those being the good old days before computers, the Internet, and all the fraud and deception that came with them.

It is still difficult for me to believe it was all so easy to do back in those days, but it really was.

CHAPTER 6:

Marlon Brando

I always thought that Betty was a level-headed girl. She always seemed to be aware of the situation and in control of the eventual outcome, but on one incredible occasion she almost lost her life because of it. Until this time, Betty had been my occasional roommate, a situational happenstance Betty alone controlled. We shared a bed whenever she wanted, but she came and went as she pleased. She didn't pay any rent and Violet didn't seem to care. I enjoyed her company when she was around, so I didn't care either. It was a situation all of us were comfortable with. Unfortunately, all of this was about to change, and as things turned out it would not be for the better.

Fate clearly ruled when the most highly revered actor of the day, Marlon Brando, moved in up on Laurel Canyon just a short distance from our place on Lookout Mountain Drive. He had lived elsewhere in Hollywood while filming *A Streetcar Named Desire* and *Viva Zapata*, and he was now in preparation for his role as Mark Antony in *Julius Caesar*. Luckily, I was one of the privileged few who witnessed Brando onstage during the original Broadway run of *A Streetcar Named Desire* when he stunned the theatre world with his electrifying performance as Stanley Kowalski. As a result, I was well aware of the great talent that lay under his skin, but I often wondered how much of his Kowalski persona was assumed and how much of it was really ingrained in his soul.

Unfortunately, Betty had her own ideas about Brando. I hadn't seen Betty in a couple of weeks when all of a sudden she arrived all atwitter with excitement. She appeared not only with her trusty handbag, which was always by her side, but with a small overnight case as well. Violet and I were in the kitchen having our morning coffee when Betty bolted in.

"Hi, all!" and a kiss on the cheek, then she disappeared up the stairwell to my room.

"Looks like Betty is going to be with us for a while," being Violet's cryptic response.

We both laughed. Betty had arrived early and then spent an hour or more in the bathroom in an attempt to get herself together. The hair, then the makeup and finally the outfit – all of it had to be absolutely perfect.

"Where are you going?" I asked innocently, "Got an interview?"

She merely replied, "Uh, huh," winked at me with a big smile and was gone. When I saw Violet a short while later, her only reaction was,

"I hope Betty knows what she's doing."

When I inquired as to what she meant, she replied,

"I just know she's heading right up the canyon to meet our new resident. I'm willing to bet on it."

And Violet was right. It never occurred to me that Betty was hell-bent on meeting Brando, but she was and she did, and when she returned she was literally flying high on cloud nine. She came in with the most quirky smile on her face, plopped down on the living room couch and just moaned. I knew then and there that our little relationship – for better or for worse – was history. Nevertheless, I was surprised I didn't feel any worse about it than I did.

I didn't see much of Betty for the next several days. My bed was always available to her, but she just seemed to come and go at odd hours during the day, keeping her evening activities strictly to herself. Finally, a week or two later, Betty came over and candidly admitted to me that she was having an affair with Brando and wanted me to meet him, insisting she told him all about me and how great a writer I was and that he told her to bring me over. I didn't believe her and I told her so, but she insisted and I finally relented. The following morning Betty came over and as we started up the canyon I remembered what Violet mentioned just a few weeks earlier about hoping Betty knew what she was doing and I repeated the warning to Betty, with emphasis.

"Betty, I really hope you know what you are doing." But Betty just smiled, took my arm and off we went.

I don't remember much about the Brando place because once we got there, we never got more than a few feet inside the front door. Betty just gave two quick knocks and pulled me in. The rest of the episode then went something like this:

"Bud, it's Betty, are you awake?"

There was no response.

"Bud, wake up, I have someone here I want you to meet. Come on, wake up."

A number of moans, groans and coughs followed. I noticed a door off to the side where all the activity seemed to be coming from, and in a moment, after much more groaning, throat clearing and other ambiguous sounds, the door was thrust open to reveal the greatest actor of our day, Marlon Brando, standing there stoically in all of his glory. To my complete surprise, however, he was stark-ass naked with his right arm thrust forward as though rehearsing for his role as Mark Antony while addressing the Roman Forum – but he voiced not a single word. All he could muster was the biggest, longest, loudest and most repellently juicy fart I had ever heard. I was totally shocked and embarrassed for him, not only for the flatulence that seemed to persist with no end, but because he was possessed with an endowment of such unremarkable size, I felt it would have been better hidden from view than exhibited in such a grossly unflattering manner. I was rendered utterly speechless.

A wave of the hand, not to Betty or me, but to the crowds of his imaginary followers out there somewhere, and the great orator was gone. A slam of the door and Brando was back in his cocoon, farting all the way as he made his exodus. A couple more moans and groans, a sneeze or two here and there, and the meeting was over.

On our way back to my place, I really didn't know what to say to Betty, and all she could say to me was,

"I'm sorry, Bobby, I guess we must have awakened him from a deep sleep."

Finally, the thought of seeing Brando standing there in front of us in such an incongruous manner got the best of me, and I burst out laughing. It didn't break the ice but it sure as hell got Betty's attention.

"Geez, Betty, he's built like a stud mouse! What in hell does he do with that little thing?"

Betty's curt response was all she could muster at the moment, but it was telling, nonetheless.

"Well, he's not built real big, Bobby, but all I can tell you is he's a good fuck – a <u>real</u> <u>good</u> <u>fuck</u>!"

"Yeah, and I bet it doesn't make any difference to you that he's a big friggin' movie star too, isn't that really it?"

There was a long pause before Betty finally answered me, and for the first time ever, I felt she finally admitted her secret predilection to me – and she did so unashamedly.

"Well, yes, it does make a difference, Bobby, and you should know that about me by now."

The following months went well for me with my career. I swore off sex for a while and had written a couple of screenplays that I had submitted to a well-known literary agent for evaluation. I felt I was finally on the right track careerwise and was not wasting my time with frivolous matters such as getting laid. I was also doing extremely well with my sound system installation business, and even hired a secretary to run the office and more technicians to do the installations. I felt I had cleansed myself of any misdeeds and was now on to new and more important matters.

It had been several months since I last saw Betty when, suddenly, one day she came bursting into my room in a hysterical state with one hand covering her face and the other pressed cautiously on her abdomen, running headlong for my bathroom and locking herself in, screaming and crying all the way. Having heard the commotion from below, Violet joined in the fray, begging Betty to open the door or to at least tell us what was going on, but her pleas went unanswered. We could hear Betty's screams and cries and her obvious extreme distress, but she still wouldn't open the door. Finally, Violet had had enough. She sensed something was drastically wrong and needed to get in to help, so she ran to her room, grabbed her master key and came back to insert the key in the lock. In a moment, the door was thrust open and Violet rushed in to help.

"Betty, what is it? What happened?"

One look and it was all we needed. There was Betty, sitting on the toilet with both arms buried between her legs, screaming in agony, her face bloody and swollen from an obvious beating.

"Oh, God! Quick Bobby, call an ambulance. This is an emergency."

I ran downstairs to the phone and made the call as directed. When I got back upstairs, Violet had maneuvered Betty to the floor by herself where she had thrust a towel between Betty's legs to stem the flow of blood. There was blood, and what I guessed to be fetal matter, everywhere. Betty was still sobbing in uncontrolled agony when I heard the siren's wail coming up Laurel Canyon, then making the left turn onto Lookout Mountain Drive. I ran downstairs again and out into the parking lot to direct the attendants upstairs to my room. Betty was given a sedative and an IV while still on the floor and then quickly transferred to a gurney for the trip downstairs to the waiting ambulance, with Violet tagging along for support.

"Bobby, this is female stuff. I'll go to the hospital with her. You stay here. I'll call you as soon as I know anything."

With the sound of the siren fading rapidly in the distance, I stopped for a moment to regain my composure. Then, avoiding the stares of my neighbors, I simply walked back in the house and upstairs to my room without offering a word of explanation to anyone, but it wasn't until I came into the bathroom and saw what was staring up at me from the bottom of the toilet bowl that I really freaked out. It appeared to be a complete human fetus with the umbilical cord and much related tissue still attached that Betty had aborted. This was a little human being and I was terribly saddened by the whole sordid mess.

I must have stared at that tiny creature for hours, or at least that is what it felt like at the time. Finally, I thought I would have to get rid of it, simply get it out of my life, but then thought better of it, decided it was not for me to do and simply lowered the lid instead.

A short while later, some attendants arrived from what I presumed to be the coroner's office to remove the remains, so I was pleased I had not disposed of the fetus on my own. After that, all that was left for me to do was to clean up the mess that remained, go to bed and try to get some sleep. I actually cried myself to sleep that night. I felt that bad for Betty and her unborn child.

Violet was the last person to have contact with Betty after this incident and the only one to see her until she was transferred out of state to a nursing home somewhere back east near her family. I never knew where that was because Betty never got into those details with me. She did tell the police she had been beaten up by some guy she had befriended in a bar, but her story and the details were so sketchy and obscure that the police never believed her. Naturally, I then became the prime suspect, but when I explained that I was not her lover and never had sex with her, their suspicions were directed elsewhere. Months later, however, Violet confided to me that Betty told her it was Brando, and that when she discovered she was pregnant, she went to him for help. He refuted her story, mischievously telling her that he was impotent and therefore incapable of impregnating her, then told her to look to her other lovers for help and threw her out. But when she returned to plead for his help a second time, he beat her up so severely she actually blacked out before slumping to the floor. The only thing she could remember after that was that he picked her up bodily and unceremoniously threw her out into the street, where a passing motorist finally offered her some help. Of course, that was Betty's story – through and through – and Violet and I had no way of knowing whether it was true or not. On the other hand, since Betty never told the police about Brando or her affair with him, there was obviously no way that they could have ever connected him to the event. In retrospect, however, I really believe her primary reason was that she was in love with Brando and didn't want to destroy his reputation. After all, she did have an affair with the greatest actor of the era – possibly the most auspicious moment of her life – and clearly, that fact was more important to her than life itself.

I never saw Betty again and as far as I know she never returned to Los Angeles. If she did she certainly didn't try to contact me, nor do I think she would have wanted to. I think she would have been much too embarrassed by the outcome of her affair with Brando to ever come see me again. Nevertheless, I will always remember Betty for all the fun times we had together and, in the end, isn't that really the best way to remember anybody? I certainly do, and when I go I hope to be remembered in much the same way.

CHAPTER 7:

The Academy Awards

On March 25, 1954, I was invited to attend my first Academy Awards presentation, which at the time was held at the RKO Pantages Theatre on Hollywood Boulevard. The event is presented annually and sponsored by the Academy of Motion Picture Arts and Sciences to award its honored Oscar statuette to Hollywood, its stars and all those participants from the various crafts who accomplished greatness on film during the previous year. As I understood it, the Academy was conducive to allowing the major talent agencies to showcase some of their more worthy new hopefuls at the event by propagating the mezzanines and galleries of the theatre with as many of their handsome, beautiful or otherwise attractive young faces as the theatre could handle. These were basically unpaid and unknown "seat fillers," many of whom had never even seen a movie star or been in the same room with one. An agent I knew obviously felt I had a future in the business – no matter that I had achieved nothing of note to date on my own – and offered me the chance to become one of the chosen few to attend this prestigious occasion, and I accepted the invitation.

My companion for the occasion, having been hand-picked for me by another agency, was a beautiful young starlet from Iceland who just happened to be in town for publicity purposes. As I understood it, she had won a beauty contest in her native country and was brought to Hollywood in the hope of representing Iceland at the new Miss Universe beauty pageant that had just been formed a couple of years earlier. Although she was introduced to me as Maia, I was never given her last name nor was I able to glean it out of her. As I soon learned, she did not speak English – nor could I speak her tongue – and neither one of us made any effort to converse through the use of sign language. As it was explained to me earlier, beautiful or talented young hopefuls from around the world were to be paired with contemporaries from the United States, and it was of no concern to the sponsors whether we could converse with one another or not. Their only intent was to make our beautiful faces available for the cameras, which, unbeknownst to me, included not only the official staff photographers on either side of the red carpet, but all the paparazzi who cared to capture our smiling faces before and after the affair was over.

Official portraits were quickly taken of each couple upon our arrival outside the theatre before we were even shepherded inside to take our assigned seats. It was all done efficiently in a military-like manner so as not to hold up the proceedings, allowing all the major stars to make their appearances last. Thus, as we were being ushered up the red carpet a whole busload at a time, one of the fans just across the tape from me thrust her arm out with a pad and pencil in her hands, poking me directly in the ribs as she spoke.

"Oh, Mr. Hudson, may I please have your autograph?"

I hate to admit it but I was shocked, then pleasantly surprised when I realized this young girl mistakenly took me for Rock Hudson, then one of the brightest upcoming new stars in the realm. Well, it was understandable, I thought. Hudson and I were both tall, dark and I was at least marginally handsome, and as a result I thought, "What the hell, I'll give this pretty young thing exactly what she wants." Responding to her request with the deepest, sexiest and most melodious movie-star-like voice I could muster, I intoned,

"Of course, sweetie, what's your name?"

The name Janet came back to me through the din, whereupon I dutifully inscribed her pad as requested, "To Janet," signing "Sincerely, Rock Hudson." Then, as I thrust the pad back in her hands I threw her a kiss, an action that so excited her, I thought she would pee in her britches. Unfortunately, my group was being pushed from the rear like a herd of stampeding elephants, and I was denied any further contact with my admirer. I merely looked at my companion, who by this time had gone into a hissy fit for having been ignored, but being unfazed by her reaction, I merely shrugged my shoulders and moved on. I tried to explain it all to her a while later, forgetting for a moment that she couldn't understand a word I was saying. What a difference, I thought, between that pretty young fan who just wanted an autograph and "Miss Iceberg" here, who reacted so poorly to her being snubbed. Sadly, she remained intransigent and unresponsive to anything I said, so I concluded that my best course of action would simply be to ignore her – and that is exactly what I did – not only then, but for the rest of the event.

During one of the lulls in the evening, I chided myself for succumbing to temptation and creating a counterfeit signature for my trustworthy young fan. Nevertheless, I soon learned that in places like Hollywood, where movie stars are often seen in public places, young, inexperienced fans often mistake lookalikes for the real thing simply because of the excitement that is created in their minds at the moment they believe a celebrity has been encountered. My adoring fan was absolutely convinced that she met Rock Hudson, and with a signature in hand to prove it, she will believe it until her dying day.

The awards that year were hosted by Fredric March and Donald O'Connor – an unlikely pair to be sure. The World War II drama *From Here to Eternity* won for Best Picture, William Holden for Best Actor and Audrey Hepburn for Best Actress, but the most memorable moment of the evening came when Frank Sinatra won the Best Supporting Actor award; it was clearly an honor that no one expected and it was greeted by tumultuous applause. What an incredible ride this guy had from obscurity, I thought, remembering back to the first time I saw him in person at the Paramount Theatre in New York upon the occasion of his first professional job as a band singer during the early '40s. His success was a prime example of exactly why people come to Hollywood in the first place – to make it as a movie star and to make it big, and that is exactly what Frank Sinatra proved on this occasion. Making it big does seem to happen to some lucky hopeful often enough to justify the entire Hollywood adventure in the minds of all those who accept the challenge.

Otherwise the awards ceremony was a boring litany of short speeches by a multitude of lesser-known recipients, as well as long breaks for Oldsmobile television commercials, from which the in-house audience was thankfully spared. Meanwhile, "Miss Iceberg" continued on in her role as the unmitigated bore. I was still mated to this wearisome woman, but I decided to accept my fate and went on to enjoy the rest of the evening's activities in silence. How sad that this beautiful example of vibrant young womanhood should be so spoiled and unwilling to participate – if only passively – in the joys of the moment. It was an enigma about certain women – and usually the most attractive ones – I was never able to fully understand.

CHAPTER 8:

The Man with the Golden Penis

I may have been new to Hollywood and its legends when I first arrived in 1952, but I quickly learned that when it came to oversize penises, Hollywood is – and always has been – awash with some of the biggest. This was true not only of the physical kind that every man carries between his thighs, but with the business variety, as well. Pity all the poor unsuspecting starlets who are deflowered by big dicks every year – and all for their talent, or lack thereof. Today we have the likes of Harvey Weinstein for allegedly raping much of the talent in Hollywood, but during the '50s Darryl Zanuck at Fox and Harry Cohn at Columbia were doing much the same. In fact, the casting couch in Cohn's office wasn't invented for anything less. Notoriously branded as the most loathsome and fearful movie mogul of all time, Cohn was known to deflower every young starlet who dared venture into his office – and then some. As a group, film producers were also commonly referred to as big pricks because it was believed they routinely fucked all of the artistic talent under their control out of their rightful compensation, and even the detestable studio bosses got into the act by screwing their employees with "creative accounting" practices that rendered most percentage deals totally worthless. One would have thought that the Buchwald v. Paramount Pictures case of the '90s would have made a difference, but it didn't. It appears that a big prick is still a big prick, no matter the consequences.

Which brings us back to the physical variety of penises. Being the gossip capital of the world, Hollywood naturally promotes rumor and raucous discussion among all its inhabitants as to who the best lay in town might be this year. Starlets from one studio or another are typically surmised to be the best candidates – and this is usually the rule because they are also generally the best fellators. Yes, cock sucking – even if described in its most formal terms – is still the preferred and most prevalent manner of sexual gratification on the casting couch. After all, the practice "gets off" innumerable Hollywood pricks each and every day without creating any lasting complications.

Sex, of course, has always been a rampant part of Hollywood history, with seemingly most of its inhabitants – regardless of their sexual preferences – actively engaged in ferreting out the best candidates. But when it comes to the overall worthiness of penises themselves, bigger has always been considered to be better, and the biggest of them all soon become legend. One of the first rumors I heard after I arrived in Hollywood was that actor John Ireland had the biggest one in town. It appeared to be the primary subject of gossip at almost every party I attended, but it didn't prove to be true to me until one day when Mr. Ireland and I happened to share adjoining fitting rooms at the Western Costume Company on Melrose Avenue. As I recall, I was being fitted with full cowboy regalia for a role I was playing in "The Return of Jubal Dolan," a TV western being shot at Republic Studios, and Mr. Ireland was being fitted for a similar role in *Gunfight at the O.K. Corral* at MGM. Our requirements being similar, we were placed in adjoining rooms to be fitted by the same dressers. Nevertheless, the giggling and raucous humor that emanated from the room next door soon made it clear to me that something worth noting had made itself available and that I was obviously missing out on it. Thus, I asked my dresser, innocently,

"What's so funny over there?"

His answer, however, was one I could have never expected.

"Oh, it's just John Ireland showing off his humongous cock."

"You're kidding me?"

"No, seriously, if you've never seen it, go on over and take a look."

Naturally, having been born with an inquisitive nature and an insatiable appetite for the bizarre, it was an offer I could not resist, and the sight of it is one I will never forget. Standing there in all his glory was John Ireland in the flesh. He was naked from the waist down, with his left foot propped up on a stool, thus allowing his oversize flaccid tool to hang down disconcertedly to the opposite knee while being attended by a most adroitly efficient dresser who was attempting to strap the thing to his right thigh. It was a sight to behold, not only because of the incredible size of his prize, but also because of the manner in which Mr. Ireland nonchalantly held court with the other dressers who had assembled in the cubicle to savor the event. Apparently the procedure of attempting to disguise this huge appendage had become a tradition of sorts, as a means for gratifying the curiosities of all those in attendance. It was a sight that even a perfectly straight man could gawk at pleasurably or, if not, at least enviously of the lucky man who was endowed with such an enormous inheritance – and apparently Mr. Ireland was always pleased to oblige. Before John Ireland, it was rumored that John Barrymore held the prize for the largest penis in town, with other mega-endowed males having come before him and since, but there can be no doubt in anybody's mind that the biggest one of them all belonged to a relatively unknown individual affectionately referred to – and forever known by – his pseudonym and alter ego, "OK Freddie."

The first time Freddie was pointed out to me was at Schwab's Drug Store, the famous Hollywood dispensary where he "hung out" to ply his trade. No, Freddie was not an ordinary street hustler or a gentleman of any sort of salacious ill repute. Freddie was a businessman of the first order and never sold anything more illicit than a quick glimpse of his incredible natural endowment. It was generally understood and accepted that Freddie possessed one of the largest penises in history, and he used it to support himself openly, without breaking the law or prostituting himself in any fashion. Freddie, in fact, was a great entrepreneur. He possessed the golden penis – the royal jewel that any man would gladly give his fortune to have been born with. Nevertheless, Freddie only displayed his member discreetly, in private and to individual customers or to small, personally approved groups. Any physical contact between Freddie's copious appendage and a customer's probing hands was strictly forbidden – at least during his ordinary everyday encounters – but what occurred with Freddie's penis socially, behind closed doors and

47

around good friends with deep pockets, was even more bizarre than any Hollywood screenwriter could imagine.

On a scale of one to ten, if Rasputin's legendary penis had been rated an incredible eleven or twelve, Freddie's would come in as an easy thirteen or more – inches, that is – and that was only while lying there, flaccid, not aroused or fully erect. For Freddie, it was truly an asset worth its weight in gold, and he soon became aware that the entire world was anxious to see it. To facilitate rapid egress of his oversize moneymaker for quick exhibition purposes, Freddie arranged to have special trousers fashioned that were replete with slits for flies and discreet flaps without buttons, zippers or other fastening devices that covered openings where his equipment could be extracted without much ado. Normally endowed mortal males can only imagine the weight of such a sizable apparatus and the difficulty of transporting it from the "tucked" position to the "untucked," for such mundane operations as would be necessary during an ordinary bathroom break or – God forbid – in the event of an erection occurring spontaneously for whatever reason one can imagine while the thing was still securely tucked away. But Freddie seemed to handle his affliction well, or at least he was never known to complain about it.

The most lucrative aspect of Freddie's unique business enterprise was the discreet exhibition of his penis at high-end Beverly Hills cocktail parties or other such social events, where the general demeanor of the attendees could be counted on to be acceptable for such a display. It should be noted that the unique manner in which Freddie devised for his penis to be revealed at such events was truly exceptional, if not spectacular. Among partygoers at the time, for an individual to be present at a venue where Freddie exhibited his jewel was considered an event akin to a rite of passage of sorts, from the proverbial squaresville to hipsville, or from being on the periphery of things to going mainstream – the viewer being "in like Flynn" after the event having occurred. It carried a magical connotation few people outside Hollywood could even grasp.

Hollywood, in fact, has always had a preoccupation with penis size. It has been universally referred to as "penis envy," and like heavy drugs, those who became obsessed by it risked being destroyed by it. For most others, however, it was like gawking at the conjoined twins in the carnival sideshow when we were twelve; it piqued the imagination and added wonderment to one's otherwise mundane existence.

My baptism into the ethereal world of the hip occurred one day at a promotional afternoon cocktail party at the home of Louella Parsons, who along with her archrival Hedda Hopper were the two most popular Hollywood gossipmongers of the day. It should be noted that Louella had been in poor health for some time and was confined to a wheelchair, but that didn't keep her from doing her thing. She was a hearty fighter and refused to give up the ghost when it came to her craft, which remained to outdo Hedda Hopper in every manner she could muster. In the case at hand, the party was actually thrown by one of the major studios in their never-ending effort to promote one of their latest releases; Louella merely supplied the premises – and the action. Established movie stars and upcoming starlets were all common fodder at such events, but the biggest star at this particular proceeding was not of the motion picture kind, all of whom were upstaged by one, little-known discovery of Louella's by the name of "OK Freddie." He volunteered that the name was actually originated by some of his earliest admirers, when during his juvenile years they would accost him and suddenly blurt out, "OK, Freddie, let's see that big cock of yours," before tossing him a couple of coins. Well, it was during the Great Depression, Freddie was hungry and there was no way he could deny his customers of their pleasure. Thus Freddie's business was born and it clearly flourished ever since.

For the event at hand, Freddie was dressed in a tuxedo not unlike Dean Martin or Frank Sinatra when on stage, but in this case he was not introduced on a stage to perform his act for all attendees to see. On the contrary, Freddie came out of the kitchen along with the other waiters carrying a large silver tray of hors d'oeuvre in front of him. The only difference between the tidbits that were laid out on Freddie's tray and those offered on the trays of the other waiters was that Freddie's extraordinarily large penis was laid out straight across the center of his. As I recall, it was lightly disguised with some fresh sprigs of parsley and the like, but other than that it was in plain sight for all to see, to savor and to salivate over. Interestingly, my first impression of the thing was that if one hadn't expected to see a man's oversize wiener so fully exposed, or in the case of a virgin who had never seen one and simply didn't know what it was, it could have easily passed for a "supersize" foot-long burrito. Hollywood legend has it that some lithesome ingénue once stuck a toothpick into it, believing it to be a morsel for her mouth alone, but try as one might, I don't believe any Hollywood harlot has ever stepped forward to claim that she could have actually serviced that prize. Even the lasciviously lovely Joan Collins, whose life story was serialized as "The Fastest Lady in Hollywood," declined to add any personal bragging rights to the legend. After all, if one says that one has had the biggest of anything, it is to brag alone, since there can obviously be no contenders. It has been widely recorded that Rasputin, Casanova and a good many other immortalized individuals possessed the largest penises in history, but none of those lucky gentlemen ever utilized their natural endowments in such a clever and unique manner as did our Freddie.

So much for the remarkable golden asset of a gentleman who made the most of his burden with a unique flair for the phenomenal – an accomplishment even Barnum would have been proud of.

CHAPTER 9:

George Hoyningen-Huene

Sometime during the early summer of 1954, I noticed the shutter on my Leica camera was sticking. It was a problem that affected accurate exposures, so I decided to take the camera in for service. Birns & Sawyer was one of the largest full-service photography outlets in the country, specializing in professional cine and still cameras and accessories. At the time, the Leica was considered the best 35mm still camera in the world, and these cameras were sold, rented and repaired by Birns & Sawyer.

When I walked into the store, it was packed, as usual, and as I waited at the counter to be served, I noticed the gentleman standing next to me was eyeing my camera. He was a tall, lean, pleasant-looking fellow with a shaved head and a touch of elegance about him that immediately propelled him out of the ordinary. This was long before bald pates and shiny scalps were the bold male fashion statement they are today, but he carried an amiable smile, possessed a distinctively calm demeanor and made instant contact with me through our static intermediary, when he asked, pleasantly, "How do you like your Leica?" My response was instant and equally as pleasant.

"I love it. It's just that I think the shutter is sticking, so I'm bringing it in to be checked."

Finally, a salesperson came up to us, picked up the Leica and reacted with a friendly query to my new acquaintance.

"Hi George, I didn't know you owned a Leica?"

"I don't," was his response, "It belongs to my friend here. I just need to rent some equipment for a portrait session next week. I'll give you the date and the delivery address. Oh, and I also need a half-dozen rolls of 220 Plus X for a shoot in Griffith Park tomorrow."

The conversation went on between the two of them for a few minutes, allowing me the opportunity to size this guy up. They spoke mainly about the specific equipment to be rented the following week, but I knew the 220 size film was a medium-format type used mainly by professionals, so I immediately speculated that I was not looking at a rank amateur like me. This, I thought, was the kind of guy I should get to know, so at an appropriate moment I simply gave him my name and introduced myself. His response was immediate and very friendly.

"Nice to know you, I'm George Huene."

Amazingly, I was totally familiar with the name Huene (pronounced "Hew-nay") and I seized the moment to tell him so.

"Is that as in George Hoyningen-Huene?" I asked.

He nodded affirmatively with a smile, and a new friendship was born. This man was one of the most famous photographers in the world, an iconic figure who along with Edward Steichen and Cecil Beaton defined fashion photography in Paris during the '30s. We shook hands, strolled out of the store together and kept talking out into the street. He asked how I knew about him and I responded that I was familiar with his work at *Vogue* magazine and as a Hollywood studio portrait photographer. I also had a few of his books that I used for reference purposes regarding his compositions and lighting techniques, and I mentioned this to him, as well.

Before long we were sitting in a local café having coffee and swapping stories about our backgrounds, interests and desires. I told him I wanted to be a screenwriter and, hopefully, a director one day, and that I was paying my day-to-day bills by installing sound systems in people's homes. He countered that he was presently doing some work in films, most recently as a color consultant on *A Star is Born* out at Warner Brothers, but now that the picture was winding down he was back doing some fashion shoots in his spare time. I mentioned that photography had been my overriding hobby and interest since I was a ten-year-old kid, whereupon he countered that if I really wanted to be a serious photographer, I needed to consider obtaining a medium- or large-format camera, as well, adding, "Admittedly, they are not as handy to carry or easy to use as a 35mm Leica, but the results are infinitely more accurate, appealing and satisfying." He finally volunteered that if I was really interested in learning more about large-format photography, he would be pleased to have me come along as an observer on one of his shoots.

We spoke for an hour or more before finally going our separate ways. What a thrill, I thought, to meet one of the greatest photographers of our time. Although George Huene was twenty or more years my senior, I felt I could be more at ease discussing the mundane matters of life with him than I would be with most of my contemporaries. I found him to be highly intelligent and extremely well spoken. He was a thoroughly interesting guy and I was pleased to have met him. As it turned out, I also remembered reading somewhere that he had a highly publicized romantic relationship with another male photographer in Paris while both worked at *Vogue*. That relationship, apparently, did not distract from Huene's talent, fame or acceptance. In fact, he was one of those extremely gifted, artistically minded people who enjoyed the admiration and respect of his peers in spite of his sexuality, at a time when homosexuality was still frowned upon in much of the outside world. Now, some twenty years later, meeting Huene and having experienced just a modicum of this incredibly talented individual's personality, I decided that his sexuality was of little concern to me, as well.

On the subject of sexuality, I soon discovered there were many other homosexual people working in Hollywood, and they were not simply limited to the obvious artistic crafts like hairdressing or costume design. To my surprise, I learned that many world-famous actors were known to be homosexual with the same-sex liaisons between megastars Greta Garbo and Marlene Dietrich on the one hand and Cary Grant and Randolph Scott on the other, all open secrets. It must be remembered that during Hollywood's golden years, homosexual relationships among Hollywood's luminaries were never written about and only rarely discussed, with only those closest to the individuals involved actually knowing whether the rumors were true. Although the homosexual lifestyle was still considered to be unorthodox, no one in the film business seemed to question it, and more surprisingly than not, no magazine or newspaper dared print anything about it. It was accepted by the industry in general, and as long as the individuals kept their noses clean, it was acknowledged that their sexual proclivities would not interfere with their work.

Sometime later, George Huene called to advise that he had a scheduled portrait sitting the following weekend and suggested that if I were free I could come and observe some of his techniques. Obviously, I accepted. Huene's studio was a spare room in an ordinary apartment complex he maintained in the Brentwood area. By the time I arrived, Huene and an assistant had set up three floodlights with reflectors, barn doors and hoods. The camera Huene had set up to handle the session was a medium-format twin-lens reflex Rolleiflex, one of the most durable and popular professional portrait cameras of the day.

As he described it, the subject of this shoot was a most beautiful seventeen-year-old girl, adding, "She is a divine creature in the first blossom of her womanhood." I thought that was the most wonderful, aesthetic manner in which to describe his subject – and, as it turned out, she was exactly as Huene depicted her. Arriving precisely on time, she proved to be an exceedingly beautiful young girl with incredibly bright green eyes and the most sensuous lips one could imagine. Unfortunately, she was burdened by artificially curled hair, tons of unnecessary makeup and a mother who knew exactly how she wanted her daughter to be photographed. Huene, however, was not about to take instruction from the likes of this woman, who obviously knew nothing about the finer points of portrait photography, and his first remark went right to the jugular.

"Madame, the girl is overdressed, overcoiffed and overdone. Get all that stuff off of her. What is all that makeup for anyway? She is a beautiful young girl. She doesn't need makeup. I want to photograph her natural beauty, not what you think she should look like. When you have her all cleaned up, dress her simply and then call me back."

Leading the mother and her charge out of the room to dismiss them, Huene's only remark upon his return said it all.

"Stage mothers are all alike. They invariably think they have another Shirley Temple in tow. They didn't make it when they were young, so now they take it out on their offspring. I feel sorry for the children, they are so vulnerable."

Huene and I continued to discuss the lighting, the camera and the manner in which he goes about getting the desired results. Then, in order to illustrate his technique, he asked me to sit in the chair as his model so that he could demonstrate how he sets up each shot. In less than an hour, Huene had snapped off a dozen or more shots of me, each time explaining the setup for that shot along with the result he was looking for. The best shot, he thought, was one of the last ones he took, with only a key light on one side and no fill light or background light to punch up the shadow areas. In parting, he asked for my address and said he would send me the prints when they came back from the lab.

A week or so later I had the results of that shoot in my hands. Most interesting was the fact that the one shot he referred to as his "best shot" of the day also turned out to be one that I consider to be the best natural portrait ever taken of me – one that only a master photographer like Huene could have visualized and brought into being. It was an amazing lesson for a rank amateur like me to experience firsthand and one I would never forget.

Over the next several weeks, Huene and I continued to maintain our informal relationship as mentor and student over the telephone, and I continued to absorb all the information he thrust upon me. I felt he was genuinely pleased to impart some of his extensive knowledge on someone who appreciated his effort, and I expressed my thanks to him for his interest in doing so.

A few more weeks passed before Huene called to ask whether I was interested in observing the screening of a series of color tests for one of the scenes from *A Star is Born*. This was the picture Huene mentioned earlier that he had been working on at Warner Brothers. He explained that principal photography for the film had been completed, but that the procedure now was to screen a number of test prints of the same scene with different color corrections in order to determine which one would fit best in the final cut. Until this point in my photography career, I had basically utilized only black-and-white film, so Huene concluded it was a good time for me to learn something about color and the many anomalies of the color system. The tests were to be screened at the Warner Brothers studio in Burbank the following morning at ten o'clock sharp. Huene volunteered to pick me up on his way out to the valley, and when we arrived at the studio we went directly to the projection room, where he told me to sit in the back row. Huene then joined a group of people gathered up front in a discussion concerning the scene about to be screened. After a few minutes the group broke up and commenced to sit down in various parts of the room, with two of the gentlemen coming back toward where I was sitting. Before I knew it, one of these gentlemen came directly over to me, looked at me glaringly and with some consternation invoked his will.

"Move over, kid, that's my seat."

My apology was ignored as he pointed to the rear corner of the room. Thus, with my tail thrust ignominiously between my legs, I moved over, dutifully, to where I was told.

When the screening was over the same group of people went back into a huddle again, but this time it was to compare notes. I had made mental notes of the various versions myself and felt I would at least be somewhat conversant in the matter were I to be asked, but I was not prepared for the encounter that followed. The gentleman who asked me to move over earlier now motioned for me to come back, and when I did, he invoked his will upon me once again.

"Tell me, which version did you like best?"

Clearing my throat in an obvious attempt to sound more convincing, I responded,

"Well, I liked number three best."

"OK, why?"

"Well, I thought number one was too red, and number two was just a little on the blue side, but it was also too light. The highlights were washed out and there were no deep dark shadows."

The second gentleman concurred.

"That's right, George, number one is too magenta and the cyan and exposure were off on number two."

While these two gentlemen were discussing the color corrections, I noticed George Huene approaching out of the corner of my eye. Huene then came up to us, apologized for not having done so earlier, and introduced me to the two men I had just been speaking with.

"Gentlemen, this is Bob Darin. He's a newcomer in town. I've been giving Bob some tips on improving his photography. Bob, this is Gene Allen, production designer on the film, and George Cukor, our director."

Oh my god, I thought to myself, this is George Cukor, one of the greatest film directors of all time. As I thrust my hand out, I honestly didn't know what I would say. Luckily for me, Cukor recognized the hesitation in my voice and came up with an instant solution, and thankfully it was on the humorous side, as well.

"Huene, this kid knows what he's doing. He tried to steal my seat back there – he's after my job already."

The laughter that followed defused the situation for me, and I felt I was back on a level playing field. Cukor then asked me the usual questions, such as where I was from and what I was intent on doing here in Hollywood, but when I told him I wanted to be a screenwriter and perhaps a director one day, he came back with a variation of the same line he used earlier,

"You see, Huene, I told you so; he really is after my job."

Cukor and I shook hands and parted company on a friendly, upbeat basis. He encouraged me to continue with my writing and even suggested I submit any screenplays I had finished to the studio for evaluation.

"And in the meanwhile, don't be afraid to take on a menial job in order to earn a living. Just remember, you're young and you've got a lot to learn."

Having met such a great director as George Cukor instantly instilled a new vigor in my being. Back in my room that evening, I dug through my files for a particular story I had written in the screenplay format that did not require additional adaptation. I submitted this screenplay to the studio the following day as Cukor suggested, then went about the business of evaluating the rest of my early writings for possible revision or future adaptation.

I had met many people within the periphery of the film business by this time, but none who could really take me under their wing or steer me in the right direction as significant and influential as George Cukor. Little did I know that the next step in my rapidly blossoming career in the motion picture industry was just around the corner and would literally come to my door with no conscious thought, determination or effort of my own. I was on my way to succeed with an incredible Hollywood career, but I had no idea how it would all come about.

CHAPTER 10:

Beverly Glen

It was about this time that I slowly became disillusioned with my life on Lookout Mountain Drive. I must mention that I loved my landlady, Violet, very much and enjoyed a good relationship with her, but to remain on Lookout Mountain any longer would bring up nothing more than bad memories about Marlon Brando, Betty and her heartbreaking and terribly unfortunate pregnancy and abortion. Months after the fact I still saw that sad little fetus staring up at me from the bottom of the toilet every time I walked into my bathroom. I was convinced that all these negative vibes put a damper not only on my creative imagination, but also on my libido. I was becoming a dull boy and I didn't like it. This was not an enjoyable avenue of thought for someone my age, when pleasant social activities and uncomplicated sex were the predominant desires in my everyday life. I finally decided I needed to get out of this house and take up residence elsewhere. It needed to be somewhere far away with a completely different aura and feel, and before I knew it, I decided that Beverly Glen, which was situated on the opposite end of town, might be a good place to start.

I had never been up Beverly Glen Canyon and knew nothing about it, except that it was located between Beverly Hills and Bel Air and extended all the way up to Mulholland Drive. The entrance was off Sunset Boulevard just east of Bel Air, Westwood and the UCLA Campus — one of the nicest and most affluent areas in Los Angeles. On the drive up the canyon I noticed a half-dozen or more homes for sale directly on the main road, but none of them exhibited the charm, potential for rebuilding and seclusion I was looking for. On the way back down, however, just a short distance before the mid-canyon shopping area, I noticed a small sign posted on a tree. All it said was "Nice" with an arrow pointing to the right. Since the purpose of the sign was not obvious from its message, I decided it was intriguing enough for me to venture a look. A quick right turn off Beverly Glen onto what appeared to be an unnamed, single-lane roadway led me though a short tree-lined lane to a dead end. The road was just a couple of blocks long and terminated into the side of a hill, and it was only then, as I came to a halt, that I noticed a second sign on a post to my right that read, "Rental with Option. Call!" This was a small handwritten sign, not a professionally printed poster from a real estate agent, and two phone numbers were scratched in pencil underneath. The house itself was hidden in trees behind the sign, so I walked up for a closer look.

The house was a single-story, wooden-frame structure with large windows and a relatively flat shingle roof. It was probably built during the '30s and had obviously been neglected. The place was empty, so I tried one of the doors and, since it was unlocked, went in. The house had two decently sized bedrooms, a single bath with a large living area and kitchen. There was no dining room, but a bar and counter between the living room and kitchen obviously served for that purpose. As expected, the bathroom and kitchen were quite outmoded and needed to be redone, but the frame structure itself appeared to be sound. All it really needed was a good cleaning, a fresh coat of paint and new fixtures throughout. Back outside, I noticed a good-sized fenced kennel with a doghouse in the rear along with an old rusty barbecue, a picnic table and some chairs off to the left – all of which had seen better days. There was a small garden area in the front of the house with a lot of cactus, but very little lawn to take care of. A quick assessment and I concluded the place would probably be undervalued because of the neglect and, if so, could probably be turned around for a quick profit with little effort.

On the way back to Beverly Glen I noticed the street sign for this road partially hidden from view by a tree. It was named Quito Lane and I made quick note of it. As soon as I came to the nearest pay phone, I called the numbers on the sign. The person I spoke with indicated he was a personal friend of and sole agent for the owner, who he indicated was living in a retirement home in Arizona. From our conversation I concluded that the owner, although not destitute, was probably in no further need of the property. As a consequence, I presumed he would probably be willing to accept almost any deal to get out from under it. The only questions I asked were the size of the lot, whether there were any liens or encumbrances on the property and the asking price. Since there was no real estate agent or selling fees involved, I made a low cash offer payable in one year with a twelve-month lease. It was an offer the agent couldn't refuse and he accepted it on the spot.

The little "Rental with Option" sign out front told the whole story. My dad, in fact, advised me years earlier that whenever making an offer to buy real estate, to do so only on a "lease with option to buy" basis. It protects both parties, but more important, it allows the buyer a way out of the deal in the event some unforeseen problems or a change in plans occurs. My only condition was for a forty-five-day grace period, allowing me time to fumigate the place, then remodel and repaint it before moving in. Naturally, I discussed my proposed purchase with Violet before signing the contract, and I told her I did not expect my move from Lookout Mountain to be a hasty one since I needed to remodel much of the place before I could occupy it. Naturally, I was pleased that Violet agreed to my plan, thus allowing us to part company on a friendly basis.

CHAPTER 11:

George Cukor

Three or four weeks had passed since I met George Cukor. I had taken his advice to send one of my screenplays to the studio for evaluation, and I had busied myself by delving into some of my other writings that had not been written in the screenplay format. I felt this was necessary in order to determine whether any of those works were worthy of being transformed for film. Since many of my works were incomplete treatments or outlines for stories requiring more work, I left them out for further development and then chose two completed works I felt showed the most promise for immediate conversion.

I had not heard back from the studio regarding the script I had submitted for evaluation, nor did I expect I would – at least not this soon. Obviously I would need to wait in line like the rest of my contemporaries for a call that might never come. It was not a pleasant thought, but there was little an unknown writer like me could do to improve upon it.

In reality, writing is a lonely profession. You lock yourself away in a room all day long with high hopes that some gem of wisdom will spring from your mind, and that is only on the good days. On most other days the writer is tormented by an obvious loss of brain function. The "writer's block," as it is generally referred to, simply renders the person functionless, and it often persists for days. Dedication, determination and resolve be damned! No wonder there are so few really good writers out there, because most "wannabes" give up the ghost too easily or yield to temptation and grind out a lot of cheap pulp crap for mass consumption, and it is all done in the name of survival.

It was one of those days when I just couldn't keep my trusty old Royal typewriter humming. I had spent the morning just doodling thoughts on my notepad with nothing really worth preserving coming to mind. I was at the bottom of my barrel and I knew it, when suddenly I heard the telephone ringing downstairs. Considering that the call might be for me, I ran downstairs to answer it – and lucky for me that I did.

"Hello?"

"Is Robert Darin in?"

"Speaking."

"Mr. Darin, this is Irene Burns, George Cukor's secretary. He'd like to speak with you."

A moment later and Cukor was on the phone.

"Bob? May I call you Bob?"

"Yes, of course."

"Bob, the studio is previewing the picture out in the valley this evening and I would like you to accompany me. Huene suggested you might like to see what a preview is all about, and I may require some help when I get there. But this has to be hush-hush, as I don't want anyone to know I'll be attending. Which reminds me, please just call me George. No last names please. I'll have another man along for help just in case we need it. I'll explain it all when I see you."

Then, as an aside to his secretary while he was still on the phone,

"Irene, please explain to Bob how to get to the house. Tell him to be there at six."

Cukor's secretary then took over with all the instructions. She explained that this was to be a sneak preview, meaning that the time and location for the showing was not to be released to the public, the hope being that the theatre patrons would be normal, every-day theatergoers and not movie people, fan clubs or members of the press. She could not tell me the name of the theatre or the location, but suggested I wear a jacket and tie and be at Cukor's house no later than six o'clock. The address was 9166 Cordell Drive in West Hollywood, just north of Sunset Boulevard off Doheny.

Cordell Drive is a narrow winding road that thrusts itself up the side of the hill like switchbacks on a mountain railroad. Cukor's property, which was near the bottom of Cordell Drive, was encircled by an imposing fifteen- to twenty-foot-high dark stone wall almost totally obscured by ivy, the result being that the house and gardens were completely hidden from view. I found a small call box built into the stone wall next to the only door I could find. When I pushed the call button, a buzzer opened the door, allowing me to enter. My initial impression after glimpsing the entranceway, gardens and house for the first time was a feeling of total euphoria. It was much like the scene in *Lost Horizon* when Robert Conway comes in through the mountain pass and first sets his eyes on Shangri-la. It was a totally unexpected view of an incredibly luxurious home from a previous era that I felt was completely alien to the otherwise mundane West Hollywood area. As I came up the first group of steps to the main ground level, a woman dressed in white service attire made an appearance through a doorway on the second-level terrace directly in front of me. I assumed this was the main entrance to the house when she pointed at me with the instruction:

"Please take the steps to your left."

After ascending as instructed, I found myself admiring a panoramic view of the entire front garden, pool area and main house. In a nutshell, this was one of the most impressive properties I had ever seen.

"I'm Myrtle, the housekeeper, please come in."

As I entered the foyer I was immediately engrossed by the classic beauty of the place. Flanked by a pair of imposing Italian Renaissance blackamoors with live flower arrangements sprouting from their heads – one placed on either side as a sort of silent welcoming committee – the entrance hall appeared more like something you would expect on a movie set and not in a private home. Directly in front of me, a set of ornate silver-gilded chairs framed a large paneled window, offering an impressive view of a small, intimate garden setting outside. To the right I noticed a beautifully appointed, richly colored, suede-paneled sitting room with fine art works adorning the walls. Multicolored parquet flooring in large squares ran uninterrupted from one room into the next.

I must have been spellbound for a moment because the

housekeeper, having noticed my hesitancy to continue, motioned me on in the opposite direction. I was directed into a carpeted study where I was offered a seat under a window on the right-hand side.

"Mr. Cukor will be a few minutes late. Please make yourself at home."

I responded with a respectful "Thank you" as the housekeeper made a discreet exit, thereby allowing me the opportunity to savor the place on my own. The room was lined with richly paneled dark oak bookshelves and cabinets on three sides. There was a long built-in, deep-seated sofa under the shelves on the left and two easy chairs placed on the right, with a small elegant side table in between. A nondescript, older-model television set occupied the lower shelf behind me. How odd, I thought, that such an incredible house would not be equipped with a more modern, state-of-the-art piece of equipment. Even the telephone, also an older model visible on a side table across the room, seemed oddly out of place. The books and their shelving, however, made the room, creating the quiet, peaceful ambiance of a small, well-stocked library. Before I could go on, however, I heard voices approaching from the adjoining hallway and, in a moment, they burst in. It was George Huene and George Cukor. After a cursory "Hello" and "Thank you for coming," Cukor deposited an armload of papers he was carrying onto a table across the room, and without missing a beat directed Huene to come into the entrance hall with him. Since the entrance hall adjoined the study where I was sitting, I could hear their entire conversation that, basically, revolved around Cukor's displeasure with the manner in which the view outside the entrance hall windows had deteriorated over the years. In his opinion, it needed a facelift, something new had to be added, perhaps a small piece of statuary, additional lighting and some new plants. Huene thought perhaps a small fountain would fit – an idea Cukor immediately embraced. Huene then suggested he contact a friend in Athens to locate some appropriate pieces. Cukor thought a small Aphrodite or Venus, not unlike the Venus de Milo at the Louvre, would do, remarking wryly,

"It would certainly add some classic charm to the scene."

Huene agreed and promised to get on it right away.

"I'll contact Maurice Bailey in the morning. I'm sure he can come up with something appropriate."

Cukor accepted Heune's offer, but from my perspective as a listener, it sounded more like they were designing a set for a stage, and as I soon found out, that was exactly what they were doing.

The meeting was over in a few minutes and the two Georges returned to the study. Huene was late for a dinner engagement, made his excuses and left. Cukor then rang for the housekeeper, informing her that there would be three for dinner, explaining that it would be an early dinner this evening because we had to leave the house no later than eight fifteen, exactly. As he hung up the phone and took a long-needed breath, I realized that he had been speaking constantly since the moment he came in. Finally, after a few more moments, he looked across the room and spoke directly at me for the first time.

"Oh, Bob, yes, thank you for coming. Would you like a drink before dinner? We can help ourselves."

Cukor then directed me to a small bar behind one of the bookshelves, which had previously been stocked with ice.

"Just make me a Dubonnet on the rocks with a lemon twist."

I complied, making the same for myself, then placed his drink on the table next to him.

"Bob, please allow me to explain the reason for all this intrigue."

Cukor took a sip from his drink, nodding his approval before continuing.

"I don't know how much Huene told you about this picture..."

But before Cukor could continue, the gate buzzer rang and another gentleman was let in, allowing Cukor to stand up and make the introductions.

"Bob, this is Ralph Jarvis. Ralph works for the government – all very hush-hush. Ralph, this is Bob Darin. Bob fancies himself a writer and wants to be a director one day."

Cukor then continued, jokingly,

"He has made moves already to take over my job if I get fired, but he doesn't know what he's in for."

We all laughed. Jarvis then explained that he didn't really work for the government but for a private company working under contract for the government. It was all top-secret stuff he was not allowed to speak about. Cukor then went on to explain what we would be in for this evening.

"Ralph, I was just explaining to Bob about this sneak preview we will be attending this evening. It's the picture I have been working on over at Warner Brothers called *A Star is Born*, with Judy Garland and James Mason. Unfortunately, there were multiple problems involved with the production – the most aggravating one for me being my desire to remain true to the script and to retain all of the scenes we were given. The studio, however, decided the picture was taking too long and costing too much money, so they sent out an overriding directive to cut as much meat and save as much money as possible. The two alternatives, unfortunately, are not compatible. I gave the studio my final cut last week and I need to assure myself that they have complied with my directions. To do this I need to see the preview tonight, but I need to do so without the world knowing it. Tonight will be the only true sneak preview, since no one is supposed to know about it; there will be a couple of regular open previews presented elsewhere later in the week, but this one, tonight, is the only important one for me. It will be held at the Panorama Theatre in Panorama City – it's out in the valley a ways. Once we arrive, I will need a seat in the back row and to assure me of that, I will need you two to hold one for me."

Cukor's directions continued throughout the dinner, which of necessity was rushed in order to get us on the road in time. Jarvis volunteered that he was familiar with the way to Panorama City, allowing that it was a few miles north of Van Nuys out in the San Fernando Valley, and he guessed it would take forty-five to fifty minutes to get there. Cukor then directed Jarvis to drive the car and have me go in to arrange for the seats when we arrived. One of his assistants, Gene Allen, whom I had met at the studio earlier, would be the go-between at the ticket booth with the passes. The preview would screen after the regular feature that was scheduled to finish around eight forty-five.

The bedlam that we encountered at the theatre, however, was not in Cukor's script. The entire street in front of the theatre was blocked with cars and a myriad of people attempting to gain admission. A carnival-type atmosphere prevailed, with small groups of fans singing various Judy Garland songs, others honking horns or throwing confetti and whatever else they had on hand out into the street. Cukor immediately realized that word had leaked out and that the theatre, to his consternation, had been taken over by die-hard Garland fans. That in itself, however, did not bother Cukor, except that he recognized it would make it more difficult for the studio to judge whether the film received a legitimate reaction. After all, the version of the film to be screened this evening was the "director's cut" – the precise way that Cukor himself visualized the script should be interpreted – and if the reception were to be anything less than expected, it might well be the last time the director's version of the film would ever be seen.

Jack Warner was the head of Warner Brothers Studio at the time, and he was the man in charge of production. Warner had been aware for months that the film was over budget, but being a businessman and not artistically gifted, his only concern was about the final cost and not the lasting value of the film Cukor had directed for him. Things went particularly bad between Cukor and Warner when the final "director's cut" was presented to Warner for his approval. Not only was the film way over budget, it was also more than an hour longer than he had first anticipated. The problem here again fell on Cukor, who, as the director, decided to include all of the musical numbers Garland had filmed, arguing they were all too good, artistically, to cut out.

"That's the stuff people are going to remember fifty years from now," he argued, "not how long the film is or how much it cost to make."

Cukor, of course, was right. The Garland fans went delirious throughout the screening and quieted down only when their goddess was performing a song. In fact, the reaction in the theatre was so overwhelming that whole lines of dialogue – even whole scenes – were drowned out by the screaming fans immediately following every Garland number. As raucous as the scene in the theatre turned out to be, Cukor was still pleased because, in his opinion, the intense reaction of the Garland fans justified his decision to include all of the footage he did, regardless of the resulting length of the film, which clearly was not commercially justifiable.

The first regular open preview of *A Star is Born* came a couple of days later in Huntington Park, California, and the last one was at the Encino Theatre, on Ventura Boulevard. The reaction in both cases was apparently as staggeringly positive as it was at the sneak preview we had attended earlier. Nevertheless, Warner was not impressed, informing Cukor that he was taking control of the project and would cut the 196-minute film down to a "workable" length – something, he explained, his distributors could handle. Cukor, on the other hand, was furious, swearing he would never work for Warner again, but in truth he realized that he had no final say in the matter. In the end, the studio prevailed. Like a Machiavellian ogre, Warner literally took scissors in hand and cut twenty-seven glorious Garland minutes out of the film, all scenes he decided were superfluous, not considering the impact those cuts would have on the continuity, flow and artistic value of what was left. That was the way of the world in Hollywood, and there was little if anything that any of the hired hands, including Cukor, could do about it.

Even in its cut form, *A Star is Born* went on to be a blockbuster, garnishing all the accolades the film justly deserved. It was a "cause célèbre" for Warner – a case of business over art – and business prevailed. In the end, Cukor and Warner finally made up and, over the years, went on to do more films together, including *My Fair Lady,* which incidentally was not only wildly successful like *A Star is Born,* but also finally presented Cukor with the highest honor Hollywood could bestow upon him, the Academy Award for Best Director – an honor previously denied him throughout his long and storied career.

As a postscript to the historical importance of *A Star is Born* and the significant contribution Cukor's direction played in its success, the shortened 1954 release version of the film was painstakingly restored in 1983 to something close to Cukor's final cut, reuniting most of the scenes so rudely excised by Warner. It might be some satisfaction to Cukor were he still with us to know that this "restored" version has been heralded by many movie aficionados as being the greatest motion picture musical in Hollywood history.

Several weeks passed before I heard from George Cukor again. *A Star is Born* was now history and all of the hoopla surrounding the picture was long gone. Like most other people in Hollywood, I discovered the sad truth that when you were not working on a picture, you were considered to be "between pictures," meaning you were unemployed and available for work. This routine was the same for big stars and top directors just as it was for everyone else. Cukor was now between pictures as well and was looking for a new project. Nevertheless, it came as a great surprise when he called me one day to ask whether I had heard back from the studio regarding the script I had submitted to them for evaluation months earlier. When I told him I had not, he suggested he would be pleased to evaluate it for me if I brought it over for him to read. I soon learned that Cukor was a voracious reader. He could digest a standard novel in an afternoon or go through a script in an hour or two and glean anything of worth or lasting value out of it. Naturally, I accepted his offer and was invited over for a luncheon meeting the following day.

Around eleven o'clock, Cukor called to confirm the time for our meeting and advised we would be having lunch outside by the pool. When I arrived at the gate I was met by a phalanx of three ferocious dogs – a standard poodle and two dachshunds. The din of their vociferous barking was outdone only by the telltale wag of their tails, so having had my own dog when I was a child, I knew immediately that I was safe. Nevertheless, when I reached down to pet the poodle on the top of his head, I was summarily attacked, albeit playfully, by the two dachshunds. Finally it was Cukor, having witnessed the scene from the pool, who came to my rescue.

"Bob, you can't show any favoritism. If you pet one you must pet all three."

Responding to the command, I petted all three, reducing the din to some friendly panting, thus allowing me to proceed to the pool without further interference.

Before asking me to be seated, Cukor abruptly introduced me to his brood. The poodle was named Sasha and he was obviously Cukor's favorite. In Cukor's words, Sasha was a prince of an animal, obviously of royal blood. I didn't doubt him. Sasha was a gorgeous creature and deserved every accolade his master could bestow upon him. The two dachshunds, however, were something else – not of royal beginnings but lovable creatures nonetheless. The older one was named Amanda and she was the mother of the younger one, her only pup, who was named Solo for quite obvious reasons. To Cukor's delight, when we sat down, all three dogs came over to sit around my chair, each vying for my attention.

"A good sign, Bob. Did you know that dogs are more intelligent than humans? Yes, they are. They have an intuitive intelligence allowing them to tell friend from foe. It is instinctive – they have it from birth."

Naturally, I agreed with Cukor's assessment. But then, how could I not? I loved animals just as much as he did and in my mind I believe I came to the same conclusion years before. Small talk between us followed for the next few minutes before Cukor picked up a small silver dinner bell from the table and rang it to summon our meal. A few moments later, Cukor's housekeeper, Myrtle Spaulding, appeared, coming down the steps with a tray in her hands, followed by a second servant, also with tray in hand. The trays were set out on a side table in the pavilion directly behind us and the plates with our food were transferred to our table. It was all done quite professionally, without interfering with our conversation.

"I see you brought some reading material for me, Bob. May I see it?"

When I presented my script to him, he immediately asked whether I had typed it up myself, and when I told him I had, he seemed genuinely pleased about it. A moment later he put it aside, commenting that he would get to it later in the day.

The rest of our conversation then revolved around me. Cukor wanted to know where I was from, my parents, my schooling, my interests, etc. He seemed particularly pleased when I told him my mother was Austrian and was born in a small town on the Austrian-Hungarian border, whereupon he volunteered that his parents were Hungarian but came from the same general region. He then quipped,

"You must know that all Austro-Hungarians are very talented."

He laughed and went on with his interrogation, including detailed questions regarding how I was taking care of myself, paying my bills, etc., and, most importantly, how much time I was devoting to my writing. I had to admit that my writing was necessarily forced to the back burner for the first year I was in town, citing that the need to support myself had to come first. His nod told me he understood. I then expanded on my assertion by reciting a litany of odd jobs I had taken on since my arrival, reading them off like clockwork from day one.

Cukor seemed genuinely pleased to hear that I possessed a variety of skills and could easily support myself should my career as a writer wane or flounder. Finally he asked about my education, where I went to school, any theatrical experience, etc., and I told him of my experiences in summer stock, college and the many plays I had seen in New York. He then mentioned his formative theatrical years in Rochester and New York before coming to Hollywood in 1929. In the end, I felt I told him all he wanted to know about me, and he seemed satisfied that I was intelligent and serious enough about my writing to be worthy of his attention.

After lunch, he stood up and walked me to the gate. Once there, and with my script in hand, he finally commented that he was always eager to help a budding young talent like me, emphasizing that if he detected any flair or gift in my writing worthy of his comment he would be pleased to let me know. I thanked him for his time and I left.

On the way home I mused over the fact that my entire conversation with Cukor was very businesslike and aboveboard. I heard rumors that he was homosexual, but he offered no hint of it. There was no joking, double entendre or innuendo of any sort to deal with. He did not attempt to feel me out intellectually or otherwise concerning my private life, girlfriends or other emotional attachments, and that pleased me because I feared I would not have known how to respond in the event he did. On the contrary, I felt my first private meeting with the great director went extremely well and I was totally pleased with the outcome.

CHAPTER 12:

Gay Hollywood

Sometime after my meeting with George Cukor, I received a call from Ralph Jarvis, the friend of his who drove us out for the sneak preview of *A Star is Born* in Panorama City. He explained that he had gone back to Florida to visit his family and just returned to L.A. He was on the way back to his job in the Far East and just wanted to say hello. He asked whether I wanted to have dinner with him that evening, but I declined, explaining that I was just moving into this new house where I planned to be working all day. I emphasized that the water and power were turned off and that there was no way for me to get cleaned up. He said he understood, suggesting that he could pick up some food on the way over and then we could just have our dinner right there at my new place. I agreed, gave him the address and went on with my work.

I had just finished painting the living room walls and was set to knock off for the day when Ralph appeared. Luckily, I had this old oak picnic table and chairs out in back that came with the house, so we brushed them off with a rag, ate our meal by the light of a candle and made the most of what Ralph had provided for us. He asked primarily about my plans for the future and where I was hoping to go from here. I explained that I had acquired the house as a "fixer-upper," intended to live in it for a couple of years and then sell it. It was all speculation on my part, but that was my plan, plain and simple. We spoke late into the evening until I finally told him I was tired and needed to get some sleep. It was only then that he asked whether he could stay the night with me, but I told him no. I explained that I had only one bare mattress and a blanket on the floor, but no sheets or pillowcases, and with no running water there was no place to bathe or clean up either.

"It's pretty slim pickin's," I told him.

He understood but explained that he needed a place to stay for a couple of nights before heading back to the Far East, so he asked whether he could bring some bedding over the following day and flop in the other bedroom. He seemed like a nice enough guy, I was too tired to argue with him, so I agreed. He thanked me, I thanked him for the dinner and he left.

I awoke early the next morning and drove to a local gym in Westwood, where one of my old scuba diving buddies had become the manager. He allowed me to shower and to utilize their facilities without paying, writing it off as a free trial. When I was finished, at least I came out feeling better than when I went in, and after donning some clean clothes I felt ready to take on the new day. My first chore was to arrange for all the utilities to be turned on at the new house and then to get some much-needed new furniture. For starters, I decided that a few new barstools might come in handy along with enough minor necessities to at least get the place operational.

My plan was to continue painting the interior until all the rooms were done, then tackle the outside later. At the same time, I had ordered all new kitchen appliances and plumbing fixtures for the bathroom that were due to be delivered by the end of the week, so imagine my surprise when I returned to the house to find Ralph on top of the ladder with paintbrush in hand and at work on the living room ceiling. There were also two big cartons out in the hallway that clearly contained a couple of beds. Additional cartons with bedding, sheets and towels were scattered throughout the house. I didn't know what to say, but when Ralph saw me come in, he looked down at me from his perch, offering me a big smile and a friendly welcome.

"Hi, Bob, welcome home. I had nothing going on today so I decided to do a little shopping, then came back here to help with the painting. I bought us a couple of beds so we'd have someplace to flop tonight. Oh, yeah, I also called the plumber and rescheduled your delivery for tomorrow. Man, we should be all set up by the weekend."

All I could do was shake his hand in thanks. I did catch his use of the word "we" – which I thought was a little brazen of him – but under the circumstances I decided to forget it. Finally, however, when I asked how much I owed him for everything he handed me some receipts, allowing the matter to be settled on the spot with a check and another broad thanks. A short while later the new refrigerator, electric range and stove arrived. All we had to do was shove the appliances in place and plug them in. By five in the afternoon, the power and the water had been turned on as well, so all the kitchen needed was the new fixture for the sink and the place would be ready to go.

By dusk, we had finished the painting, set the beds in place and sat down on the new barstools to admire our work. Finally, Ralph decided it was time for us to go out to celebrate. As he explained it, it would be the dinner he invited me out to the night before that I couldn't accept. Ralph was driving, so he took us to a nice upscale restaurant he knew in Beverly Hills. He was the perfect host, well mannered and a good tipper. We spoke of many things, including our families and backgrounds and what we expected to do with our lives, but I soon noticed that we spoke nothing about girls or sex. I just thought it was very unusual for two guys in their mid-twenties not to talk about the single major preoccupation in their young lives. On the way back to the house after dinner we came across an all-night market where we stopped to stock up the new refrigerator, but as we approached the checkout stand I noticed that Ralph had picked up a lot of beer, brats, chips and other such stuff, then went for his wallet.

"My treat, Bob. We've got to be ready for anything, right? Maybe even have a little party this weekend."

When we got back to the house, he took a couple of beers out of the pack and popped them, handed me one and put the other one to his lips. I knew the time had come for a good talk with him, and I sensed that he knew something was bothering me as well.

"What's up, Bob? You're awfully quiet all of a sudden."

I don't recall the exact wording of my message or that of his response, but I'm certain it all went pretty much as follows:

"Ralph, before I say anything, I'd like you to know that I really appreciate all the things you've done for me the past couple of days – I really do. But now, here we are, we barely know each other, and you come into my life like a roller coaster. You act like you're an old friend and that you owe me all of this, but you aren't and you don't, except that you do owe me an explanation as to why you are doing all this for me."

"Bob, I understand your concern and I'm sorry – I really am. I only hope I haven't offended you. The truth is I really like you. I think you're a great guy. You're honest, intelligent, clean cut, good looking, hard working – all the good things a guy should have going for him. I think you've got a great future ahead for you and frankly I would just like to be a part of that."

The accolades flowed like a vintage French wine out of a silver goblet and I was appreciative of that. I felt I had to give him the chance to make his case, but it all sounded much too much like a physical attraction to me and I just didn't know how to handle that sort of adulation as yet. So finally, I decided to simply take the bull by the horns and ask him straight out,

"Ralph, are you putting the make on me? Is that it?"

Although I was expecting some hemming and hawing and perhaps a couple of forced coughs to clear the throat, there was absolutely no hesitation in Ralph's answer and he presented it to me as clearly as a transcript from a written page.

"Well yeah, I guess I am – but what I'd really like to do is just go to bed with you, period. But don't worry, I'm not into hugging and kissing or any of that crap. I just think having sex with a straight guy like you is great. You know, it happens all the time, but if it doesn't happen with us, then I'd still like to be your friend – you know, like regular buddies."

No, I didn't know, and I didn't know how to answer Ralph or what to say to him. Here was this totally masculine, good-looking young guy who tells me he wants to have sex with me and if not then still be my friend – like a regular buddy – nothing else. How do you come up with an answer to that? I couldn't, I didn't and I finally told him so, but I didn't do it in a mean or oppressive manner. He was a nice enough guy and I didn't want to offend him, so I gave it back to him flippantly and with a modicum of humor attached. Frankly, it was as honest a manner as I could manage.

"Well, Ralph, you'll just have to get in line with the rest of the boys. Maybe next year or the year thereafter – who knows – but right now I'm having too much fun with the girls and that's the way it's going to stay. Besides, I never told anyone I was straight, but the truth is that I've just never had the desire to have sex with a guy and frankly don't know what I would do if I did. Please understand that I have nothing against your lifestyle or whatever you call what you do. I've been goosed, grabbed, groped and propositioned by a lot of people since coming to L.A. – including a number of guys – but I have never been approached with a proposal to match the one you just came up with and, frankly, I really don't know how to respond to it. You have to understand I did not grow up having sex with guys, so you are confronting me with a situation that is foreign to me; it is a lifestyle I am not familiar with and I know nothing about it. What I'm saying is that I cannot have you come into my life as a possible future sex partner – it simply isn't in the cards. That leaves me with the question as to what sort of relationship we could ever have. We could certainly be friends, but I doubt whether that would be sufficient for you."

Ralph took a long breath before responding. I could tell he was not a skilled orator and the words did not flow from his lips like gems of wisdom. He was ill at ease with the task I had presented to him, but to his credit he grabbed the chance to win me over and let me have it straight from the heart, and he did so in the basic street language he knew best.

"Bob, I'd like to start by telling you a little about myself. I grew up in Tampa and was still in high school when I had my first experience. I was at the beach one day when this big burly guy came over and started talking with me. The war was still on and he said he was a serviceman home on leave. I was just a skinny teenager at the time so he told me how to build up my body to become big and strong like him. One thing leading to the next, he led me behind a nearby building where he groped me. It scared the crap out of me, but when I didn't object he took my dick out and went down on me. It was the most exciting thing that had ever happened to me.

"But the most important thing I remember about this guy was not what he did but what he told me afterward. He said, 'Don't worry! This isn't going to make you queer. It's OK for two guys to do it when they are horny and there are no women around – and if you want to know the truth about it, for many of us in the service it's the only way we can get through this fucking war.' And Bob, I believed him and I don't consider myself as being gay, queer or anything else like that, because of what he did to me. I don't hug and kiss guys or swish around in women's clothing. It's just the sex I want, and I honestly feel that when two guys are buddies and close enough in all other ways that it is natural for them to do the sex part, too."

Frankly, I didn't know what to say to Ralph after that. It was the first time anyone had even used the term gay in any conversation with me and I didn't know what to make of that. I did tell him that I appreciated his baring his soul to me, but that I wanted to make certain he understood it didn't make any difference to me and that I still felt the same way about having sex with guys as I did before.

By now it should be obvious to the reader that I am not a prude – not now and not back then, when the thought of having sex with another guy was completely foreign to me. I am very liberally minded and put no one down for their lifestyle, sexual habits or personal behavior, as long as it is consensual and between adults. When I reached puberty, I was much like most other healthy males my age. I thought about sex every day and sought relief as often as possible. Since my very first sexual experience was with a member of the opposite sex, my passion naturally has always been for more of the same. Yes, vaginal sex became my penchant because that was all I had ever experienced. Since arriving in Los Angeles, however, I quickly learned to settle for oral sex whenever a willing vagina was not available.

Although I never considered myself to be a rampant heterosexual, the only real hang-up I've ever had regarding sex of any kind was the question of sodomy. I've never done it and I don't think I ever will.

While in the Navy, however, I learned that many of my shipmates preferred to sodomize their women over all other manners of sex. Old salts and new recruits alike, they all seemed to brag about their penchant for sodomy. This is an enigma to me when considering that the ultimate glory hole on a woman's body is only an inch away. Nevertheless, I believe my total disinterest in that activity is the primary reason I could never assume a homosexual lifestyle, because men simply do not possess a vagina. Even so, I have developed just as many lasting social, personal and business relationships with homosexual men as with straight ones.

To be honest, I don't have anything against two men or two women having sex with one another, regardless of which body opening they intend to penetrate. On the other hand, oral sex is androgynous and universal; it is not gender specific. It can be performed by any two people – male or female – as long as at least one of them is willing to go down on the other. Finally, there is "Madame Palm," the universally approved salvation that all men and women utilize for instant gratification when no other solution is at hand. I find all these activities understandable and acceptable. After all, we are all human and all horny at times, and whatever activity best fits the time, place and agenda will most certainly work.

But getting back to Ralph for a moment, I reiterated that we could certainly be friends and if he found that to be sufficient, then I would be pleased to allow him to stay with me for a few days whenever he came back to town. Until this point in our relationship I didn't find Ralph to be very demonstrative, but when I finished he stood up and gave me a big hug. That's all it was, just a good, solid, man-to-man bear hug, and I was pleased to accept it as such.

Interestingly, Ralph never did bring up the question of his having sex with me again. I think he finally realized that our friendship was more important to him than any potential future sex and then simply forgot about it. In the end, Ralph and I became very close friends, catering to each other's needs and bonding at least as close as any two men can get with one another.

Ralph and I had dinner at Cukor's house a couple of weeks later. To be honest, the mood was quiet and the conversation unremarkable. There were three or four other guests present besides Ralph and me. They were all men and all identified as being in the film business. Ralph later told me they were all gay, but being discreet, closeted professionals, all of the conversation was aboveboard with no homosexual connotation of any kind.

Apparently, Ralph had met Cukor some time earlier and had been to a number of his parties. I asked Ralph whether Cukor had ever put the make on him, but his answer was an emphatic no, emphasizing that Cukor was very discreet about those matters and as far as he knew, Cukor never discussed them with anybody. Regarding Cukor's so-called Sunday afternoon bacchanals everyone seemed to talk about, Ralph advised that although most of those attending the events were young homosexual men, as far as he witnessed it, the affairs were no more of a bacchanal than a dip in the pool. He insisted that he had never seen any open sexual activity around Cukor's place and that was that.

A few days later, Ralph advised that he had booked a flight for Honolulu the following Monday, that being the first leg of his flight back to his job in the Far East. He said he would be away for eight months and hoped one of the new beds would be available for him when he returned. He then left, saying he was spending the weekend in Oceanside with friends and would stop back on Monday morning to say goodbye.

Later that afternoon I ran into my next-door neighbors for the first time. I was out in the driveway washing my car when they came by to say hello. They were two very attractive young women who indicated they were nurses at the UCLA Medical Center in Westwood. They were very friendly and had a pair of miniature poodles tagging along behind them. I always loved animals so I bonded with them instantly. After the usual small talk they suggested I come down the street to meet the two guys living directly across from them. They explained that one of them was a psychiatrist at the V.A. Hospital in

West Los Angeles and the other was a high-priced divorce attorney in Beverly Hills. From the tone of their opening conversation, it was clear to me that these two girls were lesbians, their neighbors across the lane were homosexual men and (in their words) they thought Ralph and I were a gay couple as well. There was that word again and I really didn't know how to respond to it as yet. Nevertheless, when I told them we weren't, they just laughed. Surprised by their response, I inquired, innocently, as to what was so funny, but their answer surprised me even more.

"Maybe you should be. Don't you know that Beverly Glen is almost 100 percent gay?"

"If you mean homosexual by that, well, no, I didn't know that, but that's not a problem with me either. Really, I'm OK with that."

My response seemed to satisfy them and after a moment all three of us just laughed it off, then continued on with our patter before going down the lane to meet the gay doctor and his attorney lover.

Chuck and Bruce appeared to be in their mid-forties and were longtime Beverly Glen residents. They were obviously very well-off and enjoyed the fine lifestyle they had carved out for themselves. After a quick tour of their home, Chuck appeared with a fancy silver tray embellished with a wedge of Camembert cheese, fresh grapes, a loaf of French bread and a properly chilled bottle of imported Chablis. All four of these people were openly homosexual, but they were friendly, interesting, highly attractive professionals and I was pleased to have them as my neighbors. I told them I was a writer and would be living alone and would obviously appreciate their looking in on me from time to time,

"You know, just to make sure I'm OK."

They all agreed. Then, when the cheese and the wine were gone, we gave each other some friendly hugs, said our goodbyes and returned to leading our independent lives.

An interesting sidebar to all this gay talk is an episode that apparently occurred at a meeting of the board of directors of the Screen Actors Guild sometime during the tenancy of Ronald Reagan as its president. Reagan was nothing more than an occasional leading man in "B" movies throughout his film career, but he was well respected as an outspoken political advocate – a personal, likable characteristic of his that eventually led him to the White House. As the gristmills had it, Reagan caused quite a stir one day when he walked in at a board meeting and declared that he heard there were some homosexuals in the Screen Actors Guild and then formally proposed to the board to have all homosexuals banned from the union. Well, you could have probably heard a pin drop when he was finished, but as the story goes it was none other than Reagan's old buddy, Charlton Heston, who came to the rescue of every homosexual actor in town by taking Reagan aside and advising him, candidly,

"Ronnie, if we ban all homosexuals from the Screen Actors Guild, there will be no more Screen Actors Guild."

Then, when Heston gave Reagan the numbers and the overall percentages, he became so overwrought at the thought, he wept. Finally, with no support for his proposal, it was quickly withdrawn, allowing the matter to be stricken from the official record – all told, a sad but telling note in the life and social proclivities of this country's future president.

Nevertheless, this episode points out the fact that most – but obviously not all – straight people in Hollywood were aware of the grossly disproportionate share of homosexual professionals working in their midst, but that few of them ever objected to it or spoke openly about it. The list included some of the most talented individuals in the business, and most of the straights accepted that fact and were comfortable with it.

At the time, I was living in a community where most of the inhabitants considered themselves to be gay, and I finally learned that gay had become the preferred popular term to describe their lifestyle. In my case, I have always been a very active social animal and quickly learned to accept the best of what life had to offer, not only from my straight friends, but from my gay friends, as well. That is the way it was in Hollywood during the '50s. By most estimates, more than half of the artistic talent in Hollywood was gay. The only apparent difference now is that most gays have chosen to come out of the closet and are open about their sexuality.

Ralph never came back that Monday morning to say goodbye, but a gift with a goodbye note did arrive by special courier that simply blew me away. It was a beautiful German Shepherd puppy, about six months old. Naturally, it took just one look for me to fall in love with this beautiful animal. Apparently, Ralph did not consider whether I wanted an animal or how I would take care of it, but his note said it all.

"Bob, I didn't want you to be lonely up there all by yourself for the next eight months, so I thought a pet would be the perfect companion. His name is Graf. I know you will take good care of him. He will probably be full-grown by the time I get back, so please take lots of pictures. Your friend, Ralph."

Luckily, the fenced yard and doghouse from the previous owner came in very handy. Graf became my constant companion and he even took up an acquaintance with the two poodles next door. Thus, my neighbors and I traded dog chores whenever one or the other was out of pocket, and within a few weeks of my moving in, my little haven on Quito Lane became a real home – and I loved it. I locked myself in with Graf as my only roommate, and within a few weeks had accomplished more with my writing than I had been able to do since arriving in Los Angeles.

CHAPTER 13:

Vivien Leigh

One day, Irene Burns, George Cukor's secretary, called to ask whether I could come to the house for a meeting concerning my script, and naturally I agreed. As I recall, we met in the library at four o'clock. Cukor was seated on the couch with my script in hand and a small side table pushed up in front of him for his notes. As he greeted me he asked that I sit across from him. As I did I noticed Irene through an open door on the right in an adjoining room that was later identified to me as the "in house" office – the place where Irene conducted all of Cukor's affairs while he was "between pictures," which clearly was what he was at this time. In fact, Cukor's first comment to me as I sat down was about how lucky I was to get his full attention since he was not otherwise engaged in another project. That said, he got down to the gist of it, and as best as I can remember it, his comments went something like this.

"Bob, first of all I give you an 'A' for effort. This is really quite good. Not perfect, mind you, but wholly acceptable, as least as far as the basic story line goes. However, this is a war story and war stories are not my cup of tea. I know nothing about the technicalities of running a submarine and all the jargon they use to do it, so I won't comment on that. I can only tell you about the exposition, development and resolution from a literary standpoint, the character development, and your handling of the screenplay format, which, by the way, is excellent. I really have to congratulate you on that. But to get back to the heart of the matter, the main problem as I see it is the captain's motivation to surrender his ship. He must have a more noble reason than the mere fact that the war is lost and he is on the losing side. Actually you might call on the same motivation the German generals employed in their plot against Hitler in July 1944. What you should do is read *The Rommel Papers*; it is an excellent source of material for a story like this."

Cukor went on nonstop for at least another twenty minutes and I did nothing but listen to him. Frankly, I thought his comments were brilliant and I didn't dare interrupt him. Finally, the gate buzzer sounded and I could hear Irene answer the gate phone from the other room, then let someone in. Shortly thereafter the door in the entrance hall opened, interrupting Cukor's line of thought.

"Oh, it's my houseguest. Please come in, Vivien, we're just having a little script conference."

As we stood up to welcome his guest, a petite woman in a large-brimmed hat, oversize dark sunglasses and a few small packages in hand entered the room, went over to Cukor and gave him a kiss on the cheek. Then, noticing me from behind her cheaters, she motioned to Cukor, exclaiming,

"Oh, George, I'm sorry, I interrupted your conference."

"Don't be silly, Vivien, we were just finishing anyway." Then turning to me for the introduction, Cukor reprised another comic variation of the same comment he invented at the studio projection room weeks earlier.

"Vivien, I'd like you to meet the man who would like to replace me as your next director. This is Bob Darin. He is also a marvelous screenwriter. I just read his first script."

Well, you could have floored me with a feather after that, but it was only after I recovered my composure that I remember this woman taking her hat and glasses off and Cukor introducing her to me,

"Bob, please meet Vivien Leigh."

The moment her glasses came off and she looked directly into my eyes, I recognized her instantly. I remembered the first time I had seen her on the screen when she starred as Scarlett O'Hara in the most widely acclaimed film of the day, *Gone With The Wind*. Cukor was the first director on the picture and had conducted dozens of screen tests with many of the top actresses of the era, but he held out for more – for someone special – and that is what he got when he met and finally chose Vivien Leigh for the part. Vivien was in her early twenties at the time, and since she was British by birth she had to assume the southern American accent that was required for the role. Although some critics commented negatively about it, Cukor stood firmly with his choice and the studio agreed. Apparently, the Academy of Motion Picture Arts and Sciences agreed as well, awarding Vivien with her first Oscar for her interpretation of the role. Now, some fifteen years later, here I was peering into Vivien's lovely eyes. She was now a mature, fully grown woman, and her beauty was unblemished and remarkable for her age.

For the next hour or more, Cukor and his houseguest were engrossed in shoptalk concerned mainly with the type of role Cukor thought Vivien should do next. Her last film was *A Streetcar Named Desire*, for which she won her second Academy Award for Best Actress, but that was two years ago and it was clear from their conversation that Vivien was now between pictures as well. Finally the conversation came back to me. Vivien broke the ice first by proclaiming it was rude of them to keep me sitting there while the two of them were talking mainly about her. So, with a streak of tomfoolery in her voice and a dash of mischief in her eyes, she asked me, playfully, what type of role I thought she should play next. Of course, it was obvious she was jesting and I thought it best to jest back at her by suggesting, jokingly,

"It's a clear choice in my mind; you simply have to do *Gone With The Wind – II*."

We all roared with laughter, then Cukor responded with a quick,

"Well, kid, if you come up with the money we might consider it."

A phone call soon took Cukor out of the room for a few moments, leaving Vivien alone with me for the first time. Then, as he turned to go out the door, he directed me to make us all a drink.

"You know where the bar is, Bob. I'll have my Dubonnet as usual. Vivien, just tell Bob what you'd like. He's very good at mixing drinks."

As I stood up to go to the bar, Vivien followed, taking me by the arm as we crossed the room. Then, as I started to explain various drinks to her, she came right up in front of me, looked me dead in the eye and in the most sultry and enticing of voices, proclaimed,

"Surprise me; I'm totally in your hands."

Needless to say, her remark and the manner in which she delivered it dropped me dead in my tracks. Here I was alone, if only for a brief moment, with one of the most beautiful women in the world, and she was flirting with me. Worst of all, I wasn't sure whether I knew how to respond to her. Vivien was quite small and barely came up to my chin, but she had the most beguiling look on her face and the most demanding presence of any woman I had ever met. Sensing I was ill-prepared for her advance, she slowly thrust her breast into mine, then placed an outstretched index finger up to my cheek, rubbing it ever so lightly, before asking,

"Where has George been hiding you? I'm surprised he hasn't introduced us before this."

Unprepared for her question, I simply told her the truth.

"Actually, we met only recently."

Finally, after a long stage pause and a devilish smile growing ever so slowly across her lovely face, she proclaimed,

"Well, I'm pleased he allowed us to meet."

Cukor came back into the room a few moments later with a couple of scripts in hand to show Vivien. Suddenly, the titillation of a mock encounter with this beautiful creature was over and it was back to the business at hand. Since the topic of mixing drinks was not revived, I wound up making a Dubonnet on the rocks for each of us. The conversation then went back to a discussion of potential film projects for Vivien, leaving me alone on the sideline to listen. I was finally drawn back into the discussion of scripts, plots, roles, motivations, stupid producers, financial backing, and the like, from which it became clear that no matter how big of a fish a person was in Hollywood, if they were between pictures, they were on their own and basically in the same league as the lowest of the low. It was all akin to the newcomer who just got off the bus in downtown Los Angeles, or the middle-aged actor, writer or director who had been kicking around Hollywood for twenty or more years and still hadn't made a success of it. Those were the vagaries of the Hollywood system I was exposed to while listening to George Cukor and Vivien Leigh – two of the biggest names in Hollywood – discussing how they might get their next project going, as well. God, I thought, is this the kind of business I really want to get involved with for the rest of my life? These were two intelligent, grown, highly successful people, and in spite of that, they were still groveling around for their next paychecks. The idea of that happening with me really gave me pause for thought, and a career in films suddenly didn't sound so beguiling to me anymore. From Hollywood to reality, it was that euphoric yet enigmatic feeling about Hollywood and the insecurity it engendered that followed me all the days I chose to remain there. Was I being hard on Hollywood? Absolutely! Was I wrong in doing so? Absolutely not!

Vivien finally stood up to excuse herself. She said she needed to clean up and get dressed for dinner. Before departing, she took my hand and kissed me on the cheek, telling Cukor to make sure I stick with my writing, then adding as an amusing aside to Cukor, "Please have him write something for me – something brilliant."

And in a moment, she was gone. Cukor then explained that they were invited to a dinner that evening at some producer's home. I don't recall the name, but my impression was that they were on a schmoozing expedition to get Vivien some work. She hadn't done a picture in almost three years now and she was getting very anxious about it. While walking me to the door, Cukor went on to explain the overall problem with the Hollywood system and, not mincing words, he explained it exactly the way it was.

"Bob, the plain truth of the matter is that we are each only as good as our last picture, but if we haven't had a picture in a couple of years, then we aren't even in the same league anymore. We age and people's memories are short. Then you go in for an interview and it's like starting your career all over again from scratch. Not a very good prospect for some."

Back in my car and on the way home, Cukor's final remark gave me even more pause for concern. Was this rat race really where I wanted to spend the rest of my life? What would my dad say if he knew about this? Would he approve? For certain, he would not. It was the first crack in the facade I had created to make something of myself in Hollywood, and I didn't like what I was thinking.

Later that evening I was surprised by a call from Cukor. He explained that they had just returned from their dinner party and that Vivien seemed in a peculiar mood all evening. Worst of all, he quipped, "She seemed intent on leaving all her promotional activity to me, which was fine, but in the car on the way to and from, all she could do was to speak about you and how nice it was to meet someone fresh and new to the business."

I feigned being surprised, but I really wasn't; my ego and that insatiable libido of mine told me otherwise.

"She kept telling me how impressed she was with you. Frankly, Bob, I believe she is quite smitten with you. You should know that she is not very happy with her husband, Larry Olivier. He has turned out to be a terrible womanizer, unsympathetic and terribly unresponsive to her needs, so she may be in search for some outside comfort of her own. I feel she is very vulnerable to negative influences at this point in her life and is prone to depression and terrible mood swings, so please be careful."

Cukor continued by telling me he did not call to tell me what to do, only to let me know what to expect. I thanked him for his advice, but I didn't really know what else to say about it. Finally, it was Cukor who changed the subject.

"To get to the point of my call, Vivien needs an escort to take her to the Polo Lounge for lunch tomorrow. Vivien herself asked whether you were available, so of course you cannot say no. The Polo Lounge is her favorite place and it would be great exposure for you to be seen there with a star like her."

I thanked Cukor and agreed to pick Vivien up at noon. Although Cukor did not seem to sense there was anything more to Vivien's request than a childlike infatuation with someone new, I sensed from the start that she was interested in me for more serious reasons – but I had no idea how far that interest would go. I decided that the best thing for me to do at this stage of the game was to just play that tune by ear and let the notes fall where they may.

Arriving at a world-famous venue like the Beverly Hills Hotel with a world-renowned movie star on my arm was, admittedly, a new experience for me. But much to Vivien's credit, she simply thrust her arm into my crooked elbow and marched us up to the lobby like the two of us owned the place. Arriving at the front desk with all the style, self-assurance and aplomb of visiting royalty, we were welcomed by the general manager himself, who with the click of the finger assigned one of his uniformed assistants to escort us out through the hotel labyrinth to the Polo Lounge, where we were again greeted like royalty, escorted in before other guests less notable than us and marched directly to our table. The entire trip from our arrival at the hotel to our being seated was accompanied by spirited applause from those who witnessed it. Once seated, Vivien settled down in her chair like the pro she was, and with an expression of inner satisfaction developing slowly across her lovely face, tapped me on the forearm and whispered nonchalantly in my ear,

"That's the way it's done, Bobby. If you act the part and give them a little show, you can get away with almost anything."

We laughed quietly to ourselves, then got on with the pleasure of ordering our lunch.

Vivien explained that whenever she comes to a place like the Polo Lounge, she must make certain she is seen. The public expects it of her and she must comply – that being the cost of her celebrity. Her favorite table at the Polo Lounge was the one situated roughly in the center of the patio section, where more eyes were afforded the privilege of viewing her than most anywhere else in the place.

"To give them anything less would be an affront to their sensibilities. What price Hollywood, Bobby, but that's the way it has to be played."

To say that our luncheon was anything less than delightful

would be the understatement of the decade, but then, how else can one describe a pleasant culinary repast with a lovely woman who also happens to be one of the most recognizable celebrities in the world? One really can't. One can only go along with it and enjoy the experience as best as one is able. One of the most interesting aspects of our luncheon, however, was to experience, firsthand, what a true celebrity like Vivien has to go through to maintain her status as a great movie star. More specifically, it is the necessity – imagined or not – to satisfy the cravings of her fans to witness every movement and nuance of expression she can muster as she goes through the ordeal of living her life in the public eye. It was clear she felt compelled to act like the great movie star she was and to maintain that act throughout the entire time we were sitting there. Every movement of the head, the eyes and the hands was measured and calculated, all performed exactly as she would have done it had she been on a movie set and in front of a camera. In reality, of course, the whole show was for the eyes in that room that were lucky enough to be there to witness and view her performance.

I remember one particular little scene she thought up that was so beautifully executed I felt it worthy of another Academy Award nomination. The prop was one small morsel of food she had deftly cut from a larger portion. Next, she slathered it with a little sauce and then slowly raised it to her lips before holding it there motionless for several seconds, all the while describing something we had been speaking about. She kept the pose for all those inquiring eyes to savor, then glancing around the room as though seeking approval she plopped that morsel into her pretty mouth and, finally, swallowed it. It was a moment worthy of applause, but there was none to be heard. Finally giving in to reality, Vivien smiled and merely gave a little shrug as if to say, "Oh, well."

In the end, it was obvious that Vivien loved her little act just as much as all those who had witnessed it. It was a winning situation, all around, and I enjoyed playing my small part in it. The mood of the moment was broken only when Vivien finally put her hand out for mine and proclaimed stoically, "Oh, Bobby, you mustn't take me too seriously. It's all just part of this horrid game we must play, but you're an angel for putting up with it."

For the most part, our luncheon conversation was predictable but unremarkable. We spoke mainly of the parts that Cukor had advised her to pursue and those that he felt were beneath her. Not that she was in a position to refuse even the most miniscule role that might have been offered her – the only redemption being the thought of what she might do with it. That was the best and the worst of it.

"It is a terrible rat race we all must engage in. I often wonder why I keep at it. It is horrible and degrading and I hate it."

At one point I detected a very noticeable change in Vivien's demeanor and I wondered whether this could be one of those mood swings Cukor had cautioned me about. But then she would look away, change the subject or just grab my hand for support, and that seemed to comfort her.

It wasn't until we were back in the car and on our way down Sunset Boulevard to Doheny Drive that she finally broached the subject I knew would inevitably arise.

"Bobby?"

"Yes, Vivien."

She took a long pause before answering.

"George said he wouldn't be back until six. We have the entire afternoon…"

Vivien then looked up at me seductively, placed her hand on my thigh and finally murmured the invitation I expected all along.

"I need you to make love to me."

I put my arm around her shoulders and pulled her closer to me, then kissed her gently on the cheek before answering.

"Vivien, you are the most desirable woman any man could ever want. I will do everything you wish to satisfy you."

Thus, what began as a pleasant luncheon at the Polo Lounge turned out to be an even more pleasant afternoon, spending the entire time in bed together with no one to please but ourselves.

In retrospect I found Vivien to be the most kind and considerate bedmate, doing everything in her power to make my experience as pleasurable as that which I hoped I could bestow upon her. In a way, we were almost like two teenagers going at it for the first time. We checked out each other's bodies, gazing and groping and feeling our way through each moment, and apparently it worked for the both of us, as she seemed perfectly satisfied with the results.

A quick shower and we were back in bed for more of the same and it was only after the second time that I detected a definite change in Vivien's demeanor. As I expected, it all had to do with her failed marriage and how evil she felt her husband had been to her. As she described it, she had fallen in love with Olivier from the first moment she met him – her fault, not his, she exclaimed – and she had been saddled with that obsession ever since.

"What can one do," she asked, "when one makes a grievous error with one's marriage? You have to live with it – and that is what I have had to do with mine."

She then described the horrors of discovering her husband's physical shortcomings for the first time.

"Not only is he a premature ejaculator, but he is possessed with a tiny appendage that can barely hit the mark, and to make matters worse, he doesn't even realize it and considers himself some sort of a catch. You know the kind, Bobby, a sexual machine that every woman in the world is supposed to salivate over."

She finally explained that she still loved Olivier passionately, in spite of all her misgivings, but had not found a way to get him out of her mind. When Vivien finished, I was exhausted from all her anguish. God, I thought, how sad that this beautiful, vibrant woman is married to such a dolt. At least I could assure myself with the knowledge that I was a good lay and was not a premature ejaculator nor possessed of a tiny wiener, and that I was able to satisfy all the expectations her husband was incapable of fulfilling for her.

By the time we cleaned up and dressed, it was six thirty, and as was the style and procedure of the house, it was time for a libation. A couple of Dubonnets on the rocks kept us in our cups until our host arrived just a few moments later. Upon entering, Cukor came right into the library to give Vivien a kiss and then thanked me for taking care of her all afternoon. From his demeanor, it was clear he had no idea how we actually spent our time, and he didn't ask. It was our little secret and that was the way we left it.

As was his habit, Cukor picked up his messages from the end table and then went directly to his dressing room to clean up, emerging a few moments later in his lounging clothes – a loose-fitting pajama-like outfit with slippers. He explained the day had been very tiring for him and that he just needed to relax. Going through his messages for anything of interest, he informed Vivien that they had been invited for a luncheon meeting at MGM the following day with the writer and director of a film he had mentioned to her earlier, but that otherwise nothing else had come to mind. Another Dubonnet, more small talk and a quiet dinner followed. However, by the time our dessert had been consumed, it was clear that all of us were tired and eager to call it a day. Vivien was the first to make her departure, kissing both Cukor and me on the cheek before thanking us and retiring to her room. Then, as Cukor walked me to the door, he thanked me once again and simply wished me a good night. Suddenly, I felt like a lonely, abandoned puppy dog, but it was only when I arrived home, alone by myself, that I felt sort of jilted. I expected at least a little private moment alone with Vivien to give her a proper goodbye and to thank her for a most memorable afternoon. I longed for something more – but it was not to be.

Later that week, however, I did receive a surprise call from Vivien, and that made up for all my anguish. She said she was at the airport about to board a flight back to London and just wanted to call and say goodbye. I told her how thrilled I was – not only for the call but to have met her in the first place, and then the Polo Lounge and the rest of the afternoon that we spent together. She responded with the hope that she had not been too brazen with me, reiterating the fact that she really needed me, was thrilled to have had me and was even more thrilled to know I wanted her.

"At times one needs assurances. It's more than the mere physical thing — it's the proof that one is still desirable."

Vivien rattled on in short bursts of random thought. I didn't question her about it, deciding it was just better for me to let her continue on with it until she had talked herself out. Finally, she snapped out of it by herself and got back to the reality of things.

"I don't know when I might be back in Hollywood again, Bobby, but I would be pleased if you would allow me to call you."

I told her I would be thrilled, then she threw me a kiss, whispered a fond "goodbye" in my ear and hung up.

That evening, just before going to bed, Cukor finally called. He told me Vivien had left for London that morning and asked him to tell me goodbye. It was all very short and perfunctory. I didn't tell him that Vivien had already called me. I don't know why I didn't mention it — perhaps I just wanted to hear whether he might have detected something about our liaison — but he didn't. He did, however, say that Vivien had asked him whether I had an agent and when he told her I didn't, she asked him why not, suggesting that he might arrange to get one for me.

"So my reason for calling is to ask you whether you would like me to arrange this for you. I'm sorry I neglected to mention it earlier, but I believe there are many agents out there who would be pleased to handle a new untested talent like you. More important, however, I think you need someone special — someone who will give you the extra time needed to connect you with the right people."

My answer, naturally, was an emphatic,

"Yes, please do."

Cukor then suggested that he knew exactly the right person who could exploit whatever talent I had in me and get me going in the right direction.

"His name is John Darrow and I will have Irene call him in the morning."

I thanked Cukor for his help and he hung up.

Naturally, I was thrilled. All I could think about was Vivien and now, a second thrill, the prospect of getting my first real agent — and all in one fell swoop. Again, I thought to myself,

"How lucky could I have ever been?"

Irene Burns called a day or two later to inform me that Cukor had set up an appointment for me to meet John Darrow a few days later and that he requested I bring some of my writings along for his evaluation. Just the idea of preparing for this meeting took my mind off of Vivien, sex and everything else of importance in my life – and that was probably the best thing I could have had happen for me at the time.

CHAPTER 14:

John Darrow

John Darrow's office was located in a modern, upscale, single-story building in Beverly Hills, on little Santa Monica Boulevard and a mere stone's throw from the Beverly Hilton Hotel. The building had class, a fact further emphasized by its interior, which was furnished with a select mélange of fine art and elegant, color-coordinated furnishings. It was clear to me that whoever designed this place must have had class, and in a moment I found out I was right.

John Darrow had made a name for himself not only behind the scenes as one of the most successful talent agents in Hollywood, but as a leading man during the late '20s and early '30s when he was in his prime. Like other leading men who found their images waning as they approached middle age, Darrow settled on the personal talent agency business as his redemption. He was a good speaker, and a great listener, and he had an eye for talent like few people before him or since.

Darrow had known Cukor since 1929, when Cukor first came to Hollywood. At the time, Darrow was a handsome, young leading man in "B" movies, but his most telling achievement was to be chosen to play the youngest of the three star-crossed brothers in Howard Hughes' epic 1930 production of *Hell's Angels* – at the time the most expensive motion picture ever made. Now, almost a quarter century later, when this icon of early Hollywood opened the door of his office to welcome me, it was easy to see how he had made it in Hollywood and, as the saying goes, "made it big."

The gentleman standing before me was a handsome, stylishly dressed, gray-haired, middle-aged gentleman with the most distinctively craggy, tanned face I had ever seen. Obviously this guy was addicted to the sun, but he also possessed a most unique wit and personality, which he quickly displayed to me by simply introducing himself with a cheerful welcome.

"Hi, I'm Cukor's friend."

The line was delivered in a distinctive, slow, deep-throated, theatrical baritone – but I soon learned he also possessed the same kind of roguish humor that Cukor had developed – and he loved to display it. A few quips about this and that and we finally got down to business.

"So, Cukor tells me you are a writer – and a good one."

I then handed Darrow the few scripts and story outlines I had culled out for the occasion. Picking the papers up with what I interpreted as an obvious display of anticipation, he leafed through them slowly, feigning some interest, but clearly not paying enough attention to any single page to glean anything out of it. Then, after a few moments, he put them down and came out with a zinger I clearly did not expect.

"So what are you going to do with yourself while you're waiting for this stuff to be discovered? It could take years, you know, even longer. You could be an old fart before any of your work is published."

Then, leaning back in his chair, he looked me directly in the eye.

"You're a good-lookin' guy. You're still young enough to make a name for yourself in this town – and I mean in front of the cameras, not behind them. Have you ever acted?"

I told him, yes, a little, and then recited my meager résumé.

"That's OK; it's nothing to be ashamed of. We all have to start somewhere."

He then asked where I was born and went to school. I responded with, "Elizabeth, New Jersey, and Rutgers University, in New Brunswick."

Suddenly his face burst out into a broad smile.

"I knew it – I could tell by your accent. You're a Jersey jock."

Then he stood up, thrusting his hands into the air, and welcomed me into his fold.

"Well, kid, you're in good hands, because I'm from New Jersey, too."

I was quickly informed that Darrow was born in Leonia, just across the Washington Bridge from upper Manhattan and a twenty-minute drive from my birthplace in Elizabeth. Both of us started out at a summer stock company – Darrow after high school and me while still in college – and we had similar interests in art, real estate and design. By the time the interview was over, it was clear we had formed a bond and I knew I had made a new friend.

I found Darrow to be a fast-talking, sweet-tongued rascal of a guy with a great sense of humor – the kind of person you couldn't dislike – so we got along famously. He made short shrift of our joint New Jersey accents by mentioning offhand that he had to get rid of his when he first came to town, then suggesting that I had better get rid of mine, as well.

"It's distinctive but not desirable, not to mention it's not very euphonious."

I agreed to do so and he agreed to take me on as a client, and the rest, as they say, is history.

The following morning I had a call directly from Cukor, who confirmed Darrow's decision to take me on. He also mentioned Darrow's suggestion about seeing a vocal coach and getting me some acting jobs, volunteering that I could learn much about the business firsthand by simply getting involved in other facets of it.

"Darrow says he can get some bit parts for you right away and asked if I could recommend a good voice coach for you. I told him I could and I did, and if you have a pencil, you can take this down. She works at MGM and this is her number. I suggest you call her right away and make an appointment. She will call me directly with her evaluation. Darrow also suggested you get some professional photos taken, so I have arranged for that, as well. It can all be done quickly and efficiently along with your voice lessons, so please just keep me advised as to how this is all going for you."

Cukor's call was direct and quite perfunctory and I thanked him for his continued help, but he merely dismissed it with a cheerful,

"Well, if you're ever going to take over my job, I'd better make sure you are ready for it. Good luck, Bob, I'm pleased Darrow likes you. I know you will get along just fine."

Over the next several weeks, I dutifully had my photos taken, took my requisite voice lessons, rid myself of my undesirable "Joisey" accent and, in the process, satisfied both Darrow and Cukor that I was ready for anything that came along. In between these assignments, I knocked out a few more treatments, and without wasting any time decided to send them off to some new literary agents for evaluation.

Meanwhile, I received a call from George Huene asking whether I had time to help him install a fountain he had designed for Cukor's house. As he explained it, Cukor had a trip planned where he would be out of town for a couple of weeks. As such, he figured it would be a perfect time for him to build the fountain and have it operational by the time Cukor returned. He suggested I could do all the plumbing and electrical work at my leisure and help him with the masonry, as necessary. In my mind, if I were to accept the job it would be the perfect manner in which I could repay Cukor for all the help he had given me, so I accepted the job without hesitation.

Huene had received a small marble statue of an Aphrodite from his friend in Athens and picked up a perfect iridescent killer-clam shell from a small antique shop nearby. As he explained it, the design would appear much like the scene in the well-known Botticelli painting, adding stoically that it might be a little trite in some people's minds, but workable, and Cukor would love it.

Thus, on the day Cukor departed, Huene had all the masonry delivered for the pedestal and within the week we had the shell and Aphrodite installed. I did all the plumbing, then installed the water pump and ran the electric line for the accent lights overhead. Within ten days the project was done and when we turned the system on, it worked perfectly. Huene was ecstatic and thanked me for my help. When Cukor was scheduled to return, Huene asked Myrtle to turn the system on in order to surprise him with the view of the completed installation the moment he came in through the front door. It worked and, according to Myrtle, Cukor was totally overwhelmed.

Huene and I both received heartfelt thank-you calls from Cukor the following morning and, as I told Huene afterwards, it was the first time since meeting Cukor that I detected a real sense of humble pie in his voice. Huene agreed, adding,

"He really appreciates what we've done for him, Bob. Few people would have done as much, and he knows it."

Unfortunately, a drama of sorts unfolded at Cukor's house a week or two later when, on an otherwise uneventful Sunday afternoon, a sudden wind whipped up and proceeded to blow the spray from our newly installed fountain all over the entrance hall windows. It was a situation no one could have anticipated, since no high-wind condition occurred during the installation. Nevertheless, it required instant rectification in Cukor's mind, thus initiating his calling Huene and, when Huene could not be reached, in calling me. It was apparent from the tone in his voice that he required an immediate fix and that I was the only one who could provide it. As it turned out, I was working on some project at my own house and was dressed in my usual workaday uniform, a sweaty T-shirt and dirty Levi's, but when I explained this to Cukor, he simply dismissed my concern.

"That's exactly the way I need you."

He then explained that he was having people in that afternoon and needed to have the problem fixed immediately. There was no arguing with the great director, so I told him I would be right over. Imagine my surprise, however, upon arriving at his house to find the party underway with a dozen or more rowdy revelers gathered around the pool. I noticed that these were all men, and worse, they were all looking directly at me and obviously wondering who this dirty, sloppy guy was. Clearly, I did not fit in with this crowd, but it was only then that it occurred to me that I must have stumbled into one of Cukor's famous Sunday afternoon get-togethers. I didn't see Cukor right away, so I excused myself and hurried back behind the pool house to the stairway leading up to the fountain. When I arrived on scene, there was Cukor with one of his guests, both with towels in hand, trying to clean up the mess. I determined that the narrow alleyway behind the house where the fountain was located acted like a wind tunnel. Thus, with the wind being funneled in through this restricted area, it became strong enough to direct the spray from the nozzle up onto the windows. I told Cukor I would finish cleaning up the mess, replenish the system and adjust the nozzle to reduce the flow. He thanked me for coming and returned to his guests, but ten minutes later he reappeared with an untypical sheepish look on his face.

"Bob, some of my guests have expressed the desire to have you join them after you finish here. I hope you don't mind, most are just old friends and the rest are really harmless. I think they would just like to see what the wind brought in. No pun intended, but if you'd like to clean up after you're through here, I'll have a fresh shirt laid out for you in the library restroom."

I agreed, thanking Cukor for the invitation and continued on with my work. Unfortunately, I didn't have any tools with me, so I was forced to improvise a fix by placing a small pebble under the nozzle orifice to restrict the flow. It worked, reducing the spray from the nozzle by at least fifty percent. I concluded that this would suffice until Huene got back to engineer a more permanent fix, then buttoned the place up, turned on the accent lights and went in to get cleaned up.

The party, which was in full swing by the time I arrived, had grown to around twenty or more, with a half dozen or so seated around a cocktail table just outside an open dining pavilion on the right with the rest scattered in small groups around the pool. As I approached, I noticed several heads turning and glancing in my direction, but I didn't allow that to deter me. I focused my attention on finding Cukor, whom I spotted almost immediately while he was in the process of setting up the dinner table inside the pavilion with a cadre of eager helpers.

As I soon learned, these Sunday afternoon get-togethers were highly organized affairs. They were joint efforts with a half dozen or more of the invited guests acting as kitchen helpers to bring the food that had been previously prepared in the main house down to the pool area, where it was set up buffet style along a side table in the pavilion. The general mood among the guests seemed to be jovial and highly animated, but nothing, I thought, that seemed to be out of the ordinary or unusual in any way. After a moment, Cukor spotted me and it was he who spoke first.

"Oh, there you are, Bob, come with me. I'd like to introduce you to some of my guests."

Cukor wiped his hands, giving quick instructions to one of his underlings, then grasped me by the elbow and marched me over a few short steps to a small group seated around the cocktail table. I noted immediately that these were the older boys – maybe fifty years of age or more – and all those standing around in smaller groups appeared to be younger. Since the cocktail table acted as the impromptu center of activity for the moment, it gave Cukor the perfect podium from which to make a general announcement, but imagine my surprise when he reprised the same old sawhorse he had invented about me so many months before.

"Gentlemen, this is Bob Darin. I want you to take a close look at him because he is the man who wants to take my job. Yes, he does – seriously. He's a writer and a good one and he wants to direct my next film."

Well, you could have heard a pin drop for a few moments. Nobody knew what to say, least of all me. Finally, there were a couple of snickers from the crowd, a few muted laughs and then a voice from across the pool to break the silence.

"George, are we supposed to drink to that?"

The laughs that followed were spontaneous, then punctuated by raucous applause, a little more laughter and finally an exuberant din. After that, the introductions all went quickly and to the point.

The first gentleman was introduced to me as Frank Horn, a neighbor from across Doheny. All he did was shake his hand at me without a "Hi," "Hello" or other vocal utterance to break his mood. What a pompous old fuck, I thought, and I immediately took a disdainful dislike to him. I learned later that he was Cary Grant's personal manager, an occupation, I thought, that clearly could not bode well for either of them. Seated across from Horn was a younger and much more animated gentleman by the name of Grady Sutton, who stood up and gave me a cheerful "Welcome to Hollywood" salutation along with a hearty handshake. A little theatrical, I thought, but what the hell, this is Hollywood. Next in line came an older gentleman who was clearly the elder statesman of the group, one Louis Mason, who did not stand up or murmur a word but he did give me a friendly wave. In passing, Cukor mentioned that both Mason and Sutton were actors and were among his oldest acquaintances in Hollywood, punctuating his assessment of the two with a discreet warning,

"But look out for old Lou, Bob. He has the most evil, vitriolic tongue in existence."

It was about at this point that Cukor was diverted to other tasks, sending one of his assistants over to help with the rest of the introductions. I was also finally offered a drink, which, by this time, really came in handy. A little alcohol can always grease the task of meeting many new people during a short period of time, and the instant occasion was no exception. By the time we were through, I wondered to myself whether this was really one of Cukor's famous Sunday afternoon bacchanals everyone spoke about. All the guests were well dressed, cleanly shaven and nicely groomed. No beards, tattoos, T-shirts or the like. Although I assumed that most of them must have been gay, none were feminine, swishy or limp wristed as most straight people in our country at the time pictured all homosexuals to be like. There was no kissing, no hand-holding, no groping and no other displays of physical attraction, no nudity in the pool and no sexual encounters behind the pool house. I became involved in friendly conversations with several of them and generally found nothing unusual, untoward or unsavory to make note of. Overall, it was just like every other party I had attended in Hollywood to that time, the only exception being that there were no women present at this one. These were simply men who for the most part were young, attractive and masculine – the kind that no one on the outside could readily identify as being anything other than normal, red-blooded, American males.

I found all activities at the event to be aboveboard and without any negative vibes. The buffet dinner was served from the pavilion at dusk. Seating was open, with most of the guests choosing to gather at the large dining table inside the pavilion, an arrangement that allowed the participants to continue their conversations, communal style, for all to hear and participate in. The patter was generally upbeat, with comments and anecdotes thrown in at random. There were no after-dinner activities that I was aware of, and it appeared that all of the guests departed soon after all the food and drink had been consumed.

Over the next several years I attended many more of Cukor's Sunday afternoon get-togethers, and I found all of them to be much the same as the first one. All were strictly social affairs with no sexual nuance, undertone or connotation whatsoever, which is a hell of a lot more than I can say for some of the so-called "straight" Hollywood parties I had attended to that time. Naturally, I had to assume that Cukor told all of his guests to restrain themselves whenever I was asked to attend, but even with that thought in mind, I cannot conceive how any of these parties could have possibly segued into anything other than a more raucous gathering with, perhaps, some openly "slanted" remarks that my virgin ears were not used to hearing.

So where were the bacchanals, Cukor's "infamous" Sunday afternoon sexual soirees so many writers had written about? It was obvious from my observation that none of the parties I had attended could have been one of them – which begs the question in my mind as to whether any such bacchanals ever really existed. According to Scotty Bowers, in his book *Full Service* he states that Cukor's pool parties were legendary, meaning that "anyone who was anyone" was there, but he doesn't suggest that any of the parties were a sexual soiree, and in my mind Scotty would be the first person in Hollywood to know. Considering Cukor's celebrity, his stature in Hollywood and his inherent natural penchant for privacy, I would consider that any dubious liaisons he might have had over the years would have been conducted in utmost secrecy and seclusion and not under the glare of innumerable Sunday afternoon party guests who invariably possessed wagging tongues. To me, the whole idea of a scandalous sexual soiree at Cukor's house represents nothing more than a sad commentary on the motives of the many Hollywood writers who have utilized the tactic for no better reason than to enhance their own celebrity by employing it.

Such is the price of being a celebrity in Hollywood, and it seems that the truth has little to do with it.

CHAPTER 15:

The Death of James Dean

It was sometime during this period that I received a call from an agent named Dick Clayton, who was affiliated with Famous Artists, one of the largest talent agencies in the business. This was one of the agencies I had favored with some of my writings. I had met Clayton sometime earlier and although he was new at the agency business, he had already brought in the hottest new talent in town, James Dean, to Famous Artists' roster. Now on the phone with me, Clayton explained that he had been given some of my treatments to read and felt confident that he could place one of them overseas, suggesting we might have a meeting to discuss it. I agreed and we made a date to have lunch at the Brown Derby later in the week.

In the meanwhile, I called John Darrow, my primary agent, to advise him of my conversation with Clayton. Darrow said he knew Clayton well, that Clayton was an excellent agent and that if he felt he could do something with my writings, then he (Darrow) would not stand in the way.

"You couldn't have a better guy working for you. I know you will get along with him real well."

In the days before cell phones, certain good eateries like the Brown Derby that cater to celebrities recognized the need to have telephones available within easy reach of every customer. Thus, it was not unusual upon entering the Brown Derby to find a smattering of patrons engrossed in serious telephone conversations, with agents, producers, directors and stars being the most notable. Nevertheless, the best thing about the Brown Derby, as far as I was concerned, was that it was a great place to see and be seen, and the food was excellent. When I entered the main dining room and was directed to Clayton's table, I noticed that he was speaking with another gentleman seated in the adjoining booth, and as I approached them,

Clayton immediately introduced me to him. The gentleman was Paul Gregory, a large, rotund, middle-aged man with a robust personality who I soon learned was the producer of a serious television series at CBS called *Ford Star Jubilee*, and from his reaction upon meeting me, I could tell he was impressed with what he saw. Clayton picked up on the attraction as well, suggesting I might have Darrow check into that show for me. When it came to my writings, Clayton mentioned that he thought very highly of one particular treatment, adding that even though it was only in synopsis form, he couldn't put it down until he finished it.

"It was riveting, Bob – always a good sign. I think you have a real talent there."

The story he was referring to was one I simply named *The Damned*. It was basically the same age-old tale of a young boy saving his village from an impending disaster. We all remember the one about the little Dutch boy who plugged the hole in the dike with his finger, but my story was done with a new twist. I fashioned the plot around the Johnstown Flood of 1889, but I left the location open and ambiguous, allowing for the story to be adapted to almost any place on earth. Clayton advised that Famous Artists had corresponding agencies throughout the world, and he felt confident that he could place it through one of them.

Halfway through our luncheon, the waiter came over and told Clayton he had a telephone call and then placed a desk set on our table for his use. The call was from James Dean, and from the one-sided conversation I was privy to hear, I was able to glean the fact that Dean was going out of town shortly to race his new car and wanted to see Clayton before he left. Dean, apparently, was at a place named Competition Motors, the local Porsche dealer, just a couple of blocks down Vine Street from the Brown Derby. In conclusion, Clayton told Dean he would take the walk down there after lunch to meet him, adding that it would be in about a half hour. After hanging up, Clayton apologized for the interruption – repeating the gist of his conversation with Dean, and then quipped,

"If you'd like, you can tag along to meet Jimmy and see his new car."

I had never met Dean before, so naturally I was interested in doing so. Little did I know that the short walk I was about to embark on would lead me to a meeting I would remember vividly and most poignantly for the rest of my life.

It was September 1955 and James Dean was the hottest young talent in town. He had completed two very successful films and was now working on his third, an epic tale of Texas oil, greed and corruption by Edna Ferber, aptly named *Giant*, which sadly would be his last. At the time of our visit, I understood Clayton to say that Dean had finished principal photography on *Giant* but was required to be available for some post-production work and, possibly, some retakes. Dean had raced other cars while under contract to Warner Brothers, but never one as fast and powerful as his new Porsche Spyder. Jack Warner, however, was made aware of Dean's plans and, fearing the worst, summarily forbade him from participating in any racing activities until his work on *Giant* was finished. Then, as the story goes, Dean disapproved of the rebuke and confronted Warner on the telephone. Apparently, harsh words were followed by threats and accusations until Warner finally called Dean a "little bastard" and hung up on him. Not to be outdone by his boss and in a bravura display of adolescent defiance and disobedience, Dean decided to use Warner's last words to him as the name for his new car. Thus he had the words *Little Bastard* emblazoned across the car's rear cowling, just below the Porsche insignia. It was an inscription he wanted the entire world to see and be aware of.

When Clayton and I arrived at Competition Motors a short while later, it was not difficult for us to locate Dean, who, with his car, was surrounded by a number of people including his personal mechanic, Rolf Wütherich, another friend taking pictures of the new car and some helpers. The moment Dean spotted Clayton, he broke off from the pack and came directly over to us. The only word I can come up with that might describe my impression of Dean when I first laid eyes on him is that he was "ecstatic." It was like he was in another world, oblivious to everything around him and totally absorbed in the fabric of what he had woven for himself. All he could speak about was the car, the upcoming race and a somewhat jumbled strategy as to how he planned to handle it.

After a brief introduction, Dean took us over to the rear of the car, where he gleefully pointed out the *Little Bastard* inscription. I asked him a number of mundane questions concerning the car's horsepower, top speed and the like and he flipped through the answers like a pro. Then he pulled a diagram out from his pocket displaying how fast the car would go in each gear. Unfortunately, it was not clear whether Dean understood the speeds above which the gear box could not be downshifted in each particular gear – a factor peculiar to each different race car and one that would soon prove to be fatal for him. Dean then gave me a firsthand glimpse at the engine and then meticulously described all the different parts and their functions. When thinking back at that moment, I concluded he must have simply thought I was another speed freak who was interested in high-powered sports cars like he was. Finally, however, Clayton told Dean he had to get back to the office, then gave Dean a hug and wished him good luck. I shook his hand and wished him good luck, as well. Dean then pumped his fist into the air in a gutsy display of his machismo, turned on his heels and was gone.

As Clayton and I were walking back up Vine Street to collect our own vehicles, the only thing Clayton spoke about to indicate any concern was Dean's broken relationship with Jack Warner, but he did not mention the race or any possible danger that Dean might be placing himself in.

The race Dean had entered was to be held at Salinas, in central California, a good six-hour drive from Los Angeles. Since the car was brand new and had not yet been broken in, Dean's mechanic, Rolf Wütherich – who was trained at the Porsche factory in Stuttgart – suggested that instead of trucking it up on a trailer, they should drive it up themselves to make certain it was properly broken in, adding that it would also give Dean some badly needed time behind the wheel to more properly prepare him for the race. Dean concurred, thus casting the die for the fateful trip to Salinas to take place the following day, Friday, September 30, 1955, with the races scheduled to begin early the following morning.

It wasn't until around eight o'clock on Saturday morning, while washing my car, that I first heard about Dean's death. It had occurred the previous evening in an accident near Cholame, a small village about thirty miles east of Paso Robles and roughly halfway along the planned route to Salinas. I had just heard the report on my car radio, then ran back into the house to call Clayton. When he answered the phone with a cheerful "Hello," I realized instantly that he could not have heard the dreadful news as yet. I was surprised, then shocked, but all I could think of saying was,

"Dick, have you heard the news?" His response, again, was a cheerful,

"No, what news?"

"It's Jimmy, he's dead. He was killed in a car accident last evening."

For a moment there was only silence, followed by the most god-forsaken, soulful wail I had ever heard, then a whimper and a cry – a long weeping cry – and finally, silence once again. I hung up, and then realized I was weeping as well. Dick Clayton had lost his best friend and most important new client. He now had his own demons to slay and it was not for me to interfere.

On Sunday, October 2, 1955, the newspapers in Los Angeles were filled with front-page stories about the accident and all the gory details about James Dean's death. It was reported as having been a high-speed collision with another vehicle that tore the little Porsche to shreds, rendering Dean with a broken neck, massive internal injuries and multiple fractures of his arms and legs. His mechanic, Rolf Wütherich, was thrown from the car by the force of the collision but survived, also with multiple injuries. When the highway patrol responded to the scene a few minutes later, Dean was still alive and moaning audibly, but when they arrived at the nearest hospital in Paso Robles, the moaning had ceased and Dean was pronounced dead by the attending physician. It was six-twenty in the evening. On the inside pages were more stories about James Dean the person, his short life and career, with anecdotes and accounts of his early life, his loves and more, all punctuated with the sad fact of his passing at so young an age and his having been so talented. The light surrounding Hollywood's brightest rising new star had been extinguished.

"Shit," I blurted out to myself, "all of this crap in the papers sounds so fucking trite and mundane – just like a cheap Hollywood thriller."

Months after his recuperation and back in Germany, Rolf Wütherich revealed the actual reason for the accident and why it could not have been prevented. Apparently Dean was hell-bent on speeding every chance he got after departing Sherman Oaks for Salinas, but he wasn't stopped and ticketed for the offense until he reached Wheeler Ridge, the first straight, flat portion of the road north of the Grapevine. Nevertheless, that ticket did not deter him from continuing the trip at a high rate of speed in what was clearly a reckless display of his youthful bravado. As reiterated by Wütherich, some ten miles before the accident site, the Spyder crested the top of a shallow hill at a speed he estimated to be in excess of 125 miles per hour, allowing Dean to pass an entire line of cars in one swipe. However, since the car was descending the hill at such a high rate of speed, there was no way the brakes could slow it sufficiently to utilize the motor itself as a speed brake. In Wütherich's words, the Spyder had become an uncontrollable missile. The collision with an oncoming car, therefore, was unavoidable and occurred at a speed he estimated to be greater than 100 miles per hour.

I didn't hear from Clayton again for several weeks until he called one day to let me know of an offer he had received for my treatment of *The Damned*. He mentioned it was from an agent in Rome who handled accounts in many third-world countries. I told him to accept the offer and thanked him for handling it for me. He didn't offer me a word about James Dean or the funeral that followed his death and I didn't ask him about it. I considered that it would be better to simply let the matter lie. It was a closed book, and as far as I can recall, he never mentioned Dean's name to me again.

Soon thereafter, Darrow called to tell me he had received a call from Paul Gregory, the producer I had met through Dick Clayton at the

Brown Derby. Gregory indicated an interest in me for an upcoming program and told Darrow he was satisfied that I was correct for the part. Darrow was obviously pleased with the offer and thanked Gregory for his choice.

And that, I might add, is how I was given my first professional job as an actor. It was a small part to be sure, but as Darrow quickly pointed out, it was in a "premier production." *Ford Star Jubilee* was produced as a series of live productions in Studio 43 at the new CBS Television City Studios on Beverly Boulevard. The part I was given was that of a military judge in the ninety-minute live studio performance of Herman Wouk's *The Caine Mutiny Court Martial*. It starred Lloyd Nolan as Captain Queeg. The job entailed a week's rehearsals, with the show airing live on November 19, 1955. As Darrow explained it, this was very fortuitous for me because it would give me great exposure in front of the camera that could lead only to bigger and better parts. Of more importance to me, however, was the primary fact that it gave me the opportunity to join A.F.T.R.A., the American Federation of Television and Radio Artists, the required union affiliation to work in radio and television throughout the country.

"This is the real thing, Bob – you'll be exposed to stuff you could never learn at summer stock, at Rutgers or, for that matter, anywhere else."

The Caine Mutiny Court Martial came off as a huge success, enabling me to open a new chapter in my young life with the addition of a live television show now stamped in my burgeoning résumé. Well, perhaps not burgeoning as yet, but at least it gave me a start. As Darrow put it to me soon afterward,

"Everything before this point is just history, Bob. Now you have to get down to some serious business."

Well, I must have done something right, because a couple of months later, I was called back to do a second live *Ford Star Jubilee* program. This one was called *The Day Lincoln Was Shot* and it starred Raymond Massey as our 16th president. My part called for me to play President Lincoln's personal attaché, a young army officer in military uniform. Again, there would be lots of on-camera time, which, in Darrow's mind, would make the whole thing worthwhile. The expectation at the studio was that *The Day Lincoln Was Shot* was to be the most eagerly anticipated dramatic program of the season, replete with one of the most compelling historic dramas of all time. Nevertheless, quite coincidentally and more important for me was the fact that an unplanned event would occur during one of our rehearsals that would change my life and career forever.

As the fates had destined for me, the rehearsal we were involved in on this particular day proved to be very long and arduous. There was a large crowd scene that Delbert Mann, our director, was not at all pleased with. He kept going over it four or five times, calling out changes as he went along. Glitches with scenery, obtuse camera angles and confusing prop changes all complicated the matter. In the meanwhile, the studio was accumulating an excess amount of heat that the air-conditioning system wasn't capable of handling. It was a problem that finally compelled the control room to call an early lunch break to clear the studio, turn off the lights and allow things to cool down.

As I learned during earlier rehearsals, many of the cast members would take their breaks outside the emergency exits on the west side of the building. We could sit and enjoy a cigarette on the cool, shady concrete steps there, or, if we needed coffee or a snack, we could run over to Kanter's Delicatessen, a popular local beanery that was situated directly across Fairfax Avenue from the studio. Then we could enjoy our break and "shoot the shit," so to speak, as young guys are generally apt to do when left to their own resources. Without any women around as distractions, we focused mainly on chicks, tricks and politics – and not necessarily in that order. The dialogue was questionable at best and grossly crude at worst. It was during this brief respite that a couple of the guys started to tell raunchy jokes and, not wishing to be outdone, I stood up and decided to tell a couple of my own, adding the necessary pantomime and gross bodily expressions for maximum effect. To my surprise, all those present cheered and applauded when I was done, so I took an overly exaggerated comic bow with all the necessary flourishes as my way of thanking my meager audience. Unnoticed by any of us during my presentation, however, was the fact that someone else had been taking the scene in from an adjoining exit just a short distance behind me. Thus, when the cheering and applause from my little group died down, I heard a slow, steady clap of the hands followed by a hearty laugh and an offhand comment destined to be burned into my memory for all time.

"Ha, Ha, Ha! That was the funniest thing I ever heard!"

Feigning comic horror, I dared not turn around to see who my mysterious fan might be until, finally, one of my guys looked up and with his eyes bugging out of his head blurted out the answer.

"Geez, it's Jack Benny."

For a moment I must have been paralyzed in my tracks, but when I turned around for a look I found the closest adjacent exit door to ours just snapping shut and no one in view. In that brief moment, the person in question had gone back into the building and was gone.

"Are you sure it was Jack Benny?"

"Yeah, it was Benny alright. They're doing his show in Studio 33, right across the hall from us."

Turning back to resume our activities, I was overwhelmed by the thought that Jack Benny, one of the most celebrated stars and entertainers of all time, would have heard my joke and enjoyed it. The question, however, as to whether it really was Jack Benny or not became moot when, approximately ten minutes later, another gentleman came out of the same door, walked over to us and cinched it with a remark for all those present to hear.

"OK, so which one of you guys was the joker? Mr. Benny said he overheard one of you out here tell a real funny story. Which one of you was it?"

There was a moment of total silence before one, then two and finally all of my buddies jointly and with slow deliberation, brought up their index fingers and pointed them directly at me.

HARD ON HOLLYWOOD

"So you're the guy." Then, gesturing for me to follow him, he added, "OK, Mr. Benny would like to see you."

It was as quick and as simple as that. A moment later I was led into Studio 33 and introduced to Mr. Jack Benny himself. He smiled, shook my hand and then got directly to the point.

"Kid, that was the best delivery I ever heard. Where did you learn to do that? It took me thirty years to develop a delivery like that."

I professed my innocence regarding the delivery, confessing only to the fact that I relished telling funny stories and racy jokes.

"No, no, it's more than that. It's the way you developed the story and delivered the punch line, then your body language – you put it all together like a pro, but it looked like you were just ad-libbing it all for the first time. It was perfect. The joke was great, too. A little risqué though – too bad I can't use it on the show."

Benny then asked what I had done so far, what my plans were for the future and, finally, whether I would be interested in working for him. When I told him yes, obviously, that I would be, he asked for my phone number, explaining that he would like to use me on his show in some way and would call me in a couple of weeks to discuss it. He concluded with a cheerful,

"Kid, I think you've got a unique talent. Let me think about it. I'd like to see if I can fit you in somewhere."

We parted company with a warm handshake, allowing me to be back in Studio 43 before the end of the break.

Alone with my thoughts for a brief moment, I was struck dumb with the realization that, perhaps, my career was finally showing some signs of taking off. Cukor, Darrow, Clayton and now Jack Benny – I was actually working in the business, and now one of the biggest names in all of show biz appeared willing to take me under his wing. Until now, I was just another new kid on the block, standing outside on the periphery of things. Suddenly, it looked like I was finally being welcomed to come inside.

The Day Lincoln Was Shot was broadcast live on February 1, 1956. As anticipated, it came off as another huge success for the *Ford Star*

Jubilee, garnishing one of the highest viewer ratings in television history to that date. But the best offshoot of the show as far as I was concerned was the fact that it afforded me another hour or more of "on camera" time, and all at a time in my career when I really needed something positive to boost my morale. It was the exposure that got me from Point A to Point B – with "B" being the *Jack Benny Program* – making the transition and taking my career from obscurity to respectability, and all by dropping a raw joke at precisely the right place and moment in time.

I was euphoric, then mulled the matter over in my brain before wondering once again,

"How lucky could I have ever been?"

CHAPTER 16:

The Jack Benny Program

The telephone call Jack Benny promised me came through a few weeks later. It was not from Benny himself but from Ralph Levy, the director of the *Jack Benny Program*, who asked whether I had an agent. I told him yes, that it was John Darrow, and I gave him the number. A couple of days later, Darrow called to tell me of a meeting that had been arranged for us with Levy for the following week. When we arrived, Levy immediately told us about how pleased Benny was with meeting me and the fact that he wanted to find some way to use me on his show. He said Benny thought I had a great talent – a flair for comedy, adding,

"And that's exactly the kind of flair we need from someone to inject new meaning into the show."

To give us some perspective on the matter, Levy explained it as follows: "The show currently has four writers – all old friends of Jack's. Most came from the Borscht Belt or directly from the vaudeville circuit in New York, and when vaudeville died in the mid 1930s, Jack felt they would have died, too, had someone not come along to rescue them. Jack had become a big success on radio by that time and just couldn't let that happen, so he decided to hire some of the writers himself. Now, several years later, they've become so dependent on each other that Jack simply can't fire them – not that he ever would. Each of the writers are good old boys and very productive at times, but after so many years of coming up with fresh new ideas every week, they simply seem to be burned out."

Levy went on to explain that, unfortunately, they can't just hire someone to oversee the writers or give them some direction, because then they would be convinced they were going to be phased out, and that is what Jack simply wouldn't allow to happen.

Darrow then asked Levy directly for exactly what Benny thought I could do for them. Levy responded by explaining that Benny had basically thrown the ball into his corner, telling him to figure out some way to integrate me into the show without stepping on anyone's toes.

"In other words, he wants me to hire you on as a regular, to be on the set every day and to learn how the show operates and then, hopefully, come up with some fresh ideas. The problem is we can't let any of the old boys know why you are really there. So if we pull this one off, it's going to have to be done very discreetly. The three of us here and Jack would be the only ones who know."

Levy then offered that they could sign me on to a nonexclusive contract for the upcoming 1956-1957 season. To justify my presence, he thought it would be best to put me on as a regular cast member, so they could assign different parts for me to play whenever needed. This would give me legitimacy on the set and the time to get the feel of the show – to give me a better idea of what it might need to improve it. I would receive credit for each part I played, but for obvious reasons would not be credited for anything else – and especially not for any contributions I made to the scripts.

I told Levy I understood the problem and would not be offended, adding,

"Now that I have a better idea of the problem, I think I might actually have a solution for you already."

"Really? Well let's hear it."

"To begin, I know that Mr. Benny imagines me to be a stand-up comic of sorts, but I'm really not. Yes, I love telling interesting stories and funny jokes and that's what I was doing when he first laid eyes on me, but my actual primary interest is in writing short stories, doing plot outlines and simple treatments – in other words, scenarios of the basic action. That leaves the dialogue, stage direction and all the rest of it to others, which, as I see it, is exactly what you need. In other words, if I came up with the primary format for a story, that would still allow your writers to do all the lines, the jokes and all the rest, which I'm guessing is what they do best anyway."

What followed was basically a long pause while Levy and Darrow digested what I just told them; finally, Levy responded first.

"Yeah, I think that's exactly the kind of thing that might work. At least it would be worth a try."

After discussing the various parameters in more detail, Levy suggested we begin with an informal interim working arrangement where we could kick ideas back and forth and then work the final details out later.

The first show of the new season wasn't scheduled until September 23, which was still many months off, so Levy suggested we contact each other by phone once a week or so just to keep the arrangement fresh in our minds and, of course, to let him know if I came up with any ideas. Before parting, I told Levy I sincerely hoped I could make this thing work for them, if for no other reason than knowing I lived up to Jack Benny's expectations of me.

When Darrow and I arrived back at his office we were both euphoric.

"Bob, you have no idea how big this can be for you. This is an incredible coup for someone who basically has no previous experience. Benny obviously picked up on something in your personality that he liked, so whatever you did that he saw in you that day, JUST KEEP DOING IT!"

Clearly, it was a "win-win" situation for everyone involved, and that is the way I decided to handle it when the time came to get into it. Then, as if I wasn't euphoric enough with that incredible contract I was just handed by the *Jack Benny Program*, I walked into another unbelievable situation only a couple of days later.

I was doing some shopping down at the Koontz Hardware Store on Santa Monica Boulevard when I was approached by a gentleman who came up to me, thrust his finger in my face and asked hurriedly whether I was an actor. Taken by surprise but totally unfazed by his unorthodox approach, I answered him with an off-the-cuff, deadpan, noncommittal reply.

"Isn't everybody an actor?"

His response, however, simply blew me away. Thrusting his finger back at me in the most aggressive manner, he came forth with an excited response I was definitely not prepared for.

"That's it! That's it! That's exactly what we need. We're casting an episode down at ZIV tomorrow morning at eight and there's a part in it I think you'd be perfect for. If you're interested, I'll see that you get the job."

Needless to say, I showed up at ZIV at eight the following morning, the same gentleman pointed me out to the director, and the job was mine. The show was called *Frontier* – a popular new western series – and the episode was entitled "The Return of Jubal Dolan," and again, the part offered me the chance for a lot more camera time. When I called to tell Darrow about it, he quipped that I didn't even need him to get jobs anymore since I seemed capable of getting all the work I needed on my own.

"Bob, do you realize how difficult it is for most people who come to this town to get a job? Have you ever seriously thought about that?"

Shrugging my shoulders, I had to admit I had not.

"Well, maybe you should. You come along from out of the blue, you have no experience and by your own admission you don't even want to be an actor, yet you get all the jobs you can handle. It's not even fair to all the other guys out there who would give their eyeteeth for those jobs. Have you ever thought of it that way?"

Darrow went on and on and I listened to him, dutifully, as he expected I would. He had become great at lecturing me about how lucky I was in Hollywood, and all of it having come in such a short time – but this time he seemed hell-bent on going the extra mile. Naturally, it was all done with good intentions, and I enjoyed allowing him to go on with his rant as long as he wanted. After all, Darrow had become a father figure to me by this time and a major mentor to boot. He really had my best interests at heart, so a little lecture now and then was to be expected. In the end, however, I had to admit he was certainly right. Apparently I was somewhat of an anomaly in town, with more luck than any Hollywood hopeful could ever expect. My only prayer now was that my luck would hold out until some measure of higher achievement could be realized or

– God forbid – my luck would falter or my interest in the movie business waned.

The job offer at ZIV was the first of many westerns I would do over the next several years; it was also to be done on film for which I was required to join the Screen Actors Guild in order to accept it. It was a coup for me – another milestone in my career that was accomplished without any overt effort or action of my own – and I was jubilant because of it.

The *Jack Benny Program* came next. I should mention that when starting out on this project, I really knew very little about Benny other than the public persona he had generated for himself. Not surprisingly, I had seen only a few of the Jack Benny shows that were broadcast during my college years, so I was less than casually acquainted with what I would now be expected to improve upon. What I needed, I concluded, was an instant upgrade.

First and foremost in my memory of Jack Benny was the fact that he was supposed to be so cheap – a real skinflint! It was a self-deprecating gag he had invented back in vaudeville and it worked very well for him. Second was Benny's stated age of thirty-nine and the fact that he had fancied himself as being thirty-nine for the better part of his professional career. It was a great comic bit and one he had used both scripted and ad lib as often as he felt he could get away with it. The next thing I remembered about Benny was the relationship he maintained with his valet and butler, Eddie "Rochester" Anderson – a gravel-throated African-American sidekick and straight man who added much of the humor to many of their comic routines that might otherwise have fizzled had they been done with anyone else. Finally, there was Benny's old car, the Maxwell – the presumption being that Benny was too cheap to buy a new one. As far as I knew, the Maxwell was never seen. It was only mentioned, so it became the butt of many jokes and comic situations that would have waned or flopped had they concerned a vehicle of lesser antiquity.

My only concern at this point was whether any of my proposed scenarios had ever been done before, but if so, I knew that Levy, the show's director, would be the most logical person to know. Thus, I decided to call Levy and give him an idea of what I had come up with to that date. I had all my stories laid out in my head like peas in a pod, so I explained what I had for him and commenced to rattle them off one after the other until he told me to stop.

The first one had to do with Benny checking in at the airport for a flight to Hawaii, being seated next to a very beautiful woman who turns out to be a pickpocket. You can only imagine the number of possible endings to this story after she picks Benny's pocket and finds he has only two dollars in his wallet.

The second scenario had Benny waking up in the middle of the night to sounds of burglars rummaging through the house downstairs, then his attempt at waking his valet, Rochester, and trying to persuade him to go downstairs to have a look. I suggested that the possibilities for some raucous humor between Rochester and Benny in this scenario would be endless.

Levy agreed and then asked me to go on, thus allowing me to rattle off some more ideas. Somewhere along the line I offered a suggestion that had to do with Benny's old Maxwell car, which as far as I knew had never been fully exploited or used in a plot line. As I remembered it, the Maxwell was an old clunker from the early 1900s that barely ran, the premise being that Benny didn't want to get rid of it because he thought he could still get a few more miles out of it. My idea was to have someone steal the car and then have Benny go down to the Beverly Hills Police Station to file the report. I told Levy this scenario created all sorts of comic possibilities concerning the elaborate décor that might exist at the Beverly Hills Police Station, along with some unorthodox operational procedures the Beverly Hills Police Department personnel might use. Levy couldn't recall any previous show based solely on the Maxwell or the Beverly Hills Police Department, so he concluded that this scenario might have the best chance of gaining Benny's approval.

It wasn't until a month or so later that I finally received a call related to the *Jack Benny Program*, but it didn't come from Levy.

It came in to Darrow's office as a regular casting call from CBS through normal channels. It was for a minor role in an upcoming episode that I presumed was the beginning of the overall plan to get me on the set as soon as possible.

Benny was one of those incredibly talented comedians who thrived on the personal interaction that could be achieved only with a live audience. Since much of his opening routine consisted of a monologue aimed directly at that audience, he was convinced that their feedback was a necessary adjunct to get the best possible response out of him. Because of the immense popularity of live shows such as the *Jack Benny Program* at that time, CBS actually built a large studio theatre into their new Television City complex for that purpose. Studio 33, where the Benny show was broadcast, was among the largest of these, seating more than 300 people in plush Radio City Music Hall-like comfort.

During the 1956-1957 season, the *Jack Benny Program* was broadcast every other Sunday evening from September through the following April. The season consisted of sixteen shows, with most of them broadcast live from Studio 33. The usual procedure for live shows was to have a story conference scheduled for the next show as soon after the current show as possible, and this usually occurred on the Monday or Tuesday following each broadcast.

The first show I was cast in was to be broadcast on October 7, 1956, in front of a live studio audience. It was called the "George Burns/Spike Jones Show" and my part was that of an usher at Carnegie Hall, where Jack Benny was to be the featured artist. The script called for me to knock on Mr. Benny's dressing room door, then enter to announce,

"Mr. Benny, Mr. Martindale is here to see you."

It was a one-liner and I was off in a second, but as Darrow put it later,

"It's a start, so don't bitch about it."

And I didn't. Once on the set, I found the general atmosphere between all the cast and crew members to be friendly and very helpful to me. I guessed this was simply because I was the newcomer on the set, and that was comforting to me. Of course, neither Levy nor Benny would speak to me directly, because that was part of our deal. Nevertheless, only a week or two later, my first actual interaction with Benny launched me on a trial by fire I could have never expected. As I recall, I had a small part in the particular show we were doing that week. All had gone well through the rehearsal stage and we were now on set for the actual broadcast. It was twenty or so minutes before airtime and the audience was beginning to file into the theatre, when suddenly the assistant director came rushing onstage to tell Benny that Don Wilson, the show's regular announcer, was home sick in bed and would not be in. Benny, who was engaged in a conversation with others only a few steps from where I stood, reacted instantly.

"Oh, well that's not good..."

For a moment, it was obvious that he was thinking about what to do. Then, looking around the room briefly and contemplating the situation for another long moment, he looked over at me and pointed his finger directly in my face.

"You! You've got a good strong voice, you can do it. You'll have to announce the show."

It was now less than fifteen minutes to airtime and I had no idea what I was supposed to do. Basically, I was frozen in my tracks, but a moment later the assistant director grabbed me by the arm and whisked me backstage for a quick costume change, then handed me a piece of paper.

"Here, these are your lines. I'll give you your mark on stage. All you have to do is stand there and wait for the red lights to come on and then speak your lines. But make sure you have a broad smile on your face and be as upbeat as possible, OK? As soon as you finish your lines, we cue music and go to commercial. Just don't move or start to go offstage until the red lights go out. That's it. Got it?"

I nodded and he was gone.

Suddenly I realized I was all alone with nothing but my thoughts on hand. My time was fleeting, and I knew it. Then, when I looked at the clock, it was five minutes to airtime and I finally realized I hadn't even looked at my lines.

"Damn it," I thought. "You've got to do this – just <u>do it</u>."

With that miniscule amount of self-encouragement – as ridiculous as that sounds to me today – I took my lines in hand and went about the process of learning them. Then I recited them to myself, put a smile on my face and did the whole thing as upbeat as possible, just as I was instructed to do.

Two minutes to airtime and I was led up to the front of the stage and given my mark. The main stage curtain was directly behind me. The audience was all seated and all looking directly at me in anticipation of being entertained.

"You're on Camera 1, that one right there. That's where you'll get your cue. OK? Good luck."

I kept reading my lines to myself, over and over in my head, then heard the one-minute cue come over the intercom. A moment later, however, I heard another familiar voice speaking from behind the closed curtain. It was a barely audible whisper, but I understood every single word of it.

"I just heard we have more than ten-million people watching the show tonight. Isn't that great?"

It was Jack Benny's voice, and I knew immediately that it was meant specifically for me.

"Thirty seconds to airtime. Quiet please, thirty seconds."

Then, only moments later,

"Ten seconds, folks, ten seconds."

Those last ten seconds then became the most agonizing moments of my life. I kept looking for the red lights to come on. It seemed they never would. I thought my heart would just stop but it started pounding like a sledgehammer instead. Then, suddenly and miraculously, the red lights came on.

"Geez," I thought, "the red lights are on."

In that split moment, we were on the air. The camera was on me and me alone, and somehow I had to speak my lines and get off. In retrospect, I think I simply grasped the moment and ran with it, and in my best deep baritone speaking voice declared for the entire world to hear:

"LIVE FROM TELEVISION CITY IN HOLLYWOOD, IT'S THE JACK BENNY PROGRAM BROUGHT TO YOU BY LUCKY STRIKE"

The opening refrains of the music came on, we went to commercial, and the red lights went off. Bingo! It was all done in less than ten seconds. I was ushered off backstage and the moment was over and gone. The assistant director patted me on the shoulder then went on his way, but other than that the show continued without any further comment from anybody. It was only later that it really sank in that this was the first time I had ever been on camera all by myself to announce a show in front of a live studio audience with several million more viewers watching at home. My immediate thought was that I hoped they all enjoyed it. More important to me, however, was the fact I did not flub my lines, I gave my little speech the "upbeat" inflection I was instructed to give it and, hopefully, satisfied Mr. Benny by living up to his full expectations.

Later that evening when I got home and crawled into bed, I kept thinking about the event and how it all came about. I just couldn't believe that this was the way things happened on live television, but I came to the conclusion it was all deliberately planned and that the instigator was none other than Jack Benny himself. Obviously, he did it for the express purpose of proving to himself that I could handle an emergency situation in a thoroughly professional manner and, at the same time, give my presence on the set some measure of credibility. After all, isn't that exactly what Levy informed us Benny needed to pull our little stunt off?

My second and more important trial came in quick succession only a week or two later when Benny and his writers were involved in an informal discussion about a talent show they had scheduled for later in the season. As I recall, it was a long coffee break between setups and Benny was obviously trying to elicit new ideas from his people.

Again, all this dialogue just seemed to be too pat to be ad lib, so I immediately suspected it was another setup by Benny as his way of getting me involved without causing any suspicion, so I merely sat down to listen and went along with it.

Benny finally decided to postpone the talent show for lack of ideas and called for something new. Although he never looked at me directly or called on me for a response, I knew the time had come when he wanted me to act. I waited a discreet few moments each time when other ideas were presented and aired, and finally, when there appeared to be a lull in overall brain activity, I simply raised my hand. A moment later Benny invoked his will.

"It's the new kid. What do you have in mind?"

I cleared my throat first, then remembering what Levy had told me about the Maxwell scenario I got right to the point.

"Well, I was thinking. Has anyone ever thought about doing a show about the Maxwell?"

There was deathly silence. The writers looked at one another for a response, and then shrugged their shoulders. Finally it was the oldest one of the group, later identified to me as Sam Perrin, who spoke first.

"What about the Maxwell?"

"Well, Mr. Benny has mentioned his old car, the Maxwell, in any number of shows over the years, but as far as I know, the relationship between Mr. Benny and the Maxwell has never really been fully exploited. Yet, it's one of his most prized possessions."

"OK, so it's one of his most prized possessions – so what?"

"Well, let's say the Maxwell was stolen."

There was an immediate response, en masse, from the writers as a group.

"The Maxwell stolen? But who would steal the Maxwell? It's just an old junker."

"But that's just the point. Since it's so absurd that someone would actually steal the Maxwell, that fact in itself brings up an entire array of ideas I think might work."

It suddenly became very quiet as everyone was trying to digest what I had just proposed, but after a few moments of contemplation, Benny decided it was time for me to continue.

"Go on, Kid. Let's hear what you've got."

"Well Mr. Benny, the way I see it, the more absurd or preposterous an idea is, the more possibilities there are for getting some good humor out of it."

"Alright, let's hear some."

"OK, what's the first thing you would do if your car was stolen? You would call the police station to report the theft, right? Right! But this is Beverly Hills, and when you go to call the Beverly Hills Police Department, you find the number isn't listed. That's right, it's unlisted, because this is Beverly Hills and in Beverly Hills everyone has an unlisted number – including the Police Department."

Suddenly, there were some laughs and a giggle or two.

"That's very funny."

But Benny, anxious to hear what would come next, pressed me to go on.

"Don't stop. Go ahead. You're on a roll. Keep going."

And keep going I did.

"Well, as I see it, the Beverly Hills Police Department is where I think you could really get in some incredible sight gags, jokes and comic situations that wouldn't work anywhere else in the world. For starters, they wouldn't just have plain light fixtures at the Beverly Hills Police Station, they would have crystal chandeliers, and instead of standard steel office furniture they would have Louis XIV French writing desks, ornate brass ormolu-encrusted commodes, Italian Renaissance sconces on the walls and even some Greek marble statuary hovering over the entranceway. In other words, this is the Beverly Hills Police Station, the most elegant police station in the world."

A few laughs and some exuberant hand clapping punctuated my speech, but it was Benny who spoke up to seal the deal.

"Kid, I like it. I think it's just great. I think we can come up with a lot of real funny stuff to go along with that."

Then, one by one, Benny's old writers followed suit, and in a few moments all kinds of ideas sprouted forth to fill out the story. It was clear that Levy was right. The writers just needed a basic story line that showed some promise – something they could grab on to and run with. Then they could refine it, add the dialogue and do all the rest, and it was clear that Benny was pleased with the fact that his old boys picked up on it.

"Jack's Maxwell Is Stolen" aired on November 18, 1956. With no stars in the show to boost its ratings, it still garnered rave reviews as one of the best shows of the season. I was rewarded by being cast as Officer Johnson in the police station scene, where I was given some great lines along with an ad-lib dance number for good measure. When the curtain closed on that scene and we went to commercial, the entire audience broke out in spontaneous applause. From my perspective, the show was a roaring success and I felt eminently pleased to have offered the initial idea in making it so.

As a result of my success for having proposed the original idea for this show, I was rewarded with two full seasons on the *Jack Benny Program*. It wasn't until sometime during the spring of 1958 that I felt I had succeeded in my original purpose for coming on the show and decided it was time for me to go out on my own. During those two seasons, I contributed to or participated in the production of a dozen or more individual Benny episodes, all of which came off well with Benny's writers dutifully picking up the plot clues whenever I casually dropped them. In the end, the charade that Benny had initiated by hiring me in the first place went undetected by any of those he chose to protect, and after I left the show for the last time, he called and thanked me personally for having taken part in it.

In retrospect, I can truly say that I prized the time I spent on the *Jack Benny Program* and I consider it to be one of the pivotal periods of growth and learning in my early Hollywood career.

Again, all I could say to myself was,

"How lucky could I have ever been?"

CHAPTER 17:

Mulholland Drive

By 1957, with my Hollywood career on a roll and a totally successful sound installation business on the side, I felt financially secure for the first time. Quite coincidentally, I was offered a deal on my home in Beverly Glen that I couldn't refuse, so I decided to sell the property and invest my profit in a new home in the Hollywood Hills. It was located just off Mulholland Drive with a view encompassing most of Los Angeles, from the Pacific coast to the twin peaks outside Palm Springs. The two-bedroom house was older – probably built during the 1920s – but like the house on Quito Lane it offered great possibilities for a spectacular rebuild. All in all, an incredible bachelor pad and a potential gold mine for me once the renovations were completed.

The house stood in a nice quiet neighborhood with widely spaced properties on either side, offering a great deal of privacy. My nearest neighbor to the east was actor Bill Boyd, who had made quite a name for himself as Hopalong Cassidy in the film and television series of the same name. Boyd and his wife, Grace, had lived in their house for several years; they were quiet and reserved and proved to be ideal neighbors. The next house just down the street from the Boyds', however, was a rental that was leased to then teen idol Ricky Nelson, an occasional inhabitant who threw wild, noisy parties whenever he was in residence. Other motion picture and television luminaries populated the immediate area, with the Errol Flynn property just a short distance to the west. Clearly, I would finally be living right in the middle of the Hollywood milieu, and I loved it.

It was sometime during this period that my occasional friend and infrequent house guest, Ralph Jarvis, returned from his job in the Far East looking for a place to stay. As was his style, he arrived with pockets full of cash and a penchant for good places to spend it. Thus, when he came up and saw the new house for the first time, he instantly asked to move in, requesting the same sort of deal I had granted him back in Beverly Glen. Clearly, it was not an offer I could summarily dismiss. To his credit, Ralph had accumulated a significant amount of money overseas, was financially stable with a burgeoning nest egg and was not someone I would need to support. Ralph was a nice enough guy with a likable personality, and although we travelled in totally different circles and had little in common, I had no objection to allowing him to come back. He moved a few of his things into the guest room and voluntarily contributed to the burgeoning reconstruction costs and generally helped out whenever he found himself in the immediate area.

There was also the matter of Graf, the German Shepherd puppy that Ralph gave me when I moved to Beverly Glen and that he loved just as much as I did. Graf, therefore, became the bond that held our tenuous friendship together. Nevertheless, when Ralph was in town he spent his money lavishly, was always well dressed, drove a nice new car and enjoyed living the lifestyle of a rich man.

As mentioned earlier, Ralph admitted to me that he was gay, but since he appeared completely masculine I felt that few people would ever make the connection. He now explained in the most matter-of-fact manner that back in the immediate post-war years, many gay men who were freshly discharged from the military took the opportunity to use their newly found freedoms to break the chains that held them back to their hometowns, where most would still be forced to remain in the closet. Many would gravitate to New York or San Francisco, with those seeking a career in film coming to the Los Angeles area.

Ralph had a close friend who professed to meeting dozens of newcomers at the downtown Los Angeles Greyhound Bus Station. Needless to say, the singular reason for those meetings was for sexual recruitment purposes. According to the arrangement between them they would share their recruits and then pass them on to others when they were through with them. As he put it, there were many newcomers arriving in Los Angeles every day, so there was always a lot of "new talent" to go around.

According to Ralph, on one particular day in 1946, this friend brought a tall, lanky, 21-year-old guy over to Ralph's place whom he had met at the bus station a couple of days earlier. The guy was from Winnetka, Illinois, and had just been discharged from the Navy. According to Ralph, this new recruit was likable enough but had crooked teeth, acted sort of gawky and spoke with a strange Midwestern twang. After spending the night with Ralph, when asked what he was looking to do in L.A., he said that he wanted to become an actor, whereupon Ralph responded with a remark that would come back to haunt him several years later.

"You'd do better to go back to Winnetka because, frankly, you'll never make it here in Hollywood."

The two parted company on a friendly basis and according to Ralph never saw each other again. This guy, however, didn't listen to Ralph's sage advice and remained in Hollywood to seek his fortune. Over the next several years, he managed to be bedded by a few influential people, some of whom helped him mature. They also had his teeth fixed, paid for some acting lessons and sent him to a good voice coach. His name was Roy Fitzgerald, who ten years later had blossomed into the most famous movie actor in the world. The story of how Rock Hudson made it from obscurity to stardom is now legend, but according to Ralph Jarvis, the story he just told me was exactly the way it all started for him.

Naturally, my first thought was that Ralph had made the whole story up, but I had more important things to think about and quickly put Ralph and Roy Fitzgerald on the back burner. Actually, I didn't see much of Ralph at that time. He came and went as he pleased and seemed to spend more time with his friends in the San Diego area than in Los Angeles.

The first thing I did before moving into my new home was to have the place fumigated. I then took up residence in one of the bedrooms, hired a couple of out-of-work actor friends as my helpers and proceeded to rebuild the place, board by board, until it was finished. A plus for the house was the fact that it had a sizable dry basement, usable not only for storage purposes, but large enough for two additional rooms. When completed, I used one of those rooms as an office and to accommodate the bookkeeper for my sound system business, with the second room becoming a darkroom. A cement block wall with an ornamental gate out front came next, with a mélange of attractive tropical plants for the patio and front deck coming last. When it was finished, my new home was a proverbial showcase and I was justifiably very proud of it.

Albert McCleery was a TV producer from New York whom I had met socially at one of the many Hollywood parties I had attended during this period. I always liked Al and I consider that it was probably because he had a real positive attitude about things, much the same as I did. Professionally, Al had made a name for himself during the early '50s on two very successful television anthology series named *Cameo Theatre* and *Matinee Theatre*. He held producer credits on both coasts and had a very active hand in the development of new talent at the Pasadena Playhouse, one of the most successful amateur production facilities on the West Coast. Al had seen me on the *Jack Benny Program* and other shows I had done up to that time, so he was quite familiar with my work. Thus, I was not surprised when he called one day to ask that I come down to NBC for an interview concerning a particular part he thought I could play in an upcoming episode he was producing. Unfortunately, his director thought me too young for the part, so in the spirit of the moment and a flippant stab at redemption, Al invited me to a cocktail party instead, suggesting jovially,

"And bring a fun date along."

I thought the whole idea of a party substituting for a job sounded a bit bizarre to me, but then I decided, "What the hell, this is Hollywood," so I accepted the invitation. Besides, I had the perfect choice for a date, my longtime best girlfriend, Dale Sherwood, who was probably the most fun date any man could have. The evening turned out perfectly. Dale and Al got along well, we all saw each other frequently after that and – before long – I found Al had become a regular at my home, as well.

Al was married, but his wife made her home in New York, leaving him to fend for himself a good deal of the time when he was working in Los Angeles. Al was a good fifteen years my senior, but he possessed a multifaceted personality like mine that resulted in our getting along exceptionally well. His wit, swagger and wry humor added a level of sophistication to any event he attended and, frankly, I enjoyed having him around. Best of all, Al had a way of expressing himself that made one want to listen, so his presence allowed me the chance to learn much about his work in the production end of the business, which until this time had been a total void to me. At the same time, Al was aware of my wish to become a director, so he took it upon himself to mentor me as best as he could along that end of the spectrum, and I was pleased he felt obliged to do so.

In those days, when it was my turn to be "between pictures," I usually hosted a dinner party at my new home at least once a week. Naturally, most of my guests were out-of-work movie people I had befriended along the way, so the conversations were always brisk, informative and about the business. Being a successful producer and a witty raconteur, Al fit perfectly into our little group."

It was sometime during this period that Ralph came to me with the news that he had quit his government job and had taken a new job at Universal Studios. He explained that the job was not exactly an executive position – not that I expected it would be – but that it had potential and could lead to bigger and better things for him. After some requisite grilling, however, Ralph admitted, sheepishly, that it was only a desk job in the shipping department. I told Ralph that I couldn't see what kind of bigger or better thing he envisioned obtaining from a desk job in the shipping department – one I likened to being about as close to the bottom rung on the corporate ladder as one could imagine. Nevertheless, he was not deterred by my reaction, his only response being an emphatic,

"You don't give me enough credit, Bob. Just watch me. I'll make you proud of me one day."

It was about this time that I realized I had not as yet thrown a housewarming party at my new home, so I decided to throw a bash that none of us was ever likely to forget. Little did I know how prophetic that notion would turn out to be.

As a recall, I invited twenty or more of my best friends, including my agents John Darrow and Dick Clayton, my friends George Huene, George Cukor, Al McCleery (and his wife, who flew in for the occasion), Don Honrath and Violet Darling, along with my closest neighbors, Bill Boyd and his wife, Grace. Also in attendance were my two closest girlfriends, Dale Sherwood and Trudi Philion, among several others. Ralph indicated that he couldn't help out because he would be working late and not to expect him before seven. I told him that was fine and not to worry about it because I hired a couple of would-be actors in the catering business to doll up the house, do the cooking and all the rest of the preparation.

Cukor had a dinner party scheduled at his own home that evening, so he came early, had his usual Dubonnet, spent an hour or so schmoozing with the others and then left. As he was leaving, however, he took a notepaper from his pocket and handed it to me, remarking casually,

"This came for you."

I appreciated his coming, so I thanked him and walked him to the door. When I unfolded the note he handed me, I saw it was from Vivien, with her London phone number and the notation "Please call." When I looked at my watch, I realized it was the middle of the night in London, so I put the note in my pocket and decided to call her back in the morning. By seven, all of my guests had arrived except Ralph. Nevertheless, I decided we couldn't wait any longer, so I instructed the caterers to begin serving the food. About an hour later, after the last course had been served and as all of us were sitting around the living room just chatting or admiring the view, Ralph walked in with the most sheepish grin on his face. He had obviously been out drinking; his face was red, he stammered as he spoke and I really thought he might say something odd or otherwise embarrass himself. So I asked him whether he was OK, but he just waved me off and came into the living room to make his excuses.

"I'm sorry I'm late. I ran into an old friend…uh, acquaintance… he wanted to come in and say hi." Then gesturing to the kitchen, he called out, "Roy, you wanna come in?"

For a moment none of us could have guessed who Ralph's friend was. We could hear voices in the kitchen, some laughter, a couple of whoops, etc., until finally this tall lanky guy meandered out into the living room and everyone's jaw just dropped. Ralph's old friend and acquaintance was none other than Rock Hudson, in the flesh.

My first thought was that Ralph had told me the truth after all. He actually had met Rock years earlier as he had bragged, but it wasn't until Rock confirmed it himself that I was fully convinced. Rock Hudson then explained the connection in his own words.

"I have to apologize for Ralph. It's my fault he's late. I saw him walking down the street at the studio and thought to myself that I know that guy. That's the guy who told me to pack up and go back home – that I wouldn't get anywhere in this town. So I walked up behind him, tapped him on the shoulder and asked him, 'Hey, do you still think I should pack up and go home?'"

Naturally, the whole room roared with laughter, then applauded. Ralph just stood by the side with that same old sheepish grin on his face. Rock then walked around the room shaking hands with all those who cared to do so. Some exchanged niceties and others just watched. When he came around to me he thrust his hand out to take mine, and I sensed an extra-firm grip and a slight glint in his eye as he did so.

"Hi, I'm Rock, you must be Bob, Ralph told me all about you."

Then, thrusting his index finger out at me, he intoned, quietly, "I'll see you later."

With that ominous remark left for me to reflect over, he then went on to shake hands with the rest of those in the room. When thinking back at that moment, I have to remind myself that this man had just finished filming *Giant* with Elizabeth Taylor, a picture that would go on to become the most highly acclaimed movie of the year. He had made it to the cover of *Life* magazine as well as dozens of lesser publications, was voted the most handsome bachelor in Hollywood and God only knows how many other accolades. He had literally become king of the film world in every sense of the word. Every person in the room was chomping at the bit just to schmooze with him for a few moments – or for a lot more if at all possible – yet most of them had no idea what he was really there for.

As for me, I really didn't like the way he approached me with that smooth opening line of his, "Hi, I'm Rock." It was so pretentious and phony, and it just grated on me. By this time in his incredible rise to fame, I think everyone in Hollywood was aware that he was homosexual, but few people spoke openly about it. From Ralph's description of how he met Rock years earlier, I presumed that Rock was amenable to having sex with any man who would submit to his advances, but not knowing what Ralph might have told him about me, I decided I had to corner Ralph first in order to find out. Ralph had disappeared soon after Rock came in, but I quickly found him downstairs in the guest room, where he was trying to clean himself up. I never knew Ralph to be a heavy drinker, so I had to assume his surprise meeting with Rock was what prompted it.

"Ralph, you look like shit, are you OK?"

He nodded affirmatively.

"But I do feel like shit. Damn, I've never drunk so much booze in my life. He just insisted on our going out for a drink, and then it became two, three and I don't know how many more."

"Ralph, to change the subject, Rock mentioned that you told him all about me and I need to know what that is all about."

"Yeah, well, if you really wanna know, he's one horny bastard. All he talks about is sex and the first thing he asked me was who I was living with, and when I described you to him, he immediately told me he wanted to fuck you. Yeah, he said you sounded like a good fuck to him – but don't worry, you're safe! I told him you were straight and didn't do shit like that. I said I knew lots of other guys I could fix him up with and that I wanted him to leave you alone – that I didn't want him to screw things up between you and me."

Ralph then went on to explain that the only reason he even brought Rock to the house was because Rock was intent on meeting new tricks – good-looking young men for him to sodomize – and since there were none here at the party to be had, he would be obliged to drive Rock on to find a trick for him elsewhere.

Ralph then excused himself, took a quick shower and put on some fresh clothes, then came back upstairs, grabbed his old friend by the arm and marched him out of the house. Needless to say, it was not the manner in which I intended to have my party terminated, but after an exit like that, there really wasn't much more that any of us could have expected.

As Ralph admitted to me several days later, Rock was hell-bent on getting laid that evening and once Ralph told him I was not available, Rock decided it was Ralph's responsibility to get him laid with someone else. Sadly, since Rock was Ralph's newly found old friend, Ralph did not have the heart to turn him down, so he complied, becoming Rock Hudson's new procurer without his even realizing it. Worst of all, once Ralph was suckered in to satisfy Rock's prolific requirement for new sex every day, it was too late for Ralph to bow out. It was a partnership in sexual excess that Ralph would later lament over and finally apologize for, but regrettably it was also the daily practice that was primarily responsible for Rock Hudson's notorious sex life and much publicized death many years later.

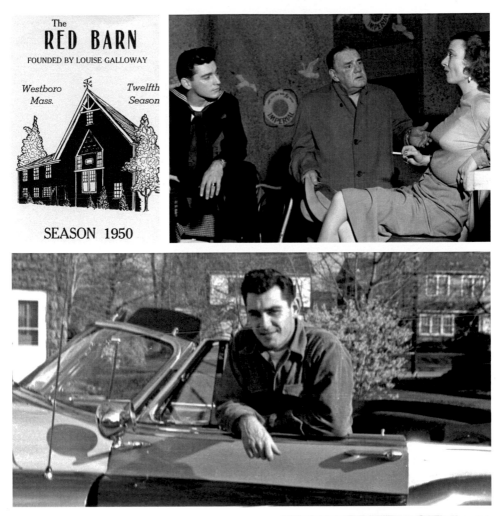

The
RED BARN
FOUNDED BY LOUISE GALLOWAY

Westboro   Twelfth
Mass.   Season

SEASON 1950

Top left: The Red Barn, my first venture into "show biz," a summer stock theatre in Massachusetts in 1950.

Top right: A scene from the Red Barn's production of Philip Yordan's *Anna Lucasta* with Teena Starr (right) as Anna, Harry Huguenot (center)as Joe and me (left) as Lester, the sailor. It was my fist stab at acting and I didn't think I was very good at it.

Middle: My Oldsmobile and me. It was the magic carpet that delivered me to an unexpected fifteen-year-long adventure in the television and movie business.

Right: This is Scotty Bowers, the first person I happened to meet upon my arrival in Hollywood. Little did I know that he was one of the most influential and important people in town.

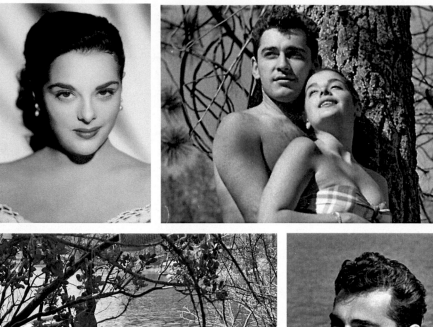

Top left: My first Hollywood heartthrob, Yvette Duguay, as she appeared in the film *The Cimarron Kid* in 1951.

Top right: Yvette and me at Lake Arrowhead.

Middle left: Yvette and Betty A getting ready for our swim at Lake Arrrowhead.

Middle right: Me, before my first early morning dip at Lake Arrowhead.

Bottom: Sammy Davis Jr. as he appeared when I first met him in Atlantic City in 1952.

Top left: Miss Iceland and me as we appeared on the red carpet at the Academy Awards ceremony in 1954.

Middle left: My ticket stub for the ceremony, note the ticket price of only $6.00.

Top right: This is Dorothy Kirsten, the world-renowned opera singer. My fortuitous introduction to her led to the formation of a new business for me.

Bottom: This is the portrait taken of me by George Huene soon after our chance meeting at Birns & Sawyer. It was a prime example of the importance of location and timing in the evolution of my budding career.

Top left: The great director, George Cukor, sharing in a laugh at a party in London in 1962.

Top right: This is me at the time I was asked to attend my first Sunday afternoon pool party at Cukor's house. Unfortunately I had not been invited to the party, only to work on a malfunctioning fountain I helped Huene to install earlier, but when some of the guests saw what the wind had blown in Cukor had no choice other than to invite me as well.

Bottom: Seated here outside the pavilion from the left are Cukor with his dog Sasha, Frank Horn (behind Cukor) and Louis Mason (on the right), with me in the center background.

Top: A reverse shot showing the main house (left), pool house (right rear) and Cukor (in right center), with his favorite dog, Sasha, a magnificent black standard poodle.

Bottom: Megastars Clark Gable and Vivien Leigh in an early production still from the most highly acclaimed motion picture of the pre-World War II Hollywood era, *Gone With The Wind*, with George Cukor, their first director on the film.

Top: Marilyn Monroe in a rehearsal still of "Heat Wave," the musical number in the film *There's no Business like Show Business* that Hal Schaefer was coaching her for at the time he brought me to her dressing room.

Bottom left: Vivien Leigh greets Marilyn Monroe at the London airport in 1957.

Middle: A casual remark from Vivien, a prompt selection by Cukor and I was rewarded with my first agent. John Darrow was one of the most respected agents in town; he was also from New Jersey and so we got along just famously. Surprisingly, he suggested I prepare myself for some acting jobs first, setting my writing career aside for later.

Bottom right: A word from Darrow, a quick phone call by Cukor and my first studio publicity shots were taken. Voice and diction coaching followed and within a few weeks my career as an actor was on its way.

Top: James Dean with his Porsche 550 Spyder. This photo was taken by one of Dean's racing friends during the time that Dick Clayton and I visited him just before his tragic death. Pictured here with Dean is Rolf Wütherich, the mechanic from the Porsche factory who was in the car with Dean at the time of the accident that took Dean's life.

Bottom left: This is my only permanent roommate, Graf, a beautiful German Shepherd puppy at our secluded little cottage on Quito Lane in 1954, allowing for one of the most productive periods of writing in my career.

Bottom right: One of my first jobs as an actor in Hollywood was the part of a settler in an episode of *Frontier* entitled "The Return of Jubal Dolan." This is a publicity shot for the series that was distributed to the press before the show was aired.

Top: My first appearance on the *Jack Benny Program* was the result of another fortuitous happenstance for me based solely on location and timing that I could have never expected to occur. Benny obviously liked what he saw in me and kept me on for two full seasons.

Bottom left: This is a frame capture from "Jack's Maxwell is Stolen." My contribution was the original premise for the show along with suggestions for much of the scenery, props and action; Benny's writers then did the rest. Seated here in the Beverly Hills Police Station scene is actor Morgan Jones as Officer Carey and me as Officer Johnson. Lyle Talbot as Sergeant Van der Meer is standing behind me while Benny, right, assumes his deadpan role as the unflappable skinflint.

Bottom right: Morgan Jones and me in a closeup from the same scene.

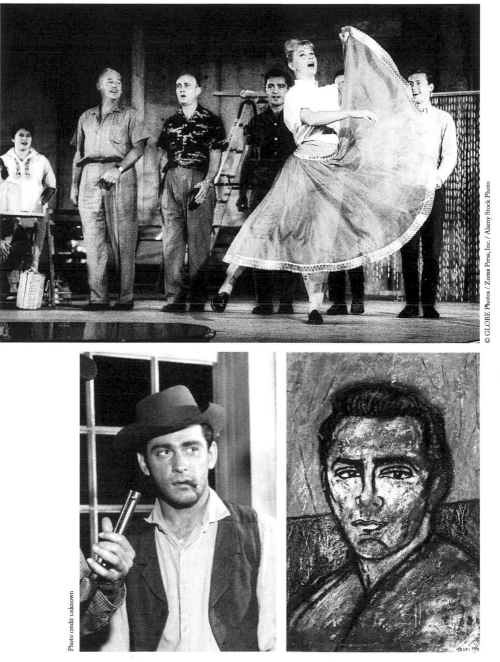

Top: From *Please Don't Eat the Daisies,* taken during our performance.

Bottom left: Here I am playing one more "mean and nasty hombre" in yet another predictable western of unremarkable origin. I felt I was playing more heavies than I cared to, but the monetary reward was too good to ignore.

Bottom right: This is the wildly impressionistic oil painting Trudi Philion did of me when we first met. It was a simple case of "artist and model" that suited us both just fine.

Below: In 1946, Ralph Jarvis met Roy Fitzgerald (later to become Rock Hudson) when both first arrived in Hollywood, then reunited nine years later with Ralph becoming Rock's instant closest pal, confidante and unwitting procurer.

Above: This is the Ralph Jarvis that I knew best. When appearing for an interview, a social affair or just a regular dinner, he was always well groomed, dressed to the hilt, drove a shiny new car, spent his money lavishly and comported himself like a successful business person. Sadly, his ill-founded loyalty to Rock Hudson changed all that, transforming his lifestyle to one that almost destroyed him.

Right: In 1959 I met Estelle Harman and soon became involved at the Estelle Harman Actors Workshop to obtain some experience with directing. The end result of that effort became *An Evening of One Act Plays* that I both directed and co-produced for Estelle. Estelle Harman alumnus Bill Bixby, pictured here in the left center, was not on our program, but he attended the event to offer his support. Bixby starred in a number of successful television series, including *My Favorite Martian* (1963-1966), *The Magician* (1973-1974) and *The Incredible Hulk* (1977-1982). Estelle Harman is pictured here in the left foreground, with me, the director, hovering over the group in the background.

My first venture into scouting locations was directed at Catalina Island, where I mistakenly assumed that many suitable beaches existed for shooting films. Since George Cukor was "between pictures" at the time, he was eager to accompany me as "my assistant" (his description, not mine), giving me more insight into the man than I could have ever gleaned in any other way.

Top: Catalina resident Fred Small was the head lifeguard at Avalon beach and a close friend who met us at the pier and arranged for our charter boat and tour around the island. Fred is shown here in his lifeguard guise with public-address horn in hand. The steamer *Catalina* that made the trip from San Pedro to Avalon every day is pictured in the background.

Middle: My "assistant," George Cukor, on our way out to the location site.

Bottom: Unfortunately, things did not pan out as I had planned. The best potential location I had envisioned had since been taken over by seals, the patriarch of which was single-mindedly determined on chasing me back into the sea and a smelly kelp bed.

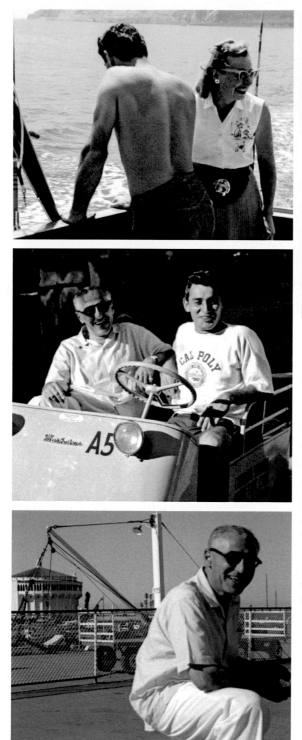

Top left: The result being that when I climbed back into the boat I stank like a dead whale. As shown here, even our guide got a big laugh out of my misfortune.

Top right: A shower and a much-needed change of clothes was the best that Fred could offer me, but it was enough to allow me to spend the rest of our trip without offending anyone – including myself.

Middle: This is George Cukor and me in one of Fred's small electric vehicles. Interestingly, these were the only rental vehicles allowed on the island and thus were the only way to get around it.

Bottom: As we waited for our plane back to the mainland, I took this photo of Cukor with the world-famous Avalon Casino in the background.

Top left: Dick DuBois, a former Mr. America winner and all-around nice guy, was just another Hollywood hopeful who finally realized he simply wasn't getting anywhere as an actor. Dick is pictured here as he appeared on his last visit to me in 1962, when he announced his intention to get out of the movie business and seek his fortune elsewhere.

Top right: This is Point Dume, a gem of a beach along the desolate California coastline just north of Malibu where we filmed the entire dream sequence for what later became the full-length feature version of *A House of Sand.*

Bottom: My first crack at film directing. Here I am upon my arrival at Point Dume with camera in hand and ready to shoot our first screen tests.

"A HOUSE OF SAND"
with MARY STATON and PHILIPPE FORQUET • Music by LES BAXTER
Produced by ROBERT DARWIN and MARIO ARAKTINGI • Written and Directed by ROBERT DARWIN

Top: During principal photography, with our star Mary Staton and Don Conley, one of the antagonists in our story.

Bottom: The object of Mary's fascination, Roland Carey, while being vamped.

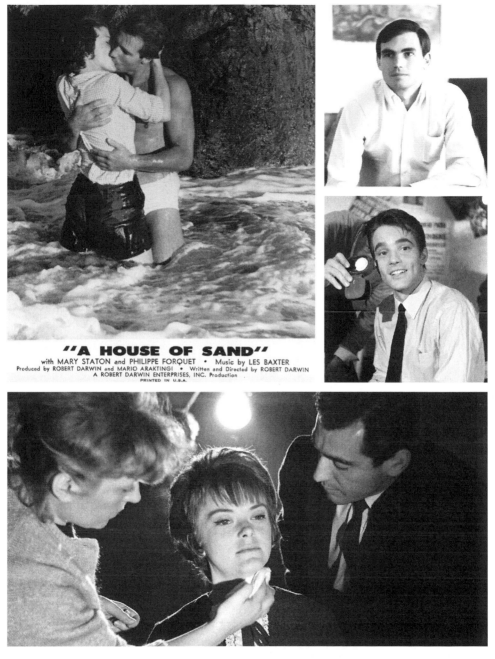

"A HOUSE OF SAND"
with MARY STATON and PHILIPPE FORQUET • Music by LES BAXTER
Produced by ROBERT DARWIN and MARIO ARAKTINGI • Written and Directed by ROBERT DARWIN
A ROBERT DARWIN ENTERPRISES, INC. Production
PRINTED IN U.S.A.

Top left: Giving Mary her reward at the beginning of the so-called "rape" scene. Of course, it was all in the eyes of the beholder, but the scene did generate enough prurient interest from Europe to garner an invitation from the Venice Film Festival, leading to the eventual production of the full-length version of the film in Paris.

Top right: Another "assistant" in name only, David Korda, became a close friend and an invaluable volunteer who helped me throughout production of the original footage at Point Dume.

Middle right and bottom: Pre-production in Paris, with Philippe Forquet in preparation for his screen test and Mary Staton during hairstyle and makeup tests.

Top left: This is me while directing our first exterior street scene with Mary and Philippe at the Au Viens Paris café.

Top right: Mary and Philippe in one of the signature photographs I took that were used in the film's publicity materials.

Middle: Here we are rehearsing for the first take in our night club scene with our script girl on my left and Dorothy Marchini, my irreplaceable one-and-only "Girl Friday," behind my right shoulder.

Left: Several takes later I was still not satisfied with the result. Additional direction and more takes followed.

"A HOUSE OF SAND"
with MARY STATON and PHILIPPE FORQUET • Music by LES BAXTER
Produced by ROBERT DARWIN and MARIO ARAKTINGI • Written and Directed by ROBERT DARWIN
A ROBERT DARWIN ENTERPRISES, INC. Production
PRINTED IN U.S.A.

"A HOUSE OF SAND"
with MARY STATON and PHILIPPE FORQUET • Music by LES BAXTER
Produced by ROBERT DARWIN and MARIO ARAKTINGI • Written and Directed by ROBERT DARWIN
A ROBERT DARWIN ENTERPRISES, INC. Production
PRINTED IN U.S.A.

Top left: Mary and her director during an obviously private moment. By the end of the shoot, I was totally confident that her performance in this film would help propel her to stardom.

Top right: Dorothy Marchini and I were clearly celebrating a moment of euphoria when we were photographed in this view. Little did we know that the worse of what was to be handed us was yet to come.

Middle left: When all the action finally fell into place, I decided to get behind the camera and shoot the scene myself. Our cameraman, left, was unperturbed, confiding that he wanted to become a director himself one day.

Middle right: Mary and Philippe pictured during the climactic moment in the film when the realities of life finally become apparent to them.

Bottom: Mary and Roland Carey during the vamp scene. Little did she know what she was getting in to.

Top left: The French Elvis, Johnny Hallyday, and his protégé, Sylvie Vartan, in 1963.

Top right: Jack Palance as he appeared at the time he confronted me – albeit playfully – on the Via Veneto in Rome. Palance was groveling around for work just like every other unemployed actor in Europe.

Middle left: The diva of all divas, Marlene Dietrich, displaying the world-famous gams that she used to derail Sylvie Vartan's performance.

Middle right and bottom: Vasso Gabriel when he attended the Cannes Film Festival in 1963, and at sixteen, when he played the lead role in *Le Petite Étranger.*

Top: Pat Curtis with his protégé, Jo Raquel Tejada, as she appeared about the time he introduced me to her. Within the year, Pat took her to Rome as I suggested, allowing for the exposure she required to garner international attention.

Right: Emerging as the world's leading sex symbol, Raquel Welsh is seen here exhibiting all of the curves and sexy demeanor that transformed her into one of the brightest stars in the Hollywood firmament.

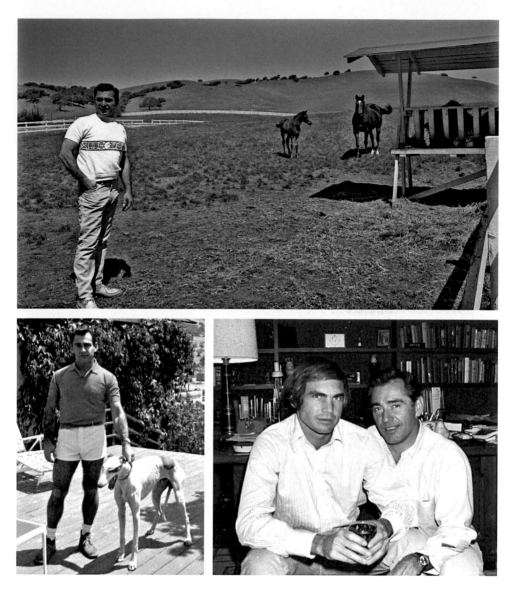

Top: The ranch in Carmel Valley where John Hernstadt and I set up our budding dynasty. From breeding horses to developing exceptional properties, we soon wound up with more projects than I had the time to handle.

Bottom left: Our luck with greyhounds, however, clearly left much to be desired. They were unpredictable, unresponsive to training and unloved by all of us.

Bottom right: David Korda and me in a photo taken in my office during David's visit to the ranch in 1971.

John Skinner photo

Top: During the late 1970s I engaged in a plethora of new projects, including seeking out new business opportunities and even committing to the writing of a new book. Here I am flying up the California coast off Big Sur in my speedy little C310 after a meeting in the Los Angeles area. Although it might seem extravagant to some, the use of a private aircraft was actually the most efficient manner for me to attend to our various interests throughout the western U.S.

Bottom: This photo of me is at Moab, Utah, while ferrying in a new airplane from Omaha to Monterey in 1979. I was fifty-three years of age at the time.

Top left: I was in my mid-sixties when this photo was taken during the early '90s, but I was still active in our business ventures, continued to possess excellent health and had no excuse not to take full advantage over the wonderful bounty nature had bestowed upon me.

Top right: Here I am relaxing between projects at a friend's home in Austin, Texas, during the mid-1980s.

Lower left: This is my passport photo in 1983 when I was fifty-seven.

Lower right: A frame from the television program *Your Town* that was broadcast live from Monterey on February 11, 2014. I was eighty-seven years of age at the time. Today, as I approach my ninety-second, I am still going strong, have all my marbles in place and possess the very essence of health, longevity and the unquenchable will to go on.

CHAPTER 18:

Vivien Leigh – Act II

Since first meeting Vivien back in 1954, I was given the pleasure of visiting with her every time she returned to Hollywood. It was a relationship based on the fondness we had developed for each other, the attention, love and devotion she did not receive from her husband and, of course, the sex, which I found to be exceptional. Consequently, I looked forward to her next visit every time she called but, unfortunately, the next time in this case was not at all what I expected.

When I called Vivien back as requested, she told me she would be returning to Los Angeles in a few days and asked that I pick her up at the airport. She explained that the trip was only to see an old friend who was very ill, adding casually that she would not be staying at Cukor's but at the Beverly Hills Hotel, remarking stoically,

"I don't want to make a pest of myself at George's – he is such a gracious host."

A few days later and Vivien was back in my life. Naturally, I picked her up at the airport, as promised. She was tired and quite bedraggled when she got off the plane, barely speaking a word. Her mood was all in stark contrast to the ecstatically engaging woman I had grown to know from her earlier visits. She explained that her friend was an old acquaintance who was quite ill and was not expected to live more than a few more days, making her visit more essential with each passing day. Otherwise, she just closed her eyes, holding my right hand tightly while snuggling up to me as closely as she dared. Just before arriving at the hotel, Vivien advised that she had prebooked her favorite bungalow, indicating it was located in the gardens off North Crescent Drive directly behind the main hotel building. She added that she did not need to check in at the front desk and could come and go as she pleased.

As expected, the bungalow had been discreetly embellished for her arrival with a display of fresh flowers and a bowl of tropical fruit to tempt the palate, but it was all of little interest to her. The moment we entered the living room, she turned toward me, flung her arms around my waist and buried her head in my chest. Then, as if acting out a little scene, she began humming to herself softly, all the while gesticulating furtively as though engrossed in a deep hypnotic trance. It was an endearing moment I felt loath to dispel, but I knew it had to be done. Picking her up bodily I carried her into the bedroom, laid her down gently on the bed, disrobed her and crawled in next to her. Not a single word was spoken; we just had sex and that was the way we remained for the rest of the day.

Vivien finally fell asleep, allowing me the luxury to go home, take a bath and tend to my own requirements. Before leaving, however, I left her a note explaining that I would be back at nine in the morning to wake her, thus allowing her the time to prepare for her visit. Much to my surprise, however, when I arrived the following morning I found that she had risen earlier, completed her toilette, enjoyed a quick breakfast and was ready to go. At that point, all I needed was the cup of hot coffee and croissant she had left for me and we were on our way.

Once on the road I sensed Vivien had set me up as her listening post, and she soon let me have it with all the fury she could muster. Predictably, all of it concerned her broken marriage to Laurence Olivier. They had been married since 1940 but had been estranged on and off since the end of the war. First, and most grievous for her, was the fact that Olivier was cheating on her and, apparently, had been doing so for years. The affairs were all surreptitious and fleeting at first, but now they were open and quite flamboyant for the whole world to witness. What Vivien didn't mention, of course, was the fact that she was doing much the same vis-à-vis her relationship with me, and I reminded her of that. Her answer, however, illustrated the difference as it existed in her mind.

"Yes, dahling, but at least I tend to keep my own affairs quite private – as I am attempting to do with you and this little fling of ours."

Needless to say, she had made her point, but it did nothing to bolster my ego. Obviously, I wouldn't have cherished the idea of being found out by her husband or being labeled as just another trick of hers, so I just kept my mouth shut. The problem of my ego, however, was clearly of no concern to her, so she just kept rattling on about her own.

Vivien's friend lived in an older, middle-class community south of Laguna Beach somewhere, a good two-hour drive down the coast from Beverly Hills. Just before arriving at our destination, Vivien became quite nervous, explaining that since this would be the last time she would likely see her friend, she wanted to be left alone with her for as long as possible. We agreed on the time for me to pick her back up, but when we arrived at her friend's house, she became very emotional and began to cry, so I simply took her by the arm, marched her up to the door and rang the bell, then walked back to the car and drove off. The entire episode, however, pissed me off and left me reeling emotionally, as well. All I could ask myself was,

"What am I doing here anyway?"

I couldn't answer that question and just fumed at myself for allowing Vivien to talk me into it. That acknowledgment left me in a state of misery and gloom, but at least I knew how to handle my anguish and would survive my misfortune – but poor Vivien could not. In fact, the visit left her devastated. She discovered that her friend not only suffered from an inoperable brain tumor but from an advanced case of dementia as well, the result being that she was incapable of even recognizing Vivien or acknowledging her presence. Thus, when I returned to pick her up at the appointed hour, I found her to be in an inconsolable state of anguish and despair. It was the ultimate insult to Vivien's fragile, overburdened sensibilities, and she reacted to it in the most wretched fashion. She cried in uncontrollable outbursts all the way back to Beverly Hills, and it was all I could do just to get her back to the hotel and put her to bed. Even so, as the fates would have it, the worst of it was yet to come. The final and ultimate assault on Vivien's capacious but bruised ego came the following evening, when after having recovered from the fitful experience of the previous day, we decided to go out for a late dinner at Scandia, a very popular upscale restaurant in the Sunset-Doheny area, where she expected to be welcomed in royal fashion. Unfortunately, it soon became clear to both of us that none of the patrons, waiters, bar people or management personnel at Scandia that evening showed any indication of recognizing her either.

Vivien stomped out of the place with all the ire and arrogance that the reigning queen of the theatre – or at least that is what she still thought she was – could muster. It was a fragile yet meaningless title she once held, but it allowed her to curse the entire business, the fans and anyone else she thought might have had a connection with it. It was her way of getting back at the powers that be, and especially all of the big movie moguls that first cater to you, make you a star, and then unceremoniously pull the rug out from under you when you show your first wrinkle.

Unfortunately, Vivien dwelt on her problem all the way to her bed, and it wasn't until I took her clothes off and thrust her naked form between the sheets once again that she recognized the fact that someone was even there for her. Grasping the moment, she thrust her arms around me as though for dear life, then realizing there was nothing she could do to change anything, took me in hand and satisfied the both of us.

I often thought about Vivien and her dilemma after that visit. I wondered over and over whether I really wanted to get involved in such a cutthroat business that disregards great talent and disposes of the remains like a used condom. It was clearly a fact of life in Hollywood that once the first blossom of one's youth was gone, any chance of maintaining the legitimate career one once had was gone with it. Unfortunately, everyone in Hollywood was aware of this fact, and there was no way it could ever be ignored or dispelled.

Over the course of the next several years, I continued to see Vivien every time she returned to Hollywood, and we continued to maintain our discreet private liaison with all the vim and vigor we could muster. The sex was great; I loved it and she made me eminently aware that she loved it, too. I put up with Vivien's grievous outbursts and misfortunate marriage as best I could; clearly, I could not allow myself to do anything less.

Unfortunately, Vivien's husband was conducting his own liaisons in a much more overt and blatant fashion. Gone was any thought of proper decorum or even the necessary propriety. He was now going at his proclivities with unabashed, shameless public exhibitions for all to see, and he was relying totally on his celebrity to get away with it. Most of his targets were young, uninitiated starlets who didn't know any better, and thus fell easily to his onslaught. According to Vivien, her husband's sexual dalliances really had little to do with her anymore, but were more the result of his own fading masculinity. What better way, she thought, for him to at least attempt to maintain the impression that he was still a virile young man the ladies all needed to reckon with.

As for Vivien herself, I had now been acquainted with her for a long enough period of time to recognize her own fading luminescence. It wasn't as though she had lost any of her innate talent as an actress, because she had not. On the contrary, what I now saw lacking was the drive for her to exhibit that talent – not only on the screen, but in her everyday life. On the whole, I found she no longer felt it necessary to display her celebrity as she did so masterfully at the Polo Lounge on our first date. Gone, also, was the necessity for her to be recognized wherever she went. I concluded that she finally accepted the fact that the celebrity that came with Scarlet O'Hara and her budding juvenile womanhood was long gone, and that she could now finally relax and resume the role of the normal human being she relinquished when she first made a name for herself on the silver screen. What a depressing descent into oblivion such a decline must be for a person like Vivien, who was once the brightest star in the firmament and was now just another fading beauty.

Needless to say, it is the way of all flesh that we humans are heir to. It is simply more difficult for those who were once the most beautiful among us. Celebrity be damned! It clearly makes the transition to normalcy that much more difficult.

CHAPTER 19:

The Rock Hudson Enigma

From the early 1950s until the mid-1980s, the most well-known gay actor in Hollywood was Rock Hudson, but what was not readily known was his incredible penchant for sex with almost any male body that was available to him. In spite of this proclivity, the fact that Hudson was an overtly practicing homosexual was never written about or publicized in any manner. It was the longest running open secret in Hollywood until 1984, when the press could no longer suppress the fact that this great star had contracted HIV/AIDS, a newly discovered, deadly, sexually transmitted disease that would take his life only months later. But it wasn't until I actually met Hudson personally that I learned what the Rock Hudson enigma was all about.

By all indications, the housewarming party at my new home up on Mulholland Drive turned out to be a huge success. No one expected a famous personage like Rock Hudson to attend the party and to schmooze with all the participants – including me. It was an unexpected experience that few of those present will ever forget. Nevertheless, I went on with my normal daily activities, not realizing that actually having met Hudson would soon become a distraction the likes of which I could have never imagined. I realized full well that my part-time housemate, Ralph Jarvis, would probably be swept away by all the new adulation, but then, after all, Rock was Ralph's newly rediscovered old friend, and I realized it would have been impossible for him not to be awed by all the attention that Rock would bestow upon him.

As I should have expected, I didn't see much of Ralph over the next several months. I socialized with my group of friends and he socialized with his. He rarely spent a weekend at the house anymore, preferring to spend the time at Rock's house or with his friends in the San Diego area. But one day I came home to find Ralph entertaining Rock in my kitchen. Rock had brought a couple of phonograph records over that he said he wanted to try on my sound system because, as he put it, he wanted to have me duplicate my system at his house. I told him I would be pleased to give him an estimate, but that I would need to inspect his house first in order to determine what was involved. He agreed, saying he had a barbecue scheduled at his place the following weekend and he thought it would be a good time for me to come over and do it, adding matter-of-factly,

"I want the best setup in town, Bob, no matter what the cost."

Rock lived at 9402 Beverly Crest Drive, in Beverly Hills. The house was a relatively modern, two-story, Spanish Revival style stucco structure with a red tile roof, located off Coldwater Canyon on a shallow bluff overlooking the cityscape below. When I arrived at the property, the scheduled barbecue party he mentioned was in full swing, with twenty or more participants drinking, carousing and milling around all over the place. I found Ralph outside on the patio after a short search and explained to him that there was no way I could do an estimate on the house with a big party like this going on, but he was too busy partying to pay me much heed. Then, as I glanced around the place to get at least an initial impression of what the installation would entail, I quickly realized this party was attended only by men – many men – with most of them being very young and very good-looking. I often wondered where all the beautiful people in Hollywood came from and then remembered what some wise old sage once intoned, namely, that there were more beautiful people per square mile in Hollywood than anywhere else on earth – and as I gazed at the crowd gathered around Rock Hudson that day, I was inclined to believe that to be true.

Rock's sexual inclinations were well known by this time and it was eminently clear he made no effort to conceal them. His forte, apparently, was to sodomize pretty teenage boys and handsome young men, and as was proven to me on this very occasion, he made no bones about surrounding himself with as many such candidates as possible, whenever and wherever he chose to do so.

As it turned out, Rock was doing the barbecuing himself that day and was clearly in no position to show me around his house – nor was I inclined to take out my pencil and pad to start measuring the place on my own. In the end, I asked Ralph to tell Rock I would return at a more appropriate time, then made my excuses and left.

I didn't see Ralph again until around eleven o'clock the following morning, when he came back to my house appearing very bedraggled and with the distinct odor of alcohol and vomit all about him.

"Geez, Ralph, what happened to you now?"

"Bob, you don't want to know."

"Look at your shirt, and your pants – you look like you fell into a toilet."

"It was worse than that. Rock made some steaks and covered them with a crappy barbecue sauce he said he made by himself. It was so bad, all those who ate it got sick, so the rest of us just started drinking an awful wine he said he got as a gift from somebody. By midnight several people had gotten ill and thrown up all over the place. When I went to help this one guy, he threw up all over me, and then I got sick from that and threw up myself. I felt so bad that I couldn't drive home, so I just found a quiet corner somewhere and went to sleep. When I woke up this morning, I found Rock crapped out upstairs in bed with two or three other guys, so I thought it best to just close the door behind me and leave."

Ralph finished by telling me I was lucky I left early. He then excused himself, went down to the guest room and went to sleep. A couple of weeks later he told me that Rock admitted to him that the culprit was the homemade barbecue sauce he had slathered all over his steaks. He didn't apologize for it, just stated that as fact. Other than that, he didn't say anything more to Ralph about the sound system he said he wanted installed at his home, and I had no intention of mentioning it to him. Ralph actually apologized to me sometime later, saying he found Rock to be very cheap and insincere, expecting others to do all kinds of things for him, and usually all for gratis. As a result, he concluded that Rock really wanted me to do the installation at his home for free, but once he realized I wasn't swept overboard by his celebrity – as so many others were prone to do – he realized it wasn't going to happen and simply abandoned the idea. Frankly, I told Ralph I didn't care about it one way or the other, because I had lots of other business and thought working for Rock would have been an extremely difficult situation for me anyway – especially when considering his sexual mores. I concluded by telling Ralph to forget it. I had bigger and better things to occupy my time than to worry about Rock Hudson.

Nevertheless, over the next several months, Rock took up the very inconvenient and unconventional habit of showing up at my home at the most inopportune times. He knew the kitchen door was never locked, so he always came in without knocking or calling in advance. It was particularly annoying for me on those occasions when I was entertaining some friends and he came barging in unannounced. Frankly, I told Ralph that I didn't care what they did together as long as he didn't just show up at my house and walk in like he owned the place. Finally, Ralph confided that Rock's procedure was to check the house out every day on his way to or from the studio, and that if there was someone's car parked out front other than Ralph's or mine, he would run in to see who it was. Naturally, if there was a good-looking young guy among my guests whom he didn't know, he would put the make on him. I told Ralph that I thought it was pretty gross of him to stalk my house like that just to find new fuckmates and that I wanted him to quit it, but Ralph admitted there really wasn't much he could do about it. Unfortunately, Rock persisted to case the house almost every day for the next several weeks, until on one occasion, he actually put the make on a straight married friend of mine who became so incensed at the proposition he punched Rock in the jaw.

That did it. I finally had my fill with Rock and gave Ralph the ultimatum I knew he would have never expected. I told Ralph if he didn't make Rock stop coming to my house, the next time he showed up I would call the police and have him arrested.

To his credit, Ralph at long last broke down, admitting to me that I was right, apologized for all of Hudson's mischievous house-stalking adventures and then, with one thing leading to the next, blurted out the whole sordid truth about the Rock Hudson enigma and the depravity that fueled his day-to-day existence. It was a story of primeval sexual wantonness that not even his closest friends knew existed – at least not at that particular time.

"Bob, you are right and, yes, I know I'm a fool for staying involved. But the truth is, I really feel sorry for the guy and I fear for what might happen to him if I deserted him. This guy is crazy; he is totally screwed up in his head and thinks about sex twenty-four hours a day. Every time we go out, all he wants from me is to find someone new for him to fuck. I've told him over and over that I don't know any more new guys for him to fuck, but he just won't listen.

"And if you think he just goes for those pretty-faced, clean-cut, young Hollywood types he has hanging around his pool, you would be wrong. The truth is, after we cruise up and down Hollywood Boulevard a couple of times, he usually has me drive him downtown, where we wind up at one of his favorite haunts, the Dover Hotel, one of the sleaziest flophouses on Main Street, where he seeks out any sexually exciting situation that might present itself. Just think about it and you can probably dream one up – gang bangs, S&M, you name it – and the worst part of it is he doesn't even wear a condom most of the time. He just rushes in hell-bent to get laid without for one moment even thinking about the consequences. He's pretty sick, Bob. I even told him so, but he just laughs me off and tells me not to be such a prude. Frankly, I don't think there's a thing anyone can do to change him. He's just that far gone already."

When Ralph was through, I suggested that he could simply drop his newly found old friend and be done with it, but he had to admit he just couldn't do that.

"I'm afraid he would be like a lost puppy dog without someone at least being there to watch over him. He may be big and tall, but he's not a fighter. I've never seen him confront anyone or stand up to a conflict."

It was apparent that Ralph was seduced by the aura and mystique of his friend's incredible celebrity. In short order he had become

Rock Hudson's closest secret friend and number one procurer. Not only that, but it appeared to me that Ralph loved the demanding position Rock had put him in, and once he had become used to it, there was no way he could give it up. It was the Rock Hudson enigma that appealed to Ralph, and once he was enmeshed in all the fame and notoriety, it became impossible for him to simply walk away from it.

Finally, however, things actually did quiet down around my house. There were no more unsolicited house calls by Ralph's friend, and I convinced myself that Ralph finally did persuade Rock to stay away from the place for good. In fact, it appeared that Ralph himself was spending more of his time elsewhere, as well – and that was fine with me, too. At least I had my house back to myself and that was the way I wanted it.

Sometime later, Ralph called to inform me that he was no longer seeing his friend, Rock Hudson. Apparently, the final altercation at my house caused a rift between them that brought their long-standing friendship and sexual procurement arrangement to a halt. Ralph admitted that he had already decided to terminate his arrangement with Rock even before my ultimatum, apologizing to me for not having done so earlier. Ralph also admitted that he was sick and tired of the entire Hollywood sex scene. Not that Ralph was overly spiritual in any manner, but in his mind the whole atmosphere in Hollywood reeked of negative influences brought about by nothing other than the town's open infatuation with sex. In his words, "If my folks ever found out about what Hollywood was really selling, and knew about the kind of thing I was doing for Rock, I think they would disown me – and God help me, but they would be right for doing so.

"Bob, I only hope you'll forgive me for all this crap you've had to endure because of Rock Hudson. If you don't hear from me for a while, don't worry, I'll be OK. I just need to get out of town and try to get my head straightened out somehow..."

To Ralph's credit, he finally did leave town, but it was not just for a short while. He called one day to inform me that he was quitting his job at Universal Studios and was moving to Hawaii. But before departing, Ralph begged me to allow him to use my guest room, if he ever had to come back to L.A. for a short visit. When considering the mood of the moment, Ralph's declaration for a life-changing move and the fact that Rock Hudson was no longer in the equation, I agreed.

In 1985, the world was stunned to hear of the death of Rock Hudson from Acquired Immune Deficiency Syndrome (HIV/AIDS), but in order to protect the great star's legacy, the primary cause of his illness was initially not revealed. Most written accounts were sanitized, with only a modicum of disturbing information concerning Hudson's deviant lifestyle ever being published. Only those who were closest to Hudson were aware of the intimate details of his lifelong perverse sexual habits and the unavoidable complications leading to his demise. But back in 1956, only his trusted friend, Ralph Jarvis, witnessed it "firsthand" and on a daily basis.

Sadly, Ralph met a similar fate as Hudson's, only a few years later. His demise, however, was not from AIDS or any other sexually transmitted disease, but from the insidious lasting effects of radiation poisoning that he acquired when working unprotected from radiation and unaware of its sinister complications while he was under contract to the U.S. Government during the initial hydrogen bomb tests at Eniwetok Atoll in 1952. That was the secret government job he was involved with when I first met him at George Cukor's home in 1954, and it wasn't until thirty or more years later that the effects of the radiation finally began to take its toll on his health. Ralph was admitted to the Veterans Administration Hospital in West Los Angeles in 1987, was diagnosed with radiation-induced cancer throughout his body and died there in abject misery on January 21, 1988.

In retrospect, and in spite of all the trauma I was forced to endure because of his relationship with Rock Hudson, I have to admit that Ralph was still one of the best friends I ever had. He was kind, considerate, overly generous and loyal to a fault, and I considered him to be a prince in his own special way. Unfortunately, the government never admitted its culpability in causing Ralph's death, nor the deaths of the hundreds of other U.S. veterans who were exposed to radiation in the same manner during the many similar government-sponsored atomic bomb tests that were conducted during the immediate post-World War II years.

CHAPTER 20:

The Post-Benny Craze

The post-Jack Benny period turned out to be both frantic and very fruitful for me. My long association with the *Jack Benny Program* on CBS created some instant openings leading to parts for me on other top CBS shows such as *Playhouse 90*, *Climax* and *The Schlitz Playhouse of Stars* – and if all that wasn't enough, it led to other casting departments at Republic, Universal and Paramount, and finally to a couple of plum roles in major motion pictures at MGM and Fox. It seemed as though I had achieved a respectable degree of success as an actor and I didn't even know it. What's worse, however, was the fact that I didn't really want it. It was a time when I had more on my plate than I could chew, but the pay was good, the times were great and for a while I really thought this sweet life I had accessed so readily would go on forever. The question, however, was not whether my life would continue and mature as it had without any conscious effort of my own, but whether I would be satisfied with the results, no matter where it led me.

It was soon after my last Benny show that I received a call from one of my old scuba diving buddies from Santa Monica. His name was Denny and it had been a year or more since I last spoke with him. We met for coffee at one of my favorite hangouts, the old Hamburger Hamlet down on Santa Monica Boulevard, when he told me about a casting call he planned to attend out at Republic Studios the following day. He said it was for a TV western, suggesting I might go and try out for it as well. I had nothing else going on that day, as I was literally "between pictures," so I agreed and then found myself outside the studio gate with Denny bright and early the following morning.

When we came onto the lot we happened to run into Lloyd Bridges, who remembered us from the day we were all scuba diving off Catalina a few years earlier. Bridges was very friendly, asked how we were doing and what we were there for, and even volunteered to speak with the casting agent for us. We gave him our names and we said our goodbyes. Ten minutes later the two of us were picked out of a lineup by name and given the parts. The entire process was over in a minute and all I knew was that I had just been given a role in a TV western and it was obvious to us that a word from Bridges was all that it took. Finally, we were told that the name of the show was *Way of the West* and my part was that of Joe. I had no idea what that part would entail, but when I expressed my concern to Denny, his only response was to just act like I knew what I was doing and to keep my mouth shut. I did exactly as he suggested and, as I hoped it would, all went well.

Sometime during that shoot I was contacted by the studio casting agent and was informed that Bridges wanted to use me in one of his upcoming *Sea Hunt* episodes, as well. Of course I was thrilled that Bridges cared enough about budding young hopefuls like me to help them out with their careers. In my case, he asked about my background, what I had done to date, even confided that he had started out in the movie business in much the same way when he was my age. When I told him I really wanted to pursue a career in writing and eventually at directing, he encouraged me to first do as much acting as I could get, then take on any other job in the business that would get me closer to the action, thereby confirming what Cukor, Darrow and so many others had encouraged me to do over the years. Finally, he introduced me to the studio casting agent with the offhand remark that this kid could go somewhere. I was thrilled by what I heard and I thanked him for his encouragement.

Over the next couple of years, I did a variety of television shows at Republic, all thanks to the casting director I had been introduced to earlier by Lloyd Bridges. Most were minor roles with few lines, but since I had dark hair and a generally swarthy complexion, I could easily pass for being a Native American. Then, with the addition of a little makeup and facial hair, I was quickly transformed to someone of Mexican or Spanish-American descent; I even did a commercial dressed as a gypsy for Gallo Wines in this guise.

By 1960 I had done three or four more westerns at Republic, all of which went well, except for one memorable event I feel compelled to exhume here if for no other reason than to pique the reader's interest.

As I arrived at the studio for this particular shoot I was fitted out in full cowboy regalia, a gun belt, spats and boots, went through makeup at the studio, and then was bussed out to the location site at the old Gene Autry ranch west of Northridge. The actual shooting site was a rough trail on rising terrain surrounded by large boulders. The camera was set up at the bottom of the draw and was angled upward, taking in the entire length of the trail from the top of the hill down to where the trail turned abruptly to the right, directly in front of the camera. I then noticed four horses being unloaded from a large trailer and corralled nearby. Finally one of the assistants came over to our bus, called out four names, including mine, and told us to go over and mount our horses, indicating our scene was being set up for the next shot.

Unfortunately, I had never been on a spirited saddle horse like this one nor had I ever intended to be. Luckily for me, however, the other riders quickly took me under their wing, showed me how to handle my horse and slowly led me out of the corral. Then, finally, we were led over to the director for an overview of the shot. Our action was to ride down from the top of the hill at a gallop, firing our weapons as we passed the camera. We were then led off to the top of the hill where loaded weapons were handed us before being lined up for the gallop. My position was number three out of the four, with one man behind me for support. But before I could even get my breath, I heard the director yell "Action," and off we went. As we came over the crest of the hill, all I could see was the abyss that lay before me as the trail dropped off precipitously into the dust thrown up by the hooves of the horses descending before me. I felt like I was on a roller coaster, so all I could do was grasp my horse's reins and hold on for dear life. As we approached the bottom of the hill where the trail turned abruptly to the right, I had no inkling as to the turn of events that were about to take place. As my horse made its turn, I kept on going straight. I had been launched headlong into space and found myself airborne in thin air. In a moment of time that seemed an eternity, I landed directly in front of the camera in a cloud of dust and I knew instantly that my life and my days as an actor were now officially over. I would be lucky, I surmised, if they just threw me off the set. Then, before I could even regain my composure, I heard the director yell "Cut," followed by some giggles and a long pause before what I knew would be the beginning of the end for my short-lived career in the movies.

"You, the guy who just fell off the horse – where in hell did you ever learn to ride a horse like that?"

It didn't take me long to respond. I stood up, brushed myself off and prepared myself for my just punishment.

"I'm sorry," I replied, "actually, I've never been on a wild horse like this one."

The laughter that followed filled the canyon for what seemed like an eternity, but in actual fact it was probably only a moment before the director responded.

"I should have guessed it. You couldn't repeat that performance if you tried. But you're lucky this time. The shot was perfect. **PRINT IT!**"

Within the week, it seemed like everybody in town had heard about my riding ability – or total lack thereof – including George Huene, who called to chide me about it, remarking gleefully that it wasn't the first time someone had taken on a role he was ill-prepared to assume. Nevertheless, he went on to explain the primary reason for his call, which was to ask whether I was interested in purchasing a complete professional motion picture camera outfit for a small percentage of the original cost. He explained it was purchased a couple of years earlier by an independent film company that had gone bankrupt and was now available through a broker friend of his for a court-ordered cash sale price of only $500. It consisted of a professional 35mm Arriflex 11 camera body, three lenses, magazines, a tripod with fluid head and all the accessories.

"With this thing, Bob, you could shoot your own movies. You could write them, direct them, and even act as your own cinematographer and editor. You could wind up being the highest-acclaimed, multi-talented whiz kid in the business, and all with no one else out there telling you what to do."

Unbeknownst to Huene, I had often thought about doing exactly as he just suggested. In fact, I had already written a number of short stories I knew could easily be modified for film, and the more he spoke about it, the more I felt that the time might have actually come for me to start doing projects like this on my own. The following morning, I went down to the bank, withdrew $500 in cash and accompanied Huene to the broker. A quick check of the equipment and it was all mine.

CHAPTER 21:

The Harvey Weinstein Syndrome

During Hollywood's golden years, no one had yet heard of Harvey Weinstein or his ruinous reputation, but it seemed as though everyone was aware that many other perpetrators of similar ilk had pervaded the Hollywood scene since its very beginnings.

As early as 1921, silent-film star Fatty Arbuckle brought the devious, sexually oriented subculture of Hollywood to the attention of the entire world when he was arrested for allegedly raping and killing a young Hollywood hopeful, Virginia Rappe, during a drunken all-night sex party at the St. Francis Hotel in San Francisco. After two mistrials, Arbuckle was acquitted of the crime, but his reputation was ruined. He died a broken man in abject shame and disgrace. In 1943, megastar Errol Flynn was arrested and prosecuted for allegedly seducing and raping another young Hollywood hopeful, and – worst of all – his victim was underage. Due strictly to his fame and incredible worldwide popularity, Flynn was acquitted of the crime, allowing him to continue his sadistic practice of seducing innocent young women until he died of acute alcoholism, drug addiction and uncontrolled sexual depravity.

After arriving in Hollywood in 1952, I quickly learned that the alleged predatory practice of control that many persons of position practiced over newcomers in the film business occurred all the time. Harry Cohn, then the studio boss at Columbia Pictures, was one of the first Hollywood moguls I heard about. Apparently, his casting couch was well known to every young "would be" starlet in town. Darryl Zanuck at Fox Studios was another mogul the girls all had to be leery about. His penchant, however, was even more devious than Harry Cohn's. He would merely enter the room in his bathrobe and unceremoniously expose himself. If any interest was shown, he would merely work up a quick erection and allow himself to be serviced. If not, the subject would be excused and the next victim allowed to enter the scene.

Although I readily admit to succumbing to the advances of any number of attractive females my age, I also welcomed the adulation of some "very select" older women whom I found to be extremely sexual and very desirable. Clearly, it is one thing to be seduced by a lovely creature in a natural social environment and quite another to be overwhelmed by an overly aggressive, unattractive, oversexed member of the human species – regardless of age or sex – who has nothing other in mind than to ravish and rape the next victim who comes along. We all know that Hollywood is and always has been the sex capital of the world, but it is also known to possess more beautiful people – male and female alike – than any other place on earth. What better place for an alleged sexual predator like Harvey Weinstein to set up shop and to satisfy his deceitful requirements. It is a no-win situation for any hopeful who submits to the advances of unsavory characters like Weinstein, but there appears to be enough willing recruits available out there on a daily basis regardless of the consequences. Unfortunately, that is the way it seems to have always been in Hollywood and most likely always will be.

I quickly learned, however, that Harry Cohn and Darryl Zanuck were not the only alleged predators a newcomer needed to avoid. Other equally unsavory men of position soon became known to me personally, resulting in a number of advances I did not wish to pursue. Only one of these, however, was underhanded and cunning enough to deserve retelling at this time.

During my prolonged association with director George Cukor, he made it a practice to introduce me to a number of successful writers in the business who he thought might help mentor or tutor me with my career, but the only one I happened to cross swords with was Noël Coward, the world-renowned British import who was in his mid-fifties at the time. In spite of his advancing age, Coward was still the darling of the theatre world in New York, where the so-called intellectuals of the day thrived on the witty, amusing and cleverly written works then in fashion by some of the most highly acclaimed writers in the business. Unfortunately, having developed a similar unrestrained sexual deportment as one of his fellow countrymen, Oscar Wilde, who shocked the world with his lurid escapades many years earlier, Coward was alleged to be a notorious, openly gay, practicing predator. He was renowned in the theatre world for his salacious liaisons with handsome young men both on and off the stage, and like Wilde, who was equally as famous and notorious during his time, he made no effort to hide it.

Coward had recently enjoyed a dramatic success of sorts with a small cabaret act in Las Vegas appropriately entitled "Noël Coward at Las Vegas," and he was still relishing the reviews. It seemed as though he was continually being praised in the press for his obvious superior intellect, wit and clever saccharine patter, but in my brief encounter with him over a sexual advance I rejected, I found him to be an unmitigated and disappointing bore.

As was Coward's style, whenever traveling the world he would always seek private accommodations at someone's home. Coward was close friends with Vivien Leigh and her husband Laurence Olivier, and all of them stayed at Cukor's home whenever they were in town and the guest room was available.

Regarding the visit in question, Coward had arrived at Cukor's home earlier that morning. Always the perfect host, Cukor had scheduled a lavish dinner party for him that evening and asked me to attend, explaining that he thought it would be a perfect time for me to meet Coward, quipping innocently,

"I told him all about you and most importantly that you were the newest writer in town and a very good one. Obviously, if he were to like some of your writings, there is no telling what kind of thing it could lead to."

He then asked me to come over beforehand to check out the decorative fountain George Huene and I had built for him earlier, explaining that it tended to get clogged with leaves and he just wanted to make certain it was working perfectly for Coward's visit.

I arrived at Cukor's house mid-afternoon, came in through the main gate and walked directly to the outside stairwell by the pool house and up to the back of the main house where the fountain was located. Unfortunately, that route took me directly past the guest room windows where – unbeknownst to me – Coward was lurking as I walked by. Apparently, he liked what he saw and immediately ran up the stairwell to the library to ask Cukor who I was. As Cukor explained it to me later, he told Coward that I was this new writer he wanted Coward to meet, but when Coward expressed an immediate sexual interest in me, Cukor claimed he then told Coward not to pursue it because I was straight and not available for that. Undeterred, however, Coward simply went back downstairs and waited at the guest room window for me to leave – and when I did, he pounced like a black widow in heat.

What occurred next was the venerable *Death in Venice* plot revisited. Not surprisingly, the theme Thomas Mann exploited so brilliantly in his novel had been repeated countless times throughout history. It was the timeless conflict between age and youth – the older man or woman and the desire for sex with a younger one. Male or female, straight or gay, it is always the same old story, each one just unique of its own accord or fashioned with a slightly different twist.

The moment Coward saw me pass his window on the way out, he rushed to the lower stairwell door and made his move. Opening the door hurriedly, he called out,

"You! You there. Please, please come here."

I turned, saw who it was and complied, dutifully, albeit with a bit of angst. Being aware of Coward's sexual proclivities, I was not about to allow myself to become engaged in any situation that was not totally open, professional and aboveboard. Nevertheless, I came to his side and exclaimed in the most friendly manner I could summon,

"Yes, what can I do for you?"

"Oh, please, please come in, I need to speak with you."

It was all pretty innocent until this point, but the more he spoke, the more he kept dragging me into the house. As a word of explanation, I should mention that the lower stairwell door in Cukor's home leads to a second door to the guest room on the left, with the stairwell itself leading upstairs to a landing with the oval room on one side and Cukor's bedroom on the other. In other words, voices spoken in the lower stairwell can easily be heard in several adjoining rooms upstairs. For me to stay on the safe side, I decided my best strategic position was to remain in the lower stairwell proper and not be coerced into the guest room, which could then be closed off from the rest of the house by the guest room door.

"Please, please, come in, you must come in. I must speak with you privately."

I countered with a friendly:

"What is it? You can speak with me here."

Finally, realizing I was not inclined to comply, and without any embarrassment whatsoever, he came right up to me, grabbed my genitals with one hand and my buttocks with the other, proclaiming for the whole house to hear,

"Oh dear boy, I must have you, I must have you."

Oh god, I thought, that is the most pathetic line I ever heard. Only an Englishman could utter that line and expect to get away with it.

For a brief moment, I genuinely felt sorry for the man. I really did. I didn't want to embarrass him by rejecting his advance in some violent manner, but by the same token, I had no wish to comply with it or offer him any hope that this encounter could reach any sort of positive conclusion. I gave him his ten-second feel – which he took full advantage of – then slowly pushed his hands away before explaining it to him as clearly and as forcefully as I could.

"Excuse me, but you don't understand. I can't comply with your wishes because I don't do or engage in what you want from me. Please understand that. It has nothing to do with you."

There was a momentary pause of disbelief, then an immediate transformation. His expression segued from a broad smile to a hideous scowl – from a look of hope to outright defiance.

"Oh, come on, now, you can't fluff me off like that. You can be had. Anyone can be had! Who do you think you are anyway? Don't you know who I am?"

"Yes, I know who you are, but I am not anyone and I cannot be had, as you put it."

"Well, if you can't be had, what do you want then? Cukor tells me you are a writer and a damn good one. I can introduce you to every important person in Hollywood, and I can do it immediately. I can give you anything you want. I can make you a celebrity, like me, even more if you do as I say. Or maybe Cukor is wrong about you and you are just another ten-cent Hollywood street hustler, a cheap trick like all the rest of them – no better than that or worse."

He rattled on with vitriolic anger for God only knows how long. Then there was a short break in the rhetoric, and finally the reality of the situation he had created. Realizing the futility of his request, he instantly assumed an obvious, overly expressive theatrical show of despair – but I didn't buy it.

"Oh god, I didn't mean that. I know you are not a street hustler, please forgive me for suggesting that – you are a dear boy – oh, please forgive me."

Then, as he moved toward me with arms outstretched in what was clearly another attempt at my crotch, I felt I had heard enough. I simply told him to back off, then slowly stepped away from him, opened the outside door and left.

By the time I returned home, I had a call waiting from Cukor, who apologized profusely for Coward's rude behavior. This was the first time that Cukor and I had the occasion to speak of anything of a sexual nature – and I could tell he was embarrassed to do so – but he felt it was so egregious an affront he simply had to make amends to correct it. He explained that he had heard everything from the oval room directly above us and was particularly offended by Coward's remark that "I could be had" – especially in lieu of the fact that Coward continued to pursue his advances in spite of Cukor's earlier admonition that I was not available. Cukor called the entire matter a sordid affair and begged me to forgive him for allowing it to occur. I assured Cukor I did not feel it was his fault but that, under the circumstances, I did not think it was in either of our interests for me to attend his dinner party for Coward that evening, and he agreed. Cukor then assured me he would never allow such an encounter to occur at his home again. He obviously felt betrayed by Coward and as far as I know never invited him to stay at his home again.

Understandably, the episode had been very painful for Cukor to endure. As a result, he never mentioned Coward's name to me again, nor did I ever hear him mention Coward to others in my presence. Nothing untoward remained as far as my relationship with Cukor was concerned, and we simply went on with our relationship as mentor and student as though the event had never occurred.

Although I never thought it was appropriate for me to discuss the matter with Cukor in any greater detail, it was simply not in my psyche to allow a rather unattractive, balding, pudgy, much older man like Coward to throw me in bed like a sack of potatoes and ravish my body as though I were a poor street urchin. It just wasn't in the cards for him and I'm only sorry that he didn't recognize that fact to begin with. Coward might not have attained the stratospheric influence in Hollywood that Harvey Weinstein achieved many years later, but he utilized the same authority that his celebrity afforded him to hopefully realize the same devious result. I might mention that I would have acted just as negatively to the approach had it been made by an older, unattractive, overly aggressive woman, because the confluence of factors would have been the same.

Unfortunately, it wasn't just the older, influential male predators who took a fancy to vulnerable young men like me, because it seemed as though there were always enough of the older female variety available to make life miserable for us, as well. The only problem in cases with female predators is that, for obvious reasons, male victims are much less likely to cry foul than female victims are – the reason perhaps being that the act might represent a weakness on the part of the man's character or actually threaten his masculinity in some malevolent fashion. Yes, I could cite a few such cases myself in situations that were just as discomforting to me as the Coward advance, but I won't, because I feel I might only embarrass myself by doing so.

I never deluded myself into believing I was the only person who was ever sexually accosted in Hollywood. I merely accepted the fact that the problem existed and went on with my life without dwelling on the consequences. Sadly, it is a situation that every attractive young aspirant in Hollywood faces on a daily basis. Considering the fact that the basic underlying component of most Hollywood films has always been sex, and to purvey sex in an ever-more interesting and pervasive manner, Hollywood has required an unending stream of good-looking, sexy young people to pull the whole charade off. As a result, it is understandable why every attractive newcomer in town involuntarily becomes fodder for the predators' unwanted advances. It is and always has been the force majeure that no unsuspecting Hollywood aspirant could avoid, and as we now know, it has been prevalent not only in Hollywood, but in our business, religious, sports and political worlds, as well.

We can only thank all the poor unsuspecting victims of major predators who have come forward in recent months to finally accuse their molesters of their heinous crimes. From Harry Cohn and Darryl Zanuck to Harvey Weinstein, Roger Ailes and the myriad of other alleged predators who have recently been brought to light, one can only hope that these revelations will ultimately put a damper on these devious practices and perhaps eliminate the stigma that most victims have been forced to carry for the better part of their adult lives.

What price Hollywood? A lot more than one can ever imagine or endure.

CHAPTER 22:

Marilyn Monroe

Hal Schaefer was a jazz musician, musical composer and vocal coach who worked in a wide variety of Hollywood films in those capacities from 1950 and on. When I met Hal in 1953, he was working at Fox as a vocal coach for Marilyn Monroe on *Gentlemen Prefer Blondes*. A year or so later, he signed on to coach Marilyn again on *There's No Business Like Show Business*. Hal was a good-looking young guy from Queens and was exceptionally talented and highly respected in the business. We enjoyed a good rapport with each other, especially when sharing our joint interests in the piano and music in general. I was just leaving the Fox commissary one day when I ran into Hal, who said he was on his way over for his daily afternoon coaching session with Marilyn. As he explained it, she was waiting for him in her dressing room, and then jokingly asked me whether I cared to come along for support. Surprised by his remark, I asked him to explain what I was supposed to support, and his response explained it all.

"Well, Marilyn is having a hard time memorizing her lyrics, so every time I see her I try to instill something new in the lesson – something to pique her interest – because once she loses it, all she can think about is sex or – in the worst case – her mother's mental illness. Not that there is anything wrong with being in bed with her. She's sensational, but when she starts in on her mother's problems, it kills the rest of the session and we never get anything done. So since you're here and if you've got the time, you could stand in as her audience of one and maybe your presence will help stimulate her to have more interest in the music – at least for a short while."

Hal went on to explain that every session seemed to work out much the same. They start out well enough with her concentrating on her singing, but within fifteen or twenty minutes her mind begins to wander, she begins fondling herself and then comes over and starts in on him.

"Naturally, we wind up in bed, and whatever I had planned for that session is over."

Without mincing words, Hal admitted that he had been having a secret affair with Marilyn for months, adding,

"The big problem is her husband, Joe DiMaggio. They're separated but he's still in love with her and he is very jealous. According to Marilyn, if he were to find out about our affair, he would have us chopped up in pieces and thrown in the ocean."

"Damn it, Hal, how did you ever get involved in a situation like that? You could get yourself killed."

"Don't remind me, I know it. Unfortunately, the studio assigned me to coach her on this picture and I've got to go through with it. My whole career is at stake here, so if you want to help me out, you could sure as hell take the load off me."

Marilyn had a four-picture contract with Fox that allowed her the luxury of enjoying a private dressing room/apartment-type trailer on the lot where she could do as she pleased. The trailer was parked a few short steps to the left and just inside the main studio gate, allowing her quick access to the commissary and all the major studio buildings. It also worked out as a makeshift private residence for her where she could rest, sleep, or do whatever she wanted.

As Hal and I approached Marilyn's dressing room, we could hear a voice wafting out at us through an open window singing along to a recording of the song "Heat Wave." The voice was unmistakable; it was Marilyn's. When we got to the door, Hal just opened it matter-of-factly and entered, motioning for me to follow. A moment later, there I stood enjoying a private, sexually provocative performance of "Heat Wave" by none other than Marilyn Monroe. Hal immediately joined in on key phrases, emphasizing certain important words with his own gestures and, in the process, indicating more force or restraint in those areas where he felt they were required. All that Marilyn had on was a simple pullover slip with no bra or other undergarment to contend with, and her breasts responded appropriately to each of her movements. It was only after the song was over and Hal sat her down for further vocal direction that I learned from their discussion that this was one of the songs she was expected to sing in *There's No Business Like Show Business*, the film she was presently working on. But there was no way to keep Marilyn quiet – she was literally squirming in her seat until she finally stood up, began fondling herself all over and continued humming the tune with every movement. It was the most sexually imbued act I had ever witnessed, almost as though she were masturbating, unashamedly, and enjoying the fact that Hal and I were watching her do it. A moment or two later, after Hal praised her for getting through a certain passage correctly, she turned, looked directly at me for the first time and asked,

"Did you like that? Did it get you hot? You know the heat wave thing? Doesn't it just get you all steamy inside?"

I responded to her inquiries with a simple,

"Yes, m'am, it sure does," along with the requisite nod.

I really didn't think I could verbalize it any better than that. Words just weren't in it for me at that moment. It was such a libidinous "come on" question I thought I might embarrass myself with a dumb answer, so I decided not to elaborate.

Marilyn then came right up to me, caressing her breasts in the process.

"It did me, too. It sure gets me hot all over."

A few moments later, the thought finally came to Hal that he had forgotten to introduce me.

"Marilyn, I forgot. This is Bob. Bob meet Marilyn."

"Hi Bob, I like the name Bob."

"Hi Marilyn, it's nice meeting you."

Hal then told Marilyn that he had asked me to sit in on the session as a way of helping her get over her stage fright, which apparently was an ongoing problem for her. The ploy worked and it seemed as though Marilyn had finally gotten down to realizing the extent of the serious work that lay ahead for her. Nevertheless, her concentration was not long lived. After a few moments, she stood up nervously, groping her body again and proclaiming she was thirsty. Then she asked Hal to call the commissary to have a bottle of champagne delivered for her, but Hal objected.

"It's too early for that, Marilyn. We've got to get a couple of hours in on this song today. We simply can't screw around with it any longer."

"But Hal, I'm thirsty. I can't think when I'm thirsty."

"OK, OK, I'll go to the commissary and get us some drinks, but the champagne is out. Marilyn, why don't you just do the song again and this time I want you to sing it directly to Bob. Remember he's your audience – your sounding board. Then, when I get back I'm going to interrogate him to see how you did."

Hal then told me to sit down and to watch every movement Marilyn made, then turned on his heels and left. In the meanwhile, Marilyn went over to fiddle with the record player, all the while quietly singing the opening strain from "Heat Wave" to herself once again.

"We're having a heat wave, a tropical heat wave..."

Marilyn was now facing away from me, exposing her entire backside for me to savor. With one line leading to the next, she was soon humping the air in front of her in an exaggerated display of orgasmic pleasure before turning around to face me, fondling her breasts passionately in the process. Oh, shit, I thought, here we go.

"The temperature's rising, it isn't surprising..."

She was now standing directly in front of me, swiveling her hips in rhythm to the music, then fingering herself in every orifice and crevasse of her body.

"Is your temperature rising, Bob? Mine is."

Indeed it was and I told her so.

"Da da da, da, da da."

Suddenly, Marilyn twisted around and flung herself to the floor. She now lay prostrate directly in front of me, pulsating with erotic energy, before continuing on with the second verse.

"She started a heat wave by letting her seat wave..."

In line with the lyrics, Marilyn waved her own seat back and forth. Then, moaning and groaning, she humped the floor with such gusto the whole trailer began to rock.

"The temperature's rising; it isn't surprising. Da da da, da, da da."

I felt my crotch was about to explode. From her very first hump to each moan and groan, I could feel the fluids begin flowing in my loins – ever so slowly at first – then begin oozing out through my jeans. I was so damn horny, I just wanted to grab Marilyn and get us both off, but I didn't dare interfere with her rant, fearing it might break her spell. Nevertheless, it was at least another long stage minute before Marilyn finally turned over to face me once again.

"Oh god, I don't know what to do with myself; sometimes I really feel like I'm losing it."

Then, looking me directly in the eye, she asked me, point blank.

"Do you think I'm pretty, Bob? Do you think I'm pretty enough to take out for dinner, or to go to bed with? Do you, Bob?"

"Yes, I do, Marilyn, very much so."

"I don't know, I wonder sometimes."

Marilyn then crawled over to me on her haunches, thrusting her arms around my calves for support, before slowly laying her head down between my knees. Naturally, I thought that she was going for my crotch and, if so, I was certainly ready for her. I had developed and maintained an erection throughout her rant that incredibly was now poking her directly in the face. There was no doubt in my mind that in a moment or two, we would finally be going at it. That Marilyn would wake up, look at me, realize I was there for her and allow me to have her.

But it was not to be. In its stead, she began to weep and then cry, and in an instant the spell of the moment was gone, and as I feared a few moments later, it was gone for good.

What followed was the most pathetic, heart-rending display of mental distress I had ever witnessed in a human being, and I felt powerless to intercede. Marilyn went on to blurt out her overriding fears from childhood on about a multitude of episodes throughout her adolescence, her mother's mental illness and the fact that she feared she had probably inherited those illnesses, as well. She just rattled on, seemingly absorbed in the process of cleansing her soul as though she was somehow speaking to her psychiatrist, or to a priest, and I just listened, spellbound, incapable of responding or appeasing her. In less than a heartbeat, Marilyn began to unload her brain with volleys of barely interconnected episodes out of her past, and the gist of her anguish overwhelmed her.

It was at least ten minutes before Hal returned from the commissary. Marilyn's head was still buried between my knees and my pant legs and crotch were sopping wet from her weeping and the oozing aftermath of my erection – and Hal knew immediately what had occurred. It was only then that Marilyn seemed aware of Hal's presence, allowing her to interrupt her thoughts and compose herself. Slowly, she wiped her eyes, got up off my knees and excused herself to go to the rest room. All Hal could do was look at the mess on my pants and shake his head.

"I'm sorry, Bob, I should have known this would happen. I'm really embarrassed about that. She's done the same with me a dozen times. It all goes well until she segues back to her childhood and all that mental crap, and when that happens I don't dare interrupt her – so I know how frustrating that can be. But she's my problem, not yours, and I apologize for that."

I told Hal he didn't need to apologize for anything. I realized she was a troubled soul and I tried to console her as best as I could. He thanked me, then suggested I just leave before she comes back, explaining that she will probably just take a handful of pills now, knock herself out, and then that will be it for the day.

On the way back home, I was so horny that I drove directly to my girlfriend Trudi's apartment and proceeded to ravish her body in a wild sexual melee from the moment I walked in on her.

"Geez, what happened to you, Bobby? I've never seen you so horny."

Obviously, when I showed her the mess on my pants and described the entire encounter I experienced with Marilyn, it was all she needed to get horned up herself. According to Trudi, my story was akin to watching good porn and that was all we needed to get us both off – and we did so in record time.

As I lay in bed that evening alone with my thoughts, all I could think about was poor Marilyn and her demons – and she had plenty of them to contend with. Nevertheless, Hal continued to coach Marilyn to the point where he felt she was as good as she could get, then unwittingly became her full-time lover, carrying on a torrid romance the whole town soon became aware of. It seemed like a winning situation for both of them until circumstances beyond their control brought their affair to an inevitable, screeching halt.

Sadly, when *There's No Business Like Show Business* was released, both Marilyn and the picture were panned, receiving the worst reviews imaginable. All in all, the project became a significant financial disaster for Fox – and Marilyn was named as the pariah who caused it all. Marilyn's fortune, it seemed, simply changed overnight, but in truth it had been waning for some time. All of the pills, booze and sex were taking their toll and Marilyn was finally beginning to realize it. Worst of all, Joe DiMaggio received word of her illicit affair with Hal and, in an act of vengeance and jealous rage, he orchestrated a mob attack that was apparently designed to rub them both out. Luckily, however, the mob went to the wrong address, allowing the lovers, who were in an adjoining apartment, to escape unharmed. Marilyn, however, finally had it with DiMaggio and, fearing for her life, filed for divorce soon thereafter.

In the end, Hal survived the event but the notoriety surrounding his unethical relationship with Marilyn cost him his job, forcing him to leave Hollywood and seek solace elsewhere. Gone was his life as one of Hollywood's finest young musical talents. His brilliant career was thus terminated prematurely, and all because of his love for sex with a woman who had more love to give than either one of them could handle.

In 1962, I was directing my first full-length feature film in Paris when I saw the headline in the *International Herald Tribune* concerning Marilyn's premature death. She was only thirty-six years of age, a sad commentary on the ultimate effects of her unorthodox lifestyle, the confluence of alcohol, anxiety and drugs, and her extremely perverse sexuality. How sad, I thought, that her demons had finally caught up with her.

When considering my short, bittersweet encounter with Marilyn, it was obvious that she was a deeply troubled soul. From basic revelations to surging primitive emotions, her entire psyche was strewn with mental flotsam going back to the earliest days of her childhood. The tragic truth being that she was incapable of handling all those disturbing memories and unable to jettison them from her mind before they overwhelmed and finally consumed her. She embodied the classic case of the psychologically disturbed, insecure beauty and, as such, was a time bomb threatening to explode at any moment; I was surprised only that it took her so long to do so.

CHAPTER 23:

The Oliviers

By 1959, Vivien Leigh's marriage to Laurence Olivier was essentially over. Oh, they still socialized together with friends and made an effort to convey the essence of a congenial relationship in public, but it was all for show. There was little chance they would ever rekindle the kind of flagship romance and respect the couple enjoyed during the late 1930s, when they were widely acclaimed as the king and queen of the theatre. Olivier was Heathcliff and Vivien was Scarlett O'Hara, and this incredible aura of royalty and invincibility existed not only on the silver screen with their Oscar-winning performances in *Wuthering Heights* and *Gone With The Wind* – their huge pre-war blockbuster successes – but in real life with all their adoring fans throughout the world.

It was now many years later, and a much more mature Laurence Olivier was in Hollywood working on another film. Although Olivier was primarily known as a stage actor – and he obviously preferred working in that medium – the real money was to be had in acting on film, even though it was more demanding on him. Nevertheless, he remained the master of his craft and quite unlike any other actor before him or since. Unfortunately, as I was soon to find out, he was just another regular human being under all his royal trappings, with faults and defects just like everyone else. Sadly, however, Olivier also found it necessary to be nasty, rude and uncommonly ill-mannered not only to his wife, but also to others who unfortunately came into contact with him.

As the events unfurled on this particular day, I had been out all afternoon and did not receive the message that Vivien had called until I arrived back home around six. Frankly, I was surprised by the call because I knew she was in town with her husband. I was aware that she was still an unhappily married woman, and as far as I knew she showed no sign of giving her husband up. I debated whether I should even call her back, but libido and lust being what they are, I just couldn't resist the enticement and the chance for yet another fling with one of the signature romances of my life – so I gave in to temptation and called her back.

Much to my dismay, Vivien gave me none of the usual small talk or even a pleasant salutation – but she did get right to the point. She explained that she was scheduled to attend a dinner at Danny Kaye's home that evening with her husband, but that someone from the studio had called to inform her that he would be working late and would be unable to attend. Vivien added,

"Well, obviously, I can't go to the affair by myself, so I need you to escort me."

It all seemed so perfunctory, yet innocent enough – at least at first glance – but my trepidations soon made me think otherwise.

"But Vivien, what if your husband shows up?"

"He won't show up, Bobby, they're shooting late. The dinner will be over long before they finish."

That was that. Try as I might, I couldn't convince Vivien otherwise. She seemed hell-bent on making an appearance at the party, and there seemed little I could do to convince her otherwise. Thus the die was cast and the confluence of regrettable events that followed became tragically unavoidable.

Danny Kaye and his wife, Sylvia Fine, were longtime close friends of the Oliviers. Kaye was a middle-aged, former comic from the Borscht Belt who had made a name for himself on radio and early television, then carved a niche in motion pictures, where he remained a star for many years. His forte, however, and his greatest gift to mankind, was his innate ability to interpret, verbally, the acrobatically clever lyrics that Sylvia composed for him, and to deliver each word in machine-gun-like, rapid-fire succession. It was a unique talent only Kaye possessed, and he refined it to a degree of excellence no pretender could ever challenge.

On a personal level, however, Kaye reigned alone in a world of his own making, and of particular note was the fact that Kaye and Olivier – to the exclusion of their wives – had exhibited such an ongoing example of primal male bonding over the years that rumor persisted they were openly gay lovers. I thought it implausible and both of them would have denied the allegations, but their overtly questionable demeanors towards each other certainly didn't help convince anyone that anything to the contrary could have been possible.

When Vivien and I arrived at the Kaye home, we were immediately ushered into the sitting room, where a few guests were already in attendance. Chins dropped amid muffled cries of "Oh!" before Vivien realized the shock effect of the situation she had created. Nevertheless, being the pro she was, she reacted instinctively and with authority.

"I'm sorry I didn't call first to explain. It was late and there wasn't time. Larry sent a message saying he had to work late and wouldn't make dinner, so I asked my friend Bob, here, to escort me in his stead."

Sylvia Fine, our hostess, was the first to react positively, coming over hastily to greet Vivien, then me, and urging the others to follow suit. Thus, I was introduced to all of those present who cared to meet me. Most were cordial and seemingly eager to learn who I was, but a big chill was yet to descend upon the room when Vivien finally realized that our host, Danny Kaye, had not as yet appeared.

"Oh, Sylvia, where's Danny? I'd like him to meet Bob."

The meeting that followed was the first real damper of the evening and clearly a precursor of things to come. I remembered seeing Kaye at the back of the room when Vivien and I first came in, but he disappeared immediately thereafter and had not reappeared. Frustrated by his absence, Sylvia apologized to Vivien and physically left the room to drag a defiant, scowling Danny Kaye out of the kitchen to make the introduction on her own. Nevertheless, Kaye barely looked at me, preferring to glance elsewhere, and his handshake – if you could call it that – impressed me as being purposefully languid and unresponsive. A moment later, I whispered to Vivien that I didn't think it was such a good idea for me to come here since our host clearly did not approve of my presence. Vivien, however, quickly dismissed my fears by grasping my hand firmly and smiling broadly, proclaiming with all due authority that Sylvia was our host, not Kaye.

Maybe so, but it was clear to me that Kaye disapproved of my escorting Vivien to the party and perhaps might even have resented Vivien for attending after Olivier informed her that he was predisposed. Who knows? It appeared to be an odd confluence of events I was not privy to, but I was sure as hell stuck in the middle of it and I knew it. In the end, I decided stoically it could only get worse – and it did.

Nevertheless, the rest of the pre-dinner activities went well. Kaye stayed out of my way as best as he could and I made every effort to avoid him. Sylvia, on the other hand, was the perfect hostess, attending to all the needs of her guests, and when we were led into the dining room to be seated for dinner, she graciously assigned the two seats flanking hers for Vivien on one side and me on the other. I surmised that Sylvia was aware of her husband's frustration with the situation at hand and would seat him at the opposite end of the table, and she did. Even so, she was clearly not prepared for the situation that was about to unfold; it was a confrontation that destroyed the evening, blowing the entire party into oblivion.

It was an entrance to end all entrances – a theatrical exhibition no one other than the world's greatest classical actor could perform, and he did so in a manner that left all of us aghast. As the door was flung open, there stood an obviously inebriated Laurence Olivier with his hair all askew, makeup residue still slathered over his forehead and neck, a sliver of lipstick smeared from his lips to the rearmost crevasses of his ear, and what appeared to be dried semen stains all over the front of his trousers. To make matters worse, however, Olivier arrived not by himself but with an equally inebriated floozy attached firmly to his arm. The vision of Sir Laurence Olivier, the once reigning king of the theatre, in such an implausible situation was one that none of us could ever hope to forget. But that in itself was not the worst of it – that part of the episode was yet to come.

Vivien just stood up, spellbound, before coming over to me and thrusting her tiny hand firmly into mine for support. Her only response, barely audible even to me, was all she could summon.

"Oh god, I never thought it would come to this."

And with that, the floodgates of evil flowed forth from Olivier's lips in a tirade no one present could have ever expected. Casting an eye at Vivien, he let her have it with both barrels.

"Oh, so the wife decided to make it here after all – and I thought my message would have kept her away. Well, so what, who cares. Who needs her, who wants her anyway?"

As Olivier staggered around the room, he circumnavigated the dining table with Danny Kaye shadowing closely behind him, and it was clear from Kaye's demeanor as to exactly where his passions lay. My first thought was that Kaye had called Olivier from the kitchen the moment Vivien and I arrived and that this present confrontation was all being orchestrated on purpose. Thus, as Olivier rounded the corner at the opposite end of the table, he spotted Vivien holding on to my arm for support, and when he focused in on the two of us together, with me standing where he used to be, I believe it was the spark that ignited the fury within him. Making his way around the table and standing just an arm's length in front of us, his eyes began rolling around wildly in his head, then unable to control his emotions any further, he began flailing his arms about in all directions, almost striking Sylvia in the process. Undeterred and unforgiving, Olivier burst into a tirade of condemnation against his wife the likes of which no person should ever be forced to endure. It was the worst exhibition of jealousy and discontent I had ever witnessed, and I was instantly determined not to hear any more of it.

"Vivien, we're leaving."

Unfortunately, however, as Vivien and I turned to leave, Olivier poked an outstretched index finger into the center of my chest and directed the rest of his condemnation against me.

"And you. Who are you anyway, her new pimp? No, let me guess – you're a paid male prostitute, I can tell – and you're probably a cheap one at that. It's exactly what she deserves."

Another poke to my chest and that was all I needed. With my

own fury now unchecked, I poked Olivier back, but not with a measly little index finger. I used the flat open palm of my hand, generating a force with my blow that was so severe, it sent him reeling backward, still gesticulating wildly, and falling into the outstretched arms of his friend, Danny Kaye, with both of them ending up in a tangled heap on the floor.

That was it and the party was over. Luckily for Vivien and me, our hostess, Sylvia Fine, was on our side and tearfully apologized for all that had occurred. As she walked us to the door, I tried to make sense out of the scene I had just witnessed and been involved in, but I could not.

Needless to say, not a word was spoken between Vivien and me all the way back to her hotel. Not surprisingly, I was so pissed off I just wanted to scream and let off some steam, but I didn't. By the time we arrived, however, I had made up my mind and decided that it was now my turn to speak up and to let Vivien know exactly where I stood. But no, I would not sully or corrupt my remarks with vitriolic outbursts against her as Olivier had done. On the contrary, I would serve them to her as calmly, honestly and determinedly as I was able.

"Vivien, before I begin, I must tell you that I love you dearly and I always will. But after that episode this evening I can't put up with any more of this ridiculous love/hatred relationship you have with your husband. Not only is it unhealthy for you, it is destructive, and now you have me involved in a potential battery situation with him and I don't like that, I don't need that and frankly, I simply won't have it!

"What is it with Olivier and you, anyway? Are you so in love with that miserable person that you can't stand to leave him? Why is that? You told me yourself how unsatisfying he is in bed and after tonight I can't imagine he could ever be much better socially. You just witnessed firsthand exactly what he thought of you – and it wasn't very pretty. How much more do you have to hear to convince yourself that your romance with him is over...gone...done with. Don't you understand, Vivien? IT'S OVER and it has been for years."

I must have gone on for five minutes or more, reminding Vivien of all the evil, negative harangue that Olivier had thrown at her, hoping to bring her to her senses – but it was to no avail. She just sat there and listened to me, dutifully, without saying a word. She kept her head bowed and her eyes closed with her arms clasped firmly in front of her. Finally, however, she came forth with her response, and it was one I can't help but remember precisely and to this day.

"Bobby, you're a sweet boy and I love you, too – believe me, I do. I know you mean well, but you simply don't understand. But then, how could you? Larry and I have been married almost twenty years, but I've been in love with him since I was a child. It is not something I can simply dismiss and forget about. I am not that sort of person. I'm sorry he brought you into the middle of it this evening. It was not my intent to involve you, and I am truly sorry for having done so. Please forgive me…"

There was a final pause and then the inevitable conclusion.

"I love you very much, Bobby, and I just want you to know that. I would never consciously do anything to hurt you, I really am terribly sorry for everything."

Vivien then reached up with her right hand to open the car door, but unaccustomed as she was to the task, she looked at me to help her. Then, as I reached over to grasp the door handle for her, I inadvertently brushed her breasts with my forearm. That brief momentary contact was all it took to set her off once again. A murmur, a brief cry, a final meeting of the eyes, and it was over.

"Goodbye, my sweet" being her last words to me, and she was gone.

I never saw Vivien again. I moved to Europe shortly thereafter and took up residence in Paris for more than five years. During that time I visited London frequently, both on business and otherwise. I still carried Vivien's phone number in my billfold and I glanced at it frequently, but I never had the heart to call her, always fearing the chance of becoming involved in her problems once again.

Over the years Vivien had developed a bipolar mental condition she seemed incapable of handling on her own. These were the mood swings George Cukor warned me about when he first introduced me to her. When this occurred in my presence, I merely handled it with all the love and understanding I could bestow upon her. My simply being there, to hold her and reassure her, seemed to make all the difference. Unfortunately, having been married to Laurence Olivier for twenty long years – with only a smattering of those years being happy ones – only seemed to exacerbate the problem for her. Thus, in 1960, Vivien and Olivier divorced, forcing her to handle her condition on her own. To her credit, she was able to garner a few choice roles, most notably in 1961 with *The Roman Spring of Mrs. Stone* and in 1965 in *Ship of Fools,* in which hers was the only memorable performance. Even so, she was never able to reap the aura of celebrity she had achieved in *Gone With The Wind* or in *A Streetcar Named Desire.* Those heady days of success were gone forever and she knew it and accepted it, attaining some sense of satisfaction in the end.

Much has been written about Vivien's death in 1967 at the age of only fifty-three, along with the extent to which Olivier grieved at her passing. All that this observer can add is that he should have been a more devoted husband to her in life. She was a wonderful, albeit complex woman with a terrible affliction who deserved more from her marriage than Olivier was able to give her. I can only grieve for the both of them. Celebrity be damned! I am amazed they couldn't allow themselves to divorce years earlier.

In retrospect, I must thank Vivien for all the wonderful times we enjoyed together and try to forget the rest of it. We were completely compatible sexually and otherwise, and I will always remember her as the vibrantly beautiful young woman who brought a new energy, direction and determination into my life, and she did so at a time when I needed it the most. Again, all I could ask myself was, "How lucky could I have ever been?"

CHAPTER 24:

The Rat Pack

I met Sammy Davis Jr. through Yvette Duguay during a trip we took back to New Jersey in 1952. At the time, Sammy was playing at the 500 Club in Atlantic City and was clearly on the road to success. Soon thereafter, he reached the pinnacle of his career, emerging as one of the most highly revered superstars of the decade, then continued on and remained as such until his passing in 1990.

Over the years, I would run into Sammy often, but never more than when he was playing at the Sands Hotel in Las Vegas with Frank Sinatra, Dean Martin, Peter Lawford and comedian Joey Bishop, then referred to jointly as the Rat Pack. The original Rat Pack was formed, quite informally, by Humphrey Bogart and a few close friends during the 1950s. All of them were disillusioned with the studio contract system in Hollywood that controlled what all the contract players could do and, by extension, what anyone not under contract to a major studio could not do, which was to obtain work. It was one of the basic injustices that existed in Hollywood at the time, and my sympathies were totally in line with theirs.

During the 1960s, and especially throughout the summer months when there was usually a lull in the production of motion pictures in Hollywood, most actors, writers, directors and others not under contract or required to remain in town for some other reason, would seek respite elsewhere. Since I was working as an actor and a writer at this time, but was not under contract to anyone, I, too, sought respite elsewhere, and one of my favorite destinations soon became Las Vegas. They had only recently begun building some nice hotels in Vegas that, along with the attendant gambling, reasonably priced meals and multitude of showgirls, soon became everyone's favorite haunt.

It was on one of these trips to Las Vegas that I arrived at the

Sands Hotel to check in. Displayed prominently in the center of the hotel lobby was a large poster proclaiming "The Sands presents The Rat Pack, Two Shows Nightly" – and there in the center of the poster was a photo of "the pack" in action with my friend, Sammy Davis Jr. prominently positioned in the middle of it. What a great coincidence, I thought. What with Sammy right here at the Sands where I would be staying, I'll give him a call and see if we can get together. Accordingly, I asked the concierge to ring Sammy Davis' room for me, but to my dismay, his response was a surprised look and a cool rebuke.

"Mr. Davis does not stay at this hotel."

Puzzled by his reply, I asked,

"Well, where does he stay? Can you give me his number?"

Without responding verbally, he wrote a number down on a scratch pad, tore off the leaf and handed it to me. I thanked him for his help and went on to sign in.

Later that afternoon, I called Sammy to say hello, and when I inquired as to the reason for his lodging elsewhere, I was clearly not prepared to hear what I was told.

"Bobby, the truth of it is that it's OK for a black person like me to entertain you white folk, but it sure as hell ain't kosher for me to mix with you socially – at least not at a white man's palace like the Sands."

He then went on to explain that all the black people who worked at the Sands, including waiters, busboys and the like, had to room "off-site" at black facilities elsewhere in town, and that even though he was a headliner at the Sands, the rule applied to him, as well. Nevertheless, he seemed loath to dwell on the negative aspects of his employment and immediately asked that I join him backstage before the show to meet the rest of the pack. Naturally, I agreed, but when I walked into the large dressing room where they were getting ready to go on, I immediately noticed that the two heavyweights in the group, Frank Sinatra and Dean Martin, were at each other's throats, taking jabs at each other and otherwise trying to get in the last word.

It was a strange negatively charged atmosphere, I thought, for these two superstars to generate between them, and all just minutes before going on to a packed house of customers who were paying good money to see them in person. Nevertheless, when Sammy took me over and introduced me to them, their mood changed only minimally and then only to get in the last word or another gratuitous dig.

"Frank, I'd like you to meet another expatriate from New Jersey…"

Sinatra immediately interrupted Sammy, inquiring,

"Where are you from, pal? What school did you go to?"

I replied that I was from Elizabeth and went to Rutgers, whereupon Sinatra remarked offhandedly and with a definite negative pitch,

"Oh, another 'Ivy Leaguer.' Shit, I was never that lucky."

Well, he was wrong about my being an Ivy Leaguer, but I didn't think it would have been appropriate for me to respond to his remark, so I just "let it ride" and went on to speak about other things. It occurred to me that he might like to know that I had been present at his first professional engagement as a band singer at the Paramount Theatre in New York back in 1941, but he was not impressed with that either, remarking caustically,

"Oh, were you one of the bobby-soxers?"

Naturally, everyone in the room laughed at the remark that was clearly at my expense. The term "bobby-soxers" was the name given to the cadre of teenage girls who congregated in front of the Paramount stage whenever Sinatra appeared and screamed in abject delight every time their idol opened his mouth. It was a phenomenon of the age that few people who witnessed it can ever forget. Sinatra clearly enjoyed the fact that he got a zinger off at my expense. Luckily for me, however, I didn't flinch, but it was Dean Martin who got the next zinger off against Sinatra, taking the onus off of me to think up a clever reply.

"No, he wasn't, he was probably just after one of the little whores like you were. You told me yourself that they were all just a pack of little whores…"

All laughed again. It was Sinatra who uttered the "check" but

213

Martin who got in the "checkmate."

The moment for playful frivolity had clearly passed and Sinatra knew it, so he changed the subject, came over to me and calmly shook my hand.

"You shouldn't pay attention to any of this crap; it goes on all the time."

Sinatra then invited me to sit down with him at his dressing table. He asked me a number of questions about Elizabeth and the general area in New Jersey where I grew up, and he seemed genuinely interested in knowing more about me instead of just getting another zinger off at my expense. He enjoyed hearing about my musical background – even my stint at the lowly Hawaiian Palms – my writings and, finally, my desire to become a film director, and before our little session was over I felt we had made a genuine connection.

"Just keep at it, Pal, and don't let any shit get in your way," being his final words of advice to me.

Over the years I ran into Sinatra a number of times and I can honestly say he always seemed genuinely pleased to see me. Each time, however, he would invariably mention the bobby-soxers or, as an alternative, simply refer to them as "his little whores" or "the little bitches." It had become a private "thing" between the two of us that clearly took the place of his having to remember my name. Obviously, we both knew what he meant by those remarks and I felt perfectly comfortable to laugh at them, as well. We always parted with a smile, a handshake or a pat on the shoulder. I had the feeling he liked me well enough, but since I wasn't one of his drinking buddies, he really didn't know where to fit me in.

I had a particularly memorable run-in with Sinatra sometime during this period at a favorite eating house of his in Los Angeles named the Villa Capri, a well-known Italian restaurant in Hollywood where Sinatra usually held his drunken male-only parties in a back room. On the evening in question, I was hosting a party of my own in the main dining room while Sinatra was boozing it up with a group of six or more of his regular drinking pals in the rear. After all, it wasn't every day you could go out to a restaurant and find yourself sharing the same rarified air with the likes of Frank Sinatra in your midst. Obviously, Sinatra did not deserve the adulation he received wherever he went, but he got it strictly on the strength of his celebrity which, at the time, was phenomenal.

As the evening wound down, the racket from the back room subsided and the Sinatra party began to exit slowly through the main dining room where, as it turned out, my group was about to leave as well. As a result, the members of both parties more or less intermingled on the way out of the restaurant and into the valet parking area out front where Sinatra and I found ourselves standing shoulder to shoulder. Suddenly, looking over at me with mock surprise, he unashamedly bellowed forth with all the gusto he could muster and for all those who were present to hear,

"My little whores. What did you do with my little whores?"

We both laughed; he got off a couple of more funny lines, then patted me on the shoulder and went on his way. He had obviously had more than enough to drink that evening and probably just couldn't think of anything else to say.

But the fates had another zinger in mind for this occasion and this time it was not at my expense. As Sinatra was walking to his car, he ran into a friend of his who had just driven up in a brand-new Mercedes-Benz sports car. As I recall, it was one of the smaller two-seater convertible types, but it gave Sinatra the chance to engage in more raucous verbalizing – all of which was clearly for the benefit of the twenty or more people who by this time had accumulated at the sight of Sinatra out in the street in an everyday Hollywood environment. In other words, he was "playing to the crowd" and was causing a commotion strictly for the sake of being noticed. What occurred next, however, was something no one present could have predicted or expected. Feigning disrespect of his friend for buying such an expensive new car like the Mercedes-Benz, Sinatra backed off a few feet and then lunged forward toward the car, kicking a huge dent into the center of the passenger door.

Gasps of disbelief ensued from everyone present. It was such a frivolous, grievous act of gratuitous destruction no one who witnessed it could believe what they had seen. Then, adding insult to injury, he followed up on the kick with the lamest possible excuse.

"Well, now it ain't new anymore. Join the crowd, pal." With that, Sinatra moved forward, got into his own car and was gone.

But the story doesn't end there. A couple of days later all of the local newspapers reported that Frank Sinatra presented a friend of his with a brand-new car. No, it was not a small Mercedes-Benz like the one he whacked in front of the Villa Capri, but a big full-size one and probably the most expensive Mercedes-Benz convertible he could find.

In retrospect, one has to wonder how anyone, celebrity or not, could contemplate such a callous and insensitive act of destruction and to do it all simply for one's own image or misguided sense of self-aggrandizement. But then, that was Sinatra at the height of his fame and relative fortune. A few years later, he was in near-bankruptcy and forced to sell off many of the possessions he had accumulated over the years.

One of Sinatra's biggest debacles occurred in 1960, when he purchased and frivolously renovated the Cal-Neva Hotel and Casino at Lake Tahoe, adding expensive, gratuitous enhancements like a celebrity showroom and a heliport on the roof. The casino, however, required the approval of the Nevada Gaming Control Board in order for it to operate and make the money that Sinatra needed to keep the place open. But because of Sinatra's ties with known mobsters and the fact that Chicago gangster Sam Giancana was actually witnessed meandering about the property, Sinatra's gaming license was withdrawn, forcing him to sell his interest in the famous facility at a staggering loss. Expensive women such as Ava Gardner and Marilyn Monroe ate up much of what was left of his fortune. Sinatra, however, was one of the most resilient celebrities of the era, going from the brink of bankruptcy to another celestial success in just a matter of months. Motion picture credits and Oscar nominations followed gold and platinum records in the whimsical and unforgiving world of pop music. His was a phenomenal career unlike any other in the twentieth century.

In 1988, years after their final Rat Pack fling, Frank Sinatra, Dean Martin and Sammy Davis Jr. – then the only remaining members of the original pack – decided to embark on a tour that threatened to end all tours – at least for these three highly self-indulgent entertainers, and as circumstances would have it, it did. The event was dubbed the Together Again tour, and after much soul-searching by Martin and much hype by the others, it got underway in Oakland, California, on March 13 of that year with Sinatra's son, Frank, Jr., conducting the orchestra. Nevertheless, Martin soon had misgivings about the whole affair and after only a few very vocal disagreements with Sinatra, the clashing egos of these two megastars simply couldn't handle it any longer. Apparently there had been a long-festering discord between the two and Martin just wasn't in the mood to hear any more of it. With tempers flaring, it was widely reported that Martin angrily flicked his lighted cigarette out into the audience – a contemptuous act on his part that angered Sinatra even more – then simply walked off the stage and quit. Martin's abandoning the tour after only four shows and in such a highly visible manner was a great blow to Sinatra's insatiable ego, since he still acted as the de facto head of the pack and, as a result, considered Martin's rebuff a personal affront to him. Nevertheless, after calming down and reassuring himself that all was not lost, he decided to continue on with Davis at least for a few more shows before the reality of the situation finally sank in. Desperate for a suitable finale that never came, Sinatra scuttled the remainder of the tour less than three weeks after Martin's departure.

Sinatra, however, was not about to allow the entire tour phenomenon to die there. He desperately needed the money a world tour generates – as did Davis – and the two of them agreed they could not let that money go. Seemingly undeterred by Martin's action – at least publicly – Sinatra then agreed to replace Martin with another tempestuous megastar, Liza Minelli. This newly formed replacement show was then named the Ultimate Event tour, and with these three uncontrollable headliners at the helm and Frank, Jr. returning as conductor, they went on with what became the most wildly successful tour they could have ever imagined, continuing uninterrupted from country to country throughout the civilized world for the better part of a year.

In the end, however, all did not go well with this tour either. Although Minelli, being the youngest of the three, seemed to weather the rigors of such a physically exhausting endeavor without any complaints, Sinatra and Davis could not. Thus, after several months on the road with little or no rest between show dates to rejuvenate them, they both collapsed under the weight of what they had created. With their bodies simply burned out and unable to continue any further, they decided to terminate the show prematurely and unceremoniously performed their last appearance together at the Sydney Entertainment Centre in Sydney, Australia, on March 4, 1989. With the arduous task of such an extended tour now behind them, Sinatra, along with his wife, his son and Sammy, departed Sidney on a private jet and, with the International Dateline in their favor, arrived at the Kahala Hilton Hotel in Honolulu later that same day. It was the last en route stop on their flight back home to California for some much-needed rest and rejuvenation.

Thus, fate allowed that I would come together with Sinatra and Sammy one last time, in Hawaii, during what was clearly the twilight of their incredible careers. I happened to be staying at the Kahala Hilton myself, having arrived a couple of days earlier. I was on a promotional tour in Hawaii regarding a very successful book I had authored about the history of the Union Pacific Railroad. As I recall, it was late in the day when Sinatra and his wife, Barbara, arrived at the hotel, checked in at the front desk and headed straight for the elevator. Concurrently, I had just returned to the hotel myself and arrived at the elevator at the same time. Sinatra and his wife shared the elevator with me for the few brief moments it took us to get to our floors. Barbara appeared bedraggled and with her hair all askew, and Sinatra was ashen, paunchy and totally unrecognizable without his signature toupee. Both were sweaty, unkempt and not unlike any other couple who might have just flown halfway around the world after a very trying experience. God, what a fall from grace, I thought, recalling that first time I laid eyes on Sinatra as a young hopeful when he made his debut at the Paramount Theatre in New York. But that was 1941 and it was now 1989. Neither Frank nor Barbara looked up at me during that brief short trip up to our rooms, so our eyes never met and I said nothing to disturb their peace. I decided that it was just not the best time for me to say "Hi, nice to see you again," or some other such drivel, so I just left them to their own thoughts.

The following morning, Sammy and I literally bumped into each other as well, and it all happened while we were both attempting to hail the same cab out in front of the hotel. Sammy instantly gave me a cheerful "Hey you, Bobby," sealing his salutation with a big warm bear hug. As it turned out, we were both going in the same direction, he for lunch at the Sheraton and I to pick up friends at the Halekulani next door, so we were pleased to share the same ride, giving us a chance to catch up on our lives. The first thing I noticed about Sammy was that he did not appear to be well. He was very thin and gaunt, with his cheeks all sunken in, not just tired and bedraggled as I had seen Sinatra and his wife the day before. He immediately began speaking about the trip, as to how arduous it was, even going back to describe the disastrous turn of events when Dean Martin decided to pull out. It was only then that I noticed how hoarse Sammy's voice sounded, and I asked him about it.

"Yeah, it's those fuckin' cigarettes. You know, Bobby, they'll probably kill me one of these days," being his curt reply.

He mentioned that he would be going in for a complete checkup after he got home, but said nothing more about it. Before long, he asked about what I was doing, where I was living, my love life, etc., and then added, nonchalantly,

"You know that Yvette passed away…"

"Oh my god! No, I didn't know," being my shocked response.

"Yeah, a couple of years ago. She had gotten pretty heavy and had a bad ticker, but she never knew it. It just conked out on her one day and that was it."

By the time we arrived at the Sheraton there was nothing more we could have said about it. I had lost one of the most memorable people in my life and there was only a deathly silence between us. Then, before Sammy got out of the cab, I looked over at his gaunt face for a brief moment and experienced a strange foreboding about his life, as well. Word of Yvette's passing cast a death knell over us, and it was as clear to me as the both of us were sitting there that death would soon have the last word with Sammy, as well. Finally, as the door of the taxi was opened for him, Sammy grabbed my arm as though for dear life and then leaned over and gave me a big comic stage kiss on the cheek before murmuring,

"You're OK, Bobby… you're a good guy."

A moment later, he was gone, and I knew in my heart that it would be the last time I would ever see him.

Sammy passed away on May 16, 1990, a little more than a year later. He had been diagnosed with terminal throat cancer soon after returning from Honolulu and, in the end, those "fuckin' cigarettes" he described to me had proceeded to kill him exactly as he predicted they would.

Sinatra would not fare much better, although he did manage to live another eight years. He left the Kahala Hilton with his wife, Barbara, and son Frank, Jr., soon after their arrival. Although Frank, Jr. could be found lounging around the hotel lobby and other public areas throughout their brief stay, Sinatra himself made no public appearances and offered no excuses. The tour, along with his earlier breakup with Martin, had obviously taken everything out of him, and from all press accounts that the public was allowed to glean of the event, it appeared that Sinatra was judged to be just as guilty for the irreparable rift as Martin was.

Upon his return home, Sinatra went into a long period of rest with a hope for recuperation, but it did him little good. He soon showed early signs of dementia, with garbled speech and the inability to remember his lyrics during live performances. It was clearly the end of his concert days, but he continued on for a short while seemingly unperturbed about it. Finally, however, as his affliction worsened, the futility of his effort could no longer be ignored, and in 1996 he made his last public appearance. After a heart attack in 1997, things quickly went downhill for him; a second one a year later was all his body could handle and he died three days later. According to the coroner's report, Sinatra had passed away due to complications from dementia, heart disease, kidney failure and bladder cancer, all of which could have arguably been caused by his excessive smoking, drinking and carousing throughout his lifetime. He was eighty-two years of age. Over the years since his death, Sinatra has been canonized as the greatest entertainer of the twentieth century, and we certainly can't say he didn't make the most of it.

I can only add that the ultimate success of any megastar proves again that people with real talent – regardless of the odds against them – can and do make it in Hollywood, and make it big. After all, isn't that what we're really here for – to hope the same success might happen to us?

CHAPTER 25:

The Beverly Hills Health Club

When I first moved to Los Angeles in 1952, I was immediately impressed with the apparent preoccupation so many people my age had with their physical attractiveness. Having grown up in a typical eastern state where the population was primarily composed of immigrant workers from varied cultures around the world, it was abundantly clear that within such a mixed environment of unrelated preoccupations, a generalized interest in physical beauty was, frankly, not a major concern. Most jarring to me was the difference in the appearance of the regular, unexceptionally developed physical specimens who populated the beaches along the New Jersey shoreline where I had grown up, compared with the stunningly beautiful iconic images one could view every day on the beaches at Santa Monica and elsewhere in Southern California. This difference was not only startling from my perspective, it was mind-boggling.

Regrettably, my first two years in Los Angeles proved to be filled with more important things to worry about than my body and, as a result, it wasn't until I was cast in *The Caine Mutiny Court Martial* in 1955 that I met someone on the set who gave me some inspiration. His name was Dick DuBois and he was a bodybuilder. Like me, Dick was not really an actor, but he got parts and made a living at it strictly on his looks. More important, however, was the fact that Dick was also a Mr. America contestant and, in fact, had won the coveted title of Mr. America the previous year.

Dick DuBois was one of those incredibly gifted guys with a body that every man in town could envy. He was handsome and possessed the most likable personality of any person I had ever met. In a word, he was a "natural" – God's gift to the rest of mankind. He was the rare, unique and exceptional type of individual some of us have the pleasure of meeting perhaps only once in a lifetime, and then only if we were lucky – really lucky.

Dick and I took up an immediate friendship that lasted for the rest of our Hollywood days. We didn't see each other often, but when we did we always got together to socialize, get involved in deep conversation or break bread whenever the occasion arose. Nevertheless, we never spoke openly about bodybuilding until he came to my house up on Mulholland one day while I was outside working on the patio, laying brick for a retaining wall I was building out front.

It was a hot, sunny Southern California afternoon. I was working shirtless and in a pair of shorts and work boots when Dick showed up, gave me a comic "knock-knock" and jokingly asked whether he could come in. Dick did not own a car. He was a deeply spiritual minimalist, relying on others to get him around, so when he arrived, he was shirtless, as well, explaining that he had just jogged the last half mile or so from where he was dropped off. His arrival called for a break in my activity, so I went in and procured some cool drinks for us before proceeding. It was during this break that Dick gave me a good hard look, then reached over and gave me a poke in the arm.

"Make a muscle, Bob. Go ahead, make a muscle."

I complied, pumping my biceps as best as I could.

"Have you ever worked out?"

His question surprised me, but since he asked, I explained that, no, I haven't, I just never seem to have the time for it.

"Well, you should. You have great legs and a good body, all you need is a little more bulk in your arms."

Dick was a great talker, capable of going on for extended periods about things that were important to him, and he always had something positive to say about anything we discussed, so his suggestion about my arms was not something I could readily dismiss. Although I was never into bodybuilding per se, I do have to admit that once he mentioned it and I then glanced over at the perfect human specimen sitting across from me, it made me feel pretty puny. Later, in passing, I asked Dick whether he had a favorite gym I could join and he immediately mentioned the Beverly Hills Health Club, adding impassively,

"It's the only civilized club in town."

"The Club," as he called it, was located on Santa Monica Boulevard in West Hollywood just east of Doheny. It was in a central location, was easy to access and offered plenty of parking where Chevies, Plymouths and Fords mixed readily with the Jaguars, Mercedes-Benzs and Rolls Royces of the club's varied clientele. Despite that, it wasn't until I actually signed up and took my first few sessions that I realized what Dick meant when he offered that the Beverly Hills Health Club was the only "civilized club" in town. It was, and the reason soon became blatantly clear. This club was not like ordinary gyms. It did not cater to the muscle beach crowd or to the serious bodybuilder at all. It was geared to the "casual" young, male client, like me, who was interested in working out only two or three times a week for an hour or two at a time and primarily for the purpose of just keeping in shape and to feel one's best.

When it came to the roster of the club's clients, it proved to be as varied and interesting as the place itself. Most noticeable among them were the movie people, the middle-level executives and the gung-ho type of young achievers. None of the clients appeared to be over thirty years of age, thus it was a young crowd and that's the way they all seemed to like it. Rich or poor, famous or not, they were all bent on looking their best and enjoying it, and that's the way it impressed me, as well.

One of the most interesting aspects of the Beverly Hills Health Club that "leveled" the crowd was the requirement that each client purchase club-issued gym shoes they would be obliged to wear whenever they were in the building. The shoes themselves were just ordinary white sneakers with rubber soles, but the unique aspect of these shoes was the name of the owner that was stenciled across the heel. Therefore, names like Newman, Hudson, Hunter and McQueen were common at the Beverly Hills Health Club, allowing for the person so named to be easily identified by even the most blasé of unsophisticated viewers.

It was sometime during this new phase in my life when I was fated to meet another one of those special people who was destined to become a lifelong friend. Our first meeting began innocently enough, but it wound up with a definite twist. One day I noticed a new kid, a lot younger than me, who began working out at much the same time as I did. I guessed he was around eighteen to twenty years of age who had not yet decided on a path for his life or had rich parents and was free as a bird to come and go as he pleased. At first we would simply say hi to each other or crank out a few remarks in passing, but after a while I began to notice that whenever I happened to glance over at him, he always seemed to be looking at me. This seemed to occur even after we went on with our activity, or when it simply did not appear to be appropriate anymore, so my immediate thought was that perhaps the kid was gay but was too shy to make an advance. Nevertheless, since young boys were not my forte – then or now – I decided the best way to solve the problem was to befriend him and see where he was coming from. The problem with my thinking, however, was that once we took up a conversation I found him to be absolutely fascinating. Not only was he from a well-known movie family, but he was smart and well spoken, and he possessed one of the most cultured speaking voices I had ever heard. His name was David Korda, and he quickly became one of my closest friends.

David was British and he grew up in a famous English household. His father, Zoltan Korda, and his uncle, Alexander Korda, were both highly successful film producers during the heyday of Hollywood, and his cousin, Michael Korda, was a world-renowned writer. Why David should pick up on me – just another guy from the gym – was a mystery to me. Thus, after our workout one day, I decided to put an end to it and simply decided, "What the hell," then asked him jokingly,

"David, you aren't gay, are you?"

Surprised by my question, his answer was an emphatic,

"No! Not that I have anything against it – because I don't – but what gave you that idea?"

"Well, it's just the way I noticed you looking at me sometimes."

"Actually, I just look at you in admiration, out of respect for your success. I think you are a great singer and performer."

"David, what are you talking about? I'm not a singer. What made you think I was a singer?"

"Well, it's on your shoes. It says 'R. DARIN' – aren't you Bobby Darin, the singer?"

Needless to say, the riddle was solved.

"No, David, I'm not. My name is Robert Darin, not Bobby, but interestingly most of my friends do call me Bobby."

"Well, that's who I thought you were. I'm sorry if I embarrassed you."

"David, you didn't embarrass me at all; it was just my salacious curiosity, nothing more."

Thus we had both clearly erred in our assumptions. We looked at each other in surprise and laughed, breaking any ice that may have still remained between us. David was pleased to inform me that his attraction was based solely on admiration, and nothing more. I apologized to him for even thinking it could have been otherwise, and he accepted my apology in the spirit of the moment.

Over the next several months, David and I developed a close personal relationship that I am proud to say we have maintained to this day. David lives in London now, where he married and has two grown children. I see David every time I go to London, and David comes to my home whenever he returns to California. It is a friendship I will cherish for as long as I live.

Sometime during this period, the singer Bobby Darin recorded a pop number called "Splish Splash." I didn't like the song but I did note that Bobby Darin was becoming quite popular by this time, and it was obvious even then that, eventually, the similar name was bound to cause a recognition problem for me. In fact, the final catalyst for a name change on my part actually occurred some months later when he recorded a blockbuster called "Mack the Knife." Clearly, I could no longer procrastinate about the matter, thus concluding that the time had indeed come for me to do it.

The following day I went down to the Screen Actors Guild

office on Sunset Boulevard and asked for a name-change form. The only problem was that I couldn't think of a new name I wanted to use. My only thought was that I wanted it to be as close to the old name as possible, but when I mentioned this to the lady behind the counter, she volunteered that she had suggested new names for other applicants many times over and that it wasn't really that difficult. Thus, with my concurrence, she began musing over the sound of the name for a few moments before coming up with some distinct possibilities.

"Let's see now…this shouldn't be too difficult. How about just adding a 'g' and we'd have Daring? If that's too pretentious, then we could do Derin? Derringer? Dorin? Darlin? Darling? (chuckle) OK, not Darling, but what about Darwin? What do you think about Darwin? That's a famous name and it's very easy to remember. All we'd have to do is add a 'w' after the 'r' and we'd have it. It's very masculine too; it suits you to a T."

I thought about it for a moment and then made my decision on the spot.

"Robert Darwin. That sounds good – I like it."

She smiled, I nodded in agreement, and that's the way my new name came about.

Sometime later I had another visit from Dick DuBois. Unlike his usual ebullient self, he seemed preoccupied with a weighty problem on this day and was clearly anxious to get it off his chest. He told me he was leaving Los Angeles the following morning and that this time he thought it might be for good. He wanted to visit some friends up north, clear his head, breathe in some fresh air and, hopefully, come up with a new plan for his future. He explained that he had been kicking around Hollywood for years, had accomplished little except for his bodybuilding titles and simply felt the time was ripe for him to move on to a new life. Like me, he detested all the time that an actor was required to waste while trying to get ahead in Hollywood, and since he was getting older and did not possess any other obvious skills to fall back on, he felt there was no reason for him to hang around any longer. Dick's thinking was clear and right to the point, and I realized there was no way he would change his mind.

Dick's plight, however, was not unlike my own. I had been kicking around Hollywood for just as many years as Dick had. True, I was still doing well and paying all of my bills with the money I was earning as an actor, but it was also true that I was no longer the optimistic twenty-five-year-old wannabe I was when I arrived in this town. My thought, therefore, was that perhaps I should get out of the acting bit as well, and to do so before impending old age proceeded to do it for me. Unlike Dick, at least I could go on with my writing and finally make an attempt at directing. After all, isn't that what I had planned on doing all along? Naturally it was, and the more I thought about it, the more I convinced myself that my window of opportunity for doing so might be just as ripe for me at that moment as it was for Dick.

Before parting, Dick and I reminisced about the old days, and we shared those moments with a final meal before saying our goodbyes. A big bear hug, the wave of his hand and he was gone. Interestingly, his final words to me were simply not to worry about him, that he would be fine, then adding dispassionately,

"God will provide, he always does."

Shortly after Dick's last visit, I did in fact abandon my acting career, concurrently launching my first attempt at film directing. Point Dume came next, then my move to Paris for five years before I finally abandoned the film business entirely and settled down in Carmel Valley to raise horses. Thus I never had the occasion to cross paths with Dick again. Years later, however, I did learn that Dick had become a preacher, and even had his own congregation down in Southern California somewhere. I was happy for him because it was clear that he had finally found his calling, which, interestingly, was the one thing that had eluded him throughout his Hollywood years.

Isn't it wonderful, I thought, when someone finally settles down and accomplishes exactly what they always wanted to do with their lives and, ultimately, is successful at it? It really reinforced the feeling that my dad was right, and that the pursuit of a lifelong ambition is a worthwhile enterprise – even after Hollywood, where the cards are definitely stacked against you.

CHAPTER 26:

The Estelle Harman Actors Workshop

During the early 1950s, Estelle Harman was an acting coach and the director of talent at Universal Studios. As such, she was responsible to teach, tutor and coach the studio's sizable cadre of contract film players who, over the course of the immediate postwar years, included such luminous graduates as Natalie Wood, Tony Curtis and Rock Hudson, among many others. Nevertheless, as the studio system began to collapse around them and their contract years came to an end, all of these talented individuals found themselves abandoned and thrust out into the harsh realm of reality to find work on their own. Not surprisingly, this included their highly respected and talented tutor and coach, the venerable and much-loved Estelle Harman, who was forced to go out into the real world on her own to form and build her own teaching facility. It was known as the Estelle Harman Actors Workshop and it operated successfully as such for many years.

I met Estelle Harman socially through a couple of her former students, actors Bill Bixby and Robert Vaughn, during my Republic Studio days, and if I could put that meeting into a proper perspective, I'd say we hit it off with a bang. I found Estelle to be a very attractive, alpha-type female with a vibrant personality and an overt gift for befriending potential talent and nurturing new relations. After all, that is what she did at Universal and, as I soon discovered, she was now doing basically the same at her own workshop on La Brea Avenue.

At the time I met Estelle, she was 44 and I was 32. How do I know that? Well, I asked her, and when I did, she responded instantly by asking me,

"Why do you ask?" Whereupon I told her,

"Because I like attractive older women."

That got me to first base alright, but it didn't get me the brass ring. This woman had obviously been around the block a few more times than I had and knew exactly how to handle a brash young upstart like me.

"Well, I like younger men – GOOD-LOOKING, YOUNGER MEN – and you certainly qualify in that department, but it won't do either one of us any good because I'm married – VERY HAPPILY MARRIED."

Oops, I guessed she got me that time. Startled by her response but undeterred, I determined to keep up the patter as long as I could before she cut me off at the pass once again – which, as it turned out, I knew she was determined to do. We went at it again, back and forth for a few minutes, but it soon became clear that I was a rank amateur and no match for my antagonist, so I finally just cut it off with the only funny line I could muster.

"Does this mean the end of our budding romance?"

We both laughed. My remark broke the ice, allowing Estelle to relax a bit, savor the moment and give me a big hug. After that, she just grabbed me by the arm and sat me down for a long chat – and by the time we were through, we knew all we needed to know about each other. Estelle and I embarked on a long and lasting friendship; it was a relationship, I might add, that would eventually offer me the chance to exit the realm of acting – as I had planned on doing all along – and put my directorial talents to the test for the very first time.

Before parting, Estelle invited me down to her workshop for a visit, then added, "But call first, and don't forget your résumé."

I agreed and did exactly as she ordered, and when I walked into her workshop for the first time and met some of her students, I was pleasantly surprised by the aura and artistic ambiance of the place and I loved it. After a basic interview, Estelle agreed to take me on for directing on the single condition that I first enroll in the school's basic acting courses that all new students were required to complete before proceeding. I agreed and we were soon on our way.

I should mention that my time at the Estelle Harman Actors Workshop was during the 1958 to 1961 period, or what I referred to previously as my "Post-Benny" years. This was a time in my life when I was still working actively and making a fine living as an actor in a variety of roles, from major studio productions to lowly television westerns. This was in stark contrast to most of Estelle's students, who had done nothing more advanced in their acting careers than a stint in a high school play or two. The result of this dichotomy was that many of my classmates looked up to me as some sort of a superior being, one who was well on the way to doing exactly what they were all still learning in acting school – and much to the consternation of some of them, I never had such an ambition and was doing well in spite of it. As a result, it was easy for them to look up to me as their director, and it simplified my job when it became time for me to do so.

The first time I was given the chance to demonstrate my skills as a director came during an annual workshop event appropriately entitled *An Evening of One Act Plays*, in which I acted as co-producer (along with Estelle) and director. It was fun, I enjoyed it immensely and I felt I had finally accomplished something along the lines of what I had been seeking. Somewhere along the way I mentioned to Estelle that I owned a professional motion picture camera and would be willing to bring it in and use it to film vignettes of each actor for introductory and publicity purposes. Estelle loved the idea. I agreed to stand the cost of the film, development, editing, etc., and Estelle agreed to contribute the use of the school premises for the project. Before long we had the place set up as a mini film studio with controlled lighting, scenery, props, the works. It turned out I had made the transition from serious amateur still photographer to an even more serious professional cinematographer and director, and I pulled it off with hardly a pause. During this process, I set up a cutting room in my basement at home, and with it the basic ingredients for the production of professional motion pictures became a reality for me.

The entire process gave me a great rush. "Damn it," I thought, "I should have done this a long time ago."

CHAPTER 27:

The Catalina Trip

One day I received an unexpected call from George Cukor. I had not spoken with him in some time and he seemed genuinely interested in hearing what I had been doing. I brought him up to date on all my activities, including the fact that I had decided to see if I could produce a little film on my own. I hastened to add that it would just be an experiment using a story line I could excerpt from one of the treatments I had written earlier, and since I had already acquired all of the camera equipment and was hell-bent on using it, I thought, "Why not?" Without hesitation, Cukor agreed, adding, "You would be a fool if you didn't."

The story I had in mind played itself out in its entirety on a secluded beach. There were only a half-dozen characters involved, so I decided it would be simple to block the action, set up the camera angles and direct it. I could probably film the entire sequence in a couple of weeks, and the only thing I needed was to find a suitable location nearby where we could shoot it. In fact, I remembered a beach out on Catalina I had seen during an early scuba diving expedition that I thought might qualify, and I told Cukor I was going back to Catalina later in the week to check it out. His response, however, was one I could have never expected.

"Wonderful! Would you allow me to sign on as your assistant? Would you?"

Obviously, I thought he was kidding, so I laughed him off.

"No, seriously, Bob, I mean it. I'm between pictures, I have nothing to do this week and I would love to accompany you on your quest."

Naturally, once I realized he really was serious, there was no way I could deny him. I told him I had a good friend who lived on Catalina and had volunteered to arrange and coordinate all the transportation, so a quick call to him was all that it took to set the trip up.

Fred Small was a longtime resident of Catalina. He was also a student at Cal Poly in San Luis Obispo, and during the summer months he resumed his job as head lifeguard and chief honcho at the municipal beach in Avalon. It was a position of some stature he had maintained since he was in high school. Fred also operated the electric car concession in Avalon – the only means of public transportation on the island – so he was a budding businessman, as well. Fred prided himself for being able to arrange whatever a visitor required, be it transportation, tours, overnight accommodations or otherwise. He was the perfect contact person for my proposed trip to Catalina and he made short shrift of all my requirements.

After explaining the purpose of my visit to Fred, he arranged for two seats on an early morning flight from Long Beach to Avalon Harbor, where he met us and introduced us to the owner of a small charter boat he had hired to take us around the island. The owner, a delightful and very knowledgeable forty-something-year-old alpha female, was also our captain and guide – and she was a good one. She knew every nook, cranny and cove on the island, and as I explained to her from the start, I needed to see every one of them; her response, however, was not that positive.

"Impossible, but at least we can check out the most logical ones on the leeward side."

Thus, beginning at the eastern tip of the island at Seal Rocks and progressing up the leeward coast to potential location sites from Willow Cove to as far north as Parson's Landing, it soon became clear that an ideal secluded white sand beach on Catalina no longer existed. Most were developed with apartments or condos down to the high-water line, and those beaches that weren't developed as yet were inhabited by whole colonies of seals or located too far from civilization to be logistically feasible. I even waded to shore through a smelly kelp bed at the one promising location I had seen during an earlier trip. My thought was to check whether there was enough room for a campsite and storage facilities for the equipment, but I was rudely accosted by a huge bull sea lion with his family in tow that instantly changed my mind for me. This beach was his turf now and he wasn't about to give it up, chasing me all the way back into the water before returning to his brood.

When I climbed back on board our boat, I suddenly realized the stupidity of having waded through a stinking kelp bed, because I now reeked like a putrid sewer. Then, to make matters worse, Cukor and our guide both decided that even if the problem with the animals could be solved, the place was too isolated to work as a filming location. I was then informed that sites on the windward side would all be too cold, too windy and even more remote than any we had seen on this side. It soon became clear that my decision to use Catalina as a likely location site was ill-founded, bringing my Catalina expedition to a screeching and ignominious halt.

By the time we returned to Avalon, I not only stank like a toilet, but my emotions were in the toilet as well. Holding his nose in a comic pretense of disgust, Fred directed me to the nearest shower, then loaned me a clean set of clothes consisting of one of his Cal Poly sweatshirts and a pair of shorts. Some food and a quick tour around Avalon in one of Fred's little electric cars followed, and after some obligatory picture taking to commemorate the visit, we thanked him for his help and headed back down to the pier for our flight back to the mainland.

Once in the air, Cukor instinctively picked up on my funk and wasn't about to let it go on without interceding.

"Bob, you needn't feel bad about this failed venture. I can't even begin to tell you how many scouting trips I've taken with similar results. It's all in the vagaries of the system and we must accept it as such. Nevertheless, I can tell you this. I think you did admirably today and handled the entire trip in a very professional manner. I overheard the manner in which you were giving instructions to our guide. You did so with a full understanding of what you were seeking, and then handled the matter with great authority and control – all attributes required of a good film director."

"Thank you, George; I wasn't aware you were listening."

"Well, I was, and I can tell you this, I have no doubt that you will become a great director one day. Your performance today proved it."

When we landed in Long Beach it was almost six o'clock, so Cukor suggested we stop off for an early dinner in downtown Los Angeles. He explained that he knew of a great restaurant in Chinatown called Little Joe's that had some of the best food he had ever eaten, so it took no coaxing on his part to get me to concur.

After our dinner – which really was as good as he indicated it would be – Cukor changed gears and turned his attention back to the primary problem at hand, namely, a suitable location for my shoot.

"Bob, in my view, since you are funding this entire project on your own, I would suggest you make it as simple as possible and shoot it as close by as you can. Ask Darrow about it. He is usually very good at solving things like this and, being a beach bum himself, he might just have the solution at his fingertips."

I thanked Cukor for his tip and the following morning called Darrow, exactly as Cukor had suggested.

In retrospect and thinking back at the Catalina trip and its unremarkable outcome, I couldn't help but marvel at the fact that one of the greatest film directors of all time actually came along to assist me in my mission. Even more amazing is the fact that he restrained himself from giving any direct orders to Fred, me or our guide – commands or simply instructions as he would have certainly given on a project of his own. Finally, I realized that George Cukor, like John Darrow, had slowly segued into a father figure for me and that there was actually no way I could have curbed his eagerness to assist. It was in his psyche to tutor and help newcomers in the game who he felt had some chance of reaching the heights like he did. My only part in the equation was the fact that he thought me worthy enough to spend his valuable time on me, and that is a fact I simply cannot ignore.

Again, all I could say to myself was, "How lucky could I have ever been?"

CHAPTER 28:

Doris Day

It was one of those clear, sunny, Southern California Saturday mornings when I woke up to confront an entirely new set of problems. I had voluntarily decided to abandon my livelihood as a working actor, a profession I had maintained successfully in Hollywood for more than seven years, and embark on a new life into the unknown realm of producing a motion picture. First things first, however, it was eminently clear that I could not go forward until we found a suitable location. The script I had chosen called for a secluded beach for all the action, and since I had already scouted Catalina Island with negative results, my next thought was to check out the California mainland. Obviously, anything from Santa Monica to the south would be too inhabited for our use, so the answer had to lie to the north.

I usually spoke with my agent, John Darrow, at least once a week, whether I had any work-related activities pending or not. Darrow owned a beach house in Malibu where I often spent the weekend. Being a good agent, he was totally aware of my proposed independent moviemaking project and was quite eager to help bring it to fruition. But when Cukor told him we had been to Catalina and had not found a location as yet, he suggested I come out to his place for the weekend, adding,

"I think we should take a drive up the coast a few miles. There's a place I know of up there that might just be ideal for you."

The only problem as Darrow quickly described it was that heading northward from Malibu, the coast highway quickly separates from the coastline, making access to any beach that much more difficult and, in some cases, nearly impossible. There was one spot, however, only a few miles up the coast from his house that he indicated was off the highway, surrounded by tall cliffs on all sides and was thus very secluded – perhaps ideal – for what I was seeking. He hastened to add, however, that it was also a formidable trek to access, speculating it was a good quarter-mile walk from the highway through tall brush to the top of the cliff, then a circuitous route down the side of the cliff to the beach. The place was called Point Dume, and although it was difficult to access, he felt it would be worth my while to check it out.

Naturally, after Catalina, I was quite pessimistic about ever finding an ideal site near Los Angeles, but once I laid eyes on Point Dume my elation soared. Locationwise, this place was ideal. Depending on traffic and the time of day, it was roughly only forty-five minutes to an hour's drive from Hollywood. It was picturesque, secluded and contained one of the most beautiful clear sand beaches I had ever seen. All we needed was two to three weeks of clear, Southern California weather, and our picture would be "in the can." One quick look with Darrow that day and I was sold on it. I was euphoric and ecstatic, and now that the location problem was settled, I couldn't wait to get on with the project.

The next morning, I awoke early and decided to take a quick swim in the ocean before heading back to town. The water was cool but inviting, and when I came out I noticed this young blond woman coming over to greet me from the house next door. I noticed a couple of people playing volleyball on a makeshift court between the two houses, but when the woman came closer and I could see her face, I recognized her instantly to be none other than a very friendly and ebullient Doris Day.

"Hi, we're just setting up a volleyball match next door. We need a fourth, so why don't you come over and join us?"

Frankly, I don't remember exactly how I reacted to her request, but I do remember her taking me by the arm and literally marching me over to her place. The mood was light and jovial and in the spirit of the occasion I was pleased to join in their play.

In this section of Malibu the beach area was private and continuous between the houses. It was also relatively flat in the upper section above the high-water mark, so it was a natural place in which to set up a volleyball court. As instigator and high priestess of the event, Doris quickly barked out her orders for all to follow:

"OK, we can play doubles now," then pushing me by the arm, gave me my instructions.

"You go over there with Ernie and I'll double over here with Nat."

As things progressed, there was no time for introductions or small talk. Ernie and Nat were heavy into the game already and kept at it even after Doris and I joined in the field. The opening play started out fast and furious, and it wasn't until after the first score that I could even take a moment out to look over and see who our playmates were. Chomping on his ever-present cigar in my corner was a very animated Ernie Kovaks, who was spewing quick one-liners across the net in machine-gun-like fashion. Nat, who was flanking him in the opposite corner, was the king of croon himself, Nat King Cole. So at the first appropriate break in the action, I merely looked over at Ernie, stuck out my hand and proclaimed,

"Hi, I'm Bobby."

Undaunted but appreciative of the reminder, Doris quickly echoed back with a perfunctory,

"Oh, and Nat, that's Bobby over there."

Both of Doris' guests gave me a quick wave of the hand, I waved back and the game was on in full force.

In the end, I couldn't say that anyone actually won the game because, frankly, no one seemed interested in keeping score. It was simply a fun way to get in a little exercise and, for those so inclined, to chat, sound off or simply let off some steam. Nat and Ernie each had their own hit television shows back in 1957 and both had their share of clinkers to complain about, thus allowing the banter and bitching between the two of them to go on unabated. Unexpectedly, Ernie picked up on my speaking voice and asked whether I had ever done any announcing, and when I told him about my standing in for an ailing Don Wilson on the *Jack Benny Program* one day, he quickly barked back,

"You've got a hell-of-a-lot better voice than Don Wilson has. Benny should have kept you on instead of him."

Doris then joined in on the conversation, seemingly agreeing with Kovaks until finally, with the game no longer a priority, she asked all of us to come in for some refreshments, where the banter between Ernie Kovaks and Nat King Cole went on nonstop for the rest of the morning. Eventually, Darrow came over to join in the scrimmage and contribute some quips of his own. Darrow was a great raconteur, and once he got going on a subject there was little anyone could do to stop him. Finally, I reminded myself that my time in the sun had to come to an end. I had to get back to town, so I thanked Doris for a very fun morning, made my excuses and departed.

An interesting outcome of this little event occurred a couple of weeks later when Darrow called to inform me that I was asked to appear for a casting call over at MGM. The part was for the lead singer/dancer in a faux-amateur musical production number with Doris Day in her new picture, *Please Don't Eat the Daisies*. As he explained it,

"After you left, Kovaks mentioned your voice again and, when asked, I explained that you also had a great singing voice and could dance too."

Darrow then added, sheepishly,

"I guess Doris just picked up on that."

Darrow, however, never did explain exactly how I got the part or whether Doris had anything to do with it, but in my mind I convinced myself that she did. The fact is, I did have a good singing voice and it fit in perfectly for the production depicted in the picture.

Doris Day was gracious to me throughout the shoot, so much so, in fact, that at one point I even felt comfortable enough to ask her whether she remembered meeting me back at the NBC studios in New York when she first began singing with Les Brown. Her response was positive – sort of – but I really felt she did not recall it. How could she have? I was just the kid sitting next to her in the rehearsal hall and she was a bright new singing personality on her way to stardom.

It was also during this mandatory period of transition in my life that I was cast in the plum supporting role of the project commander's adjutant in *Men in Space*, one of the first space-related dramas to surface as a television series. My role entailed a good deal of dialogue in which I was required to explain much of the technical jargon to others involved in the project and, by extension, to the television audience, who in those days was not quite as savvy about space as they are today. Although this show seems overly primitive when compared with the digitally generated, megaspectacular images we are all used to seeing today, it was all we had in those days and the best that the industry could produce. Bill Lundigan was the star of the show, with my part continuing from episode to episode throughout the season. Like the *Jack Benny Program* before it, *Men in Space* promised to offer continuous employment for me for at least the balance of the current season, if not the run of the show. But because of my prior commitment to produce and direct my own first motion picture – which necessarily took precedence for my time – it forced me to bring my involvement in *Men in Space* to an end after only a few of the episodes had been produced.

Thus, *Men in Space* became the last acting job I ever accepted. My time as an actor in Hollywood had come to a rapid, self-imposed end. My mind had been made up to concentrate all of my time and effort on directing, and there was no way I would allow myself to ever turn back.

CHAPTER 29:

A House of Sand

The evening of one-act plays I had directed at Estelle Harman's workshop was now behind me and I was hell-bent on getting on with my new career. Although my first directorial effort was on the stage and not on film, I had already been involved in enough film projects as an actor to realize that the process of directing for film was quite different, presenting the director with a myriad of problems that simply do not exist on the stage. In my case, however, the act of directing my actors would be a multifaceted endeavor that would encompass more of the arts and sciences of moviemaking than any regular director had ever attempted. Being a one-man production team, I would also be required to perform all of the usual duties required of the jobs I intended to perform, including those of the director along with the writer, producer, cinematographer and editor. Most would be first-time efforts, but being quick of mind and physically able to perform the required tasks, I was confident I could accomplish all of them.

Nevertheless, the primary problem with shooting my own first film was that I would be obliged to pay for all the expenses myself – a disheartening prospect to be sure. In spite of Cukor's earlier admonition about never investing in one's own film project, it seemed the only way for me to go. Thus, after much soul-searching, a modicum of concern and a serious calculation as to what I imagined the project might cost me, I decided I would allow myself the luxury of expending only a certain fixed amount of my own money. Then, if that did not prove to be sufficient to complete the project – and if no angel happened along to assist – I would abandon it and go on with my life. In deference to my dad, I decided I would not dip into the trust he had set up for me when I was a child, so the obvious solution was to shoot something that would be inexpensive to do – a quickie – and to do it on the sly with no permits, no unions and no temperamental stars to contend with. I also realized it would be best to do it on location, with the camera handheld for the most part and preferably with little or no dialogue – a combination of factors making it easy to process and edit. In a nutshell, it would be an experiment, a sort of screen test or audition of any latent talents I might possess that, in the event the resultant film was well received, could propel me on to the next level of acceptance. At that point, it might allow me to be in a better position to venture forth with my career, solicit investors and do a full-blown movie on a professional level for the whole world to evaluate.

I had written a suitable script sometime earlier about a group of young people out on the beach entitled *A House of Sand*. It required a lot of pantomime, had little dialogue and, as a result, fit the bill perfectly for this project. With the location issue behind us, my primary interest now was to settle upon the right actors – all unknowns, of course – to tell the story and help me pull the whole thing off. Luckily, Estelle's workshop harbored a sizable cadre of young hopefuls, and although some were simply too new or inexperienced at the game to fit the bill, others appeared to be quite talented and eager to prove their worth. Thus, individual interviews, readings and tryouts came next.

Among the many problems I encountered, however, were the sexual mores of the nation that in 1960 were not exactly what they are today. As an example, the main female character in my story was required to portray a spontaneous orgasm without the necessary physical contact normally required for the event – a feat that might be considered passé in film today but was unheard of at the time. Although most of the major studios tended to conform to the strict Motion Picture Production Code that still existed in 1960 – albeit reluctantly at times – a number of free-based independent filmmakers worldwide were simply no longer inclined to comply with it. Unwilling to be burdened by the code's dated morality and awkward enforcement procedures, a "new wave" of intellectual self-expression by motion picture directors advocated the premise that film was an art form and, thus, was inherently free from the burden of censorship. The theory was generally referred to as auteurism – an anglicized derivative of the French word "auteur," which literally translated means "creator of an artistic process," such as the author of a book, the composer of a musical composition or, as in the case at hand, the director and creative architect of the filmmaking process. In my case, I had not as yet made any commitment to the process, so I was not under any delusion to advocate or adhere to it. I decided to stick with the existing code as much as possible and merely attempt to maneuver my script around the obvious hurdles. After all, the film was still a big experiment for me at this juncture and I didn't think I was in any position to rattle official heads either statewide, nationally or on an international level.

I conducted numerous interviews over the ensuing weeks, shot screen tests of those actors I felt were particularly qualified, and before long I had all of the parts cast. Most important for me was the casting of the lead role, the part of Mary, an impressionable young girl hung up on her life experience because of a premature sexual encounter. Since the story is basically about Mary, her hang-ups and her continuous need for acceptance, the part required an actor who was capable of conveying the multiple feelings of sexual insecurity, emotional immaturity and the contradictory signals related to physical desire and revulsion, and who was capable of doing it all for the camera – both convincingly and with her utmost inner feelings exposed for all to see. It was not a role just any young hopeful could play, but I felt I had hit the mark with a bright young student at the workshop by the name of Mary Staton. Mary was the right age for the part and was pretty enough physically to be convincing, but she was not a raving beauty and that is the way I wanted it. In my mind, the character required more of a Julie Harris than an Elizabeth Taylor – she would simply be more believable that way.

There were a few other plum roles to be cast, including the key part of the handsome young seducer. That role went to Roland Carey, a young Swiss actor with credits in Europe who was just visiting friends in Los Angeles when I met him. The other roles went to Donald Conley, Vance Gillespie, Jill Janssen and Ted Morgan, all previously known to me from my time at the workshop and all eminently qualified to fill the bill.

With the casting procedure now behind us, I still hadn't given thought to the biggest problem still remaining unsolved. It was the logistical feat of transporting the entire company and all the equipment from Hollywood to Point Dume, then hauling everything down to the beach, setting it all up for each shot, tearing it all down at the end of the day and hauling it all back home, and to do so every day until all the principal photography had been completed. Worst of all was the fact that our little company of fledgling actors would be obliged to do all this by themselves and all without a crew. On a professional film these tasks are all normally performed by thirty or more people who are all trained and qualified in their particular crafts. In the end, however, one willing volunteer did come forth to offer his help. It was my newly found English friend from the Beverly Hills Health Club, David Korda, and the primary reason he chose to do so was because he had an inherent incentive of his own. David was a bright, young kid who, having been born into one of the most successful families of motion picture producers in the business, was eager to add his own name to the family slate and prove his mettle, as well. David signed on as my assistant – a title he jokingly held in name only – but the job did offer him the opportunity to haul camera cases, film cans, tripods, reflectors and screens up and down the cliffs of Point Dume every day, and he did so enthusiastically and without a whimper. He was invaluable to me in the physical sense, but he also supplied the necessary incentive that allowed me the essential freedom from being burdened by extraneous undertakings during the crucial time when I needed to concentrate on the task of directing the picture and, hopefully, hold the whole project together.

The primary understanding among all of the project's participants was that they realized, accepted and appreciated the fact that this was an amateur production in which they would be working on their own initiatives, at their own expenses and with no guarantee that they would ever be paid, praised or compensated for their contribution in any way. Basically, they were interns learning their crafts, and they were well aware that I was there under the same pretext, to learn my crafts, as well.

The first rehearsals were conducted at my home and then at our actual location at Point Dume. Most rehearsals went well, but it was only after our first dry runs out on the beach that the vagaries, uncertainties and difficulties of location filming came to light. As I expected from the start, the primary difficulty was always the weather and, as we soon discovered, early fall at Point Dume was one of the worst times of the year. Mornings were almost always covered with a thick layer of fog – a low overcast that often remained entrenched until noon. A second problem, however, was even more intrusive, that being the early morning sun worshippers who seemed to arrive at the crack of dawn and remained as mobile background statuary throughout the day. Luckily, most offenders responded favorably to our requests for privacy on the set and agreed to relocate to more remote locations outside our field of view, leaving the weather as the most unpredictable source of concern throughout our stay.

In the end, we completed our principal photography in fourteen shooting days spread out over a two-month period. Generally, I was satisfied with the actors and their overall responses to my direction. We didn't experience any of the temper tantrums, hissy fits or other displays of bruised egos that often plague major productions with temperamental divas and overpriced stars. Everything considered, I concluded we all came out of our little experience quite unscathed.

Until this point, all I had seen of the action my actors had given me was what I observed through the camera's viewfinder, with each scene laid out in dozens of little bits and pieces that only allowed my mind the luxury of visualizing how it might look as a single interconnected entity. Now, if all went well, that action would come to life for me in the cutting room as all those pieces were meticulously cut and spliced together to form a cohesive whole or – in the worst-case scenario – if the parts didn't fit they might wind up, proverbially, on the cutting-room floor.

In anticipation of this portion of the process, I rented a Moviola projector, an editing table and associated equipment from Birns & Sawyer, which we set up in my basement. It was a tight squeeze to be sure, but I believe the close quarters invoked an even more intimate sense of oneness between the project and me. It had clearly become my baby, but because it was still in the womb – so to speak – I wouldn't have any idea what it would look like until all the elements were fit together, allowing for a unified print to be born.

It took less than a month for me to cut, splice and assemble the first rough cut of the film, which now became our work print. I was able to accomplish this task in spite of the fact that I was new at the job and had never done this kind of work before. Nevertheless, I had good responsive hands, possessed excellent coordination and, with George Huene's patient "over-the-shoulder" mentoring on all the intricacies of handling, cutting and splicing film, I completed the task at hand quickly and with no negative complications.

With the rough cut of the picture now in the can, the time to consider the audio tracks had to come next. Although I had recorded a wild track of voice, surf and miscellaneous sound effects while out at the beach, all these various sounds had to be laid in and synchronized with the picture, and this was one job I knew I could not handle on my own. It required a professional sound man and a fully equipped recording stage to complete. Accordingly, I contracted with one of the better-known independent studios in town, where all the tracks were laid in with expert precision.

With the picture, voice and effects tracks now behind us, I was faced with the most arduous task of all – that being the daunting question of what to do about a music track. Everyone knows that a movie has to have a music track, and this one could obviously be no exception. Until now, I was too involved with the actual production of the visual elements to be much concerned about it; however, being a one-man production team placed the burden of obtaining a suitable music track squarely on my shoulders and, frankly, I had no idea as to how

I was to proceed. As luck would have it, however, I experienced yet another fortuitous chance meeting, and this one was with one of the movie music giants of the day.

Les Baxter was one of the three most prolific composers and conductors of film scores in the business who, along with Lalo Shifrin and Henry Mancini, scored most of the bigger films then being produced in Hollywood. For me to meet a composer with the stature and respectability of someone like Baxter at such an opportune time for my project was more than I could have ever expected. Yet the meeting occurred, not because of any effort or perseverance on my part, but rather because of a short mention in *Daily Variety* observing the fact that principal photography for *A House of Sand* had been completed. How lucky could I have been to be invited to a cocktail party and be introduced to Baxter himself by a mutual friend who just happened to be one of those Hollywood diehards who devoured every item in *Daily Variety* the moment it hit the stands? With a background like that, just one mention of the picture to Baxter was all it took.

"I think you two should get to know each other. Bob, this is Les Baxter. Les, this is Bob Darwin. Bob just finished shooting *A House of Sand* out on the beach, and I'll bet my cajones he needs you to score it for him."

Indeed I did, and I told Baxter so. Surprisingly, he was very receptive to my need and immediately asked to see my work print, which I then made available for him to screen at a local projection stage. Soon thereafter, Baxter called to tell me he liked the film and agreed to sign on as music director. Bingo! The deal was done. It was that simple and that quick.

As Baxter explained it, he maintained a handpicked group of forty studio musicians he employed to score all his films. These forty musicians composed the core of his orchestra, which could be enlarged or reduced in size depending on the need. Naturally, all of Baxter's musicians were members of the American Federation of Musicians, and since I still held my own membership card in that union from my days as the lowly piano player at the Hawaiian

Palms back in New Jersey, I was well aware of what a score with forty or more professional union musicians was going to cost me. Nevertheless, I didn't flinch! My unfettered enthusiasm for the project did not wane. I accepted the fact that whatever the cost, I would be obliged to bear it. As uncharacteristic as it was of me to go through with a project like this without thoroughly examining every aspect of it beforehand, I gave Baxter the go-ahead without even a second thought.

A few weeks later Baxter presented me with an open reel audio tape of the music he had composed for the picture. If I approved it, he would then arrange and score the film. Baxter's music included what he called the main theme – a song he composed expressly for the picture – a stand-alone melody complete with lyrics he explained he thought could make the charts on its own merits, with or without the picture for support.

At this point in the process, I became so euphoric about the film's ultimate success that I gave no further thought of turning back. I became so hyped just listening to the music Baxter had composed that I decided it would be ludicrous to entertain any thoughts of abandoning the project now. I concluded that it was simply no longer an option. I told Baxter to book the studio and let me know the date. A couple of days later I signed the AFM contract for the musicians, and I was now committed to the deal.

Later that afternoon I played Baxter's tape of the main theme over and over, and the more times I played it and ran it through my head, the more I convinced myself that we really did have a winner on our hands.

The first preview of the completed film was held at the Screen Director's Theatre on Sunset Boulevard on June 4, 1962, to generally positive reviews, the best of which appeared in the *Hollywood Reporter* with the headline:

A HOUSE OF SAND SUITABLE FOR ART THEATRE AUDIENCES
Robert Darwin Film a Good First Try

A few excerpts from the review follow:

"Another would-be filmmaker has solved his problems by writing his own story, producing and directing himself, and taking camera directly into his own hands to complete the assignment. Robert Darwin is the one-man production staff who has made *House of Sand* a promising effort, if not wholly successful. Darwin displays a gift for cinematic storytelling…He creates some memorable images and indicates a knowledge of framing and cutting…"

On the negative side, this reviewer felt that the all-important rape scene was too explicit, complaining that the point of it was almost lost in the manner in which I chose to portray it. Actually, I considered his use of the word "explicit" to be a backhanded compliment, but I was not at all convinced he phrased himself correctly to express what he meant.

On the other hand, *Variety* was not so kind, generally criticizing the film as a "medley of sexy charades on the beach." Nevertheless, the reviewer did manage to offer me a glimmer of hope with a positive review of my directorial skills by declaring matter-of-factly,

"Darwin shows a flair for dramatic photography, relying almost exclusively on the storytelling virtue of the lens, accompanied by an absolute minimum of dialog. There is great mobility in his camerawork and visual impact in some of his Eastman Color compositions, although a third of the footage seems to consist of flesh, the other two-thirds water."

Interestingly, this tenuous narrative pertaining to sex on the one hand versus water on the other resulted in generating a much more positive reaction from Europe than it did at *Variety*, eliciting a response from one of the largest theatrical agencies in Rome requesting a print of the picture for screening at the Venice Film Festival later that summer. Needless to say, I was thrilled at the prospect of exhibiting the picture at one of the greatest film venues in the world, in spite of the fact that I knew it would cost much more money than I had available. Nevertheless, Darrow, Cukor, Huene, Clayton, McCleery and every other movie professional I queried were all thrilled at the idea and urged me to accept the invitation. Darrow, in fact, summed it up beautifully in the most succinct manner he could summon:

"It's a once-in-a-lifetime opportunity, Bob, don't fuck it up."

The festival, however, was still three months in the future, which in my mind was plenty of time in which to make a final decision. Unfortunately, I was wrong, and my decision to wait would soon come back to haunt me. In the meanwhile, however, I previewed the picture a couple more times in California, first at the Los Feliz Theatre in Los Angeles and then at the Loma Theatre in Coronado. Both screenings were in front of regular theatre audiences and both drew acceptably high positive responses. Nevertheless, Darrow's reaction in both cases was still the same.

"SEND THE FILM TO VENICE, AND DO IT NOW!"

Finally I agreed, convincing myself that the cost be damned, it simply wasn't fair for any of the participants if I didn't go. Packing and shipping came next, and within the week the film was on its way to my new agents in Rome.

I had never been to a film festival, so I wasn't really familiar with the procedures, but from gleaning all the information I had on hand, I concluded it would be a four- to five-day affair, with screenings followed by cocktail parties and meetings where arrangements could be made to sell or distribute the product. Then, regardless of whether the reception was good or bad, one way or the other, within a week or ten days I would be back home with some sort of a deal in my pocket. Naturally, my overriding hope was that it might foster the careers of my actors and me, that being the ultimate reward for our having become involved in the project to begin with.

It was now mid-August and the festival was still a couple of weeks off, so I decided to fly to Europe a week or so early in order to visit my cousin, Inge, who was then living in Munich. Inge, who was born in Salzburg, Austria, in 1922, was one of those rare natural beauties who exhibited all the attributes required of stardom on film at a very early age. Thus, in 1937, when she was only fifteen, she was discovered while riding her bicycle to school, given a screen test and signed by UFA, then the largest film studio in Germany, to a long-term contract. Unfortunately, by the time Inge finished high school, World War II had begun and all thoughts of a film career became history. Now, more than twenty years later, I found her to be a beautiful mature woman, a refined version of the raving beauty she had been in her youth.

After as few pleasant days with my niece, I contacted my agents in Rome to arrange for my accommodations in Venice, but was greeted by the most distressing news. I was told that the film had arrived in Rome, but was still being held in Customs at the Rome airport. Apparently the shipment was lacking the proper importation documentation and, thus, was impounded. The only solution now was for me to fly to Rome myself to correct the deficiency and have the film shipped off to Venice as soon as possible.

Needless to say I was on my way to Rome on the next plane, but it was only after my arrival at the Customs office that it became clear my troubles had just begun. Aside from the previously mentioned documentation problems, I was informed that the film had also been imported illegally and I would need to post a bond to clear it.

Obviously, this was not a problem I could handle on my own, so I called my agency in Rome for assistance. Luckily, they assigned a gentleman familiar with the process to accompany me back to the Customs office to negotiate the matter for me, but it still took three long days to arrange for the bond, post it and wrangle with the Customs people to accept all the corrected documentation. In the end, however, all of our efforts were for naught. By the time the film was released by Customs, retagged, shipped and delivered to the festival offices in Venice, the time to present the film for competition had run out.

I was devastated, and worst of all, I realized it was entirely my own fault. Had I shipped the film earlier when Darrow first suggested it, none of this would have occurred. Here I was, all by myself in a foreign country, with little money in my pocket and no plans for what to do. My first thought was to junk the whole project, get back on the first plane to Los Angeles and simply forget about it.

Luckily for me, however, cooler heads prevailed. The following morning I called the festival office to arrange for the film to be shipped back to the U.S., but when I did, I happened to speak with a gentleman who was well aware of the film, had seen the reviews in *Variety* and the *Hollywood Reporter* and wisely suggested a simple alternative for me.

"Mr. Darwin, why not just have the film shown out of competition?"

There was a long pause before I responded. Having no idea what he was talking about, I simply asked him for an explanation.

"It happens all the time. Every year several films are rejected from participating in the competition, or as in your case, were received too late. Many of these are simply rescheduled to be shown out of competition, meaning they would not be official entries and therefore could not be considered for a prize, but they would still be shown and reviewed by the press. After all, isn't that what the festival is really all about?"

I must have seemed pretty stupid to this gentleman because I honestly never knew this alternate route existed, but when I discussed this possibility with my agency, they concurred, I agreed to the plan and the rest, as they say, is history. I asked the agency to make all the necessary arrangements for the screenings and to find a place for me to stay nearby. What a fortuitous change of events for me. All of a sudden, a disastrous end for my project had been averted, and before the day was out, I was on my way to Venice on the next plane.

Again, I mused to myself,

"How lucky could I have ever been?"

CHAPTER 30:

The Venice Film Festival

I was greeted at the Venice airport by my agents, Agencia Roma, and was whisked away via water taxi to the Grand Island of the Lido, where most of the principal screenings and related activities for the festival were scheduled to occur. They also arranged for a small pensione for me near the theatres where the film was to be shown. It was convenient to access festival activities, was inexpensive and offered me all the amenities I felt I required.

Thus, barely three months after our first preview in Los Angeles, the film was screened out of competition at the Venice Film Festival. The date was September 1 and the place was the Cinéma Excelsior on the Venice Lido. Attendance was moderate but the reaction was more than I could have anticipated, with the first inquiry coming from an official with the French Ministry of Foreign Affairs, Philippe Erlanger, who requested a meeting over lunch at the Excelsior Hotel the following day. A quick call to my contact at the festival committee offices confirmed that Monsieur Erlanger was indeed with the Ministry of Foreign Affairs. He also advised that he was a founder and member of the jury of the prestigious Cannes Film Festival and possessed all of the authority, recognition and standing required to promote any film, person or entity to instant acceptance, not only in France but throughout the entire motion picture world. Naturally, I was pleased with the report and, accordingly, accepted Monsieur Erlanger's invitation.

The Excelsior was one of those huge palace hotels from the late Victorian era that can still be found in most of the principal tourist cities in Europe, and it possessed all the grandeur and style one would expect from one of its kind. It would be unthinkable to cross paths with anyone associated with one of these trophy establishments who did not speak fluent English and – more importantly for me at the time – didn't know how to recognize an American upon first laying eyes on one. Thus, I was addressed in English the moment I arrived at the front desk to request directions.

"Good morning, sir, may I be of assistance?"

"Yes, thank you. I'm meeting Philippe Erlanger in the restaurant for lunch. Could you direct me to his table?"

"But of course Mr. Darwin. Monsieur Erlanger advised earlier that you would be joining him."

Now that's what I call service. The gentleman assisting me then introduced himself as one of the assistant managers. He offered me his card and advised that in the event I required any facilities for a meeting, press conference or the like, to please just give him a call. I was pleasantly surprised by the offer and accepted it as graciously as the moment allowed.

A few steps later I was whisked through the dining room to a quiet corner table where I was formally introduced to Erlanger himself.

"Monsieur Erlanger, Mr. Darwin."

"Mr. Darwin, it's so nice of you to come."

My host was a very pleasant, mild-mannered, middle-aged gentleman with a slightly balding pate, a propensity for the rotund and what appeared to be a mischievous smile. Erlanger spoke perfect English with only a modicum of his French heritage peeking through. Reeking of the grand lifestyle as only a true purveyor could do, he raised his hand for mine, then offered me the seat next to his. Our introductory patter was friendly but brief, allowing my host little time to get directly to the point.

"Mr. Darwin, you must be very pleased with the reception your film received yesterday. I'm sorry the print was not received in time to be entered into the festival competition, because I feel confident it could have easily won an award."

Erlanger went on to praise me for taking on so much of the production burden by myself, suggesting jokingly that other talented filmmakers might quickly learn to follow suit. Then, when mentioning the review he had seen in the *Hollywood Reporter* that panned the rape scene as being too explicit, he added that he felt I had handled the scene with great taste, sensitivity and restraint, congratulating me on the result. He went on to dissect the scene in minute detail, covering the manner in which I decided to frame it and shoot it handheld, emphasizing the low angle with the waves crashing all around. In essence, he felt the scene was "brilliant cinema" and the best depiction of a sexual encounter he had ever seen. It goes without saying that I agreed with him wholeheartedly, but I kept my enthusiasm to a discreet inner roar I was hopeful he would not detect. It soon became clear, however, that Erlanger obviously loved to hear himself speak and, as a result, probably did not pick up on many of my nuances. He was an incredible raconteur who seemed capable of covering a half-dozen independent thoughts before coming up for air, but since he was speaking primarily about *A House of Sand* and me, I decided it would be best to simply allow him to continue with his lecture and to keep my mouth shut as much as possible. Finally, he seemed to change gears in midstream, segueing from praise of what I had accomplished to thoughts of what I might do now and in the immediate future.

"Have you given any thought to distribution? Has anyone in the U.S. shown an interest?"

I had to admit that we had the chance to screen the film only three times in the U.S., with two of those showings qualifying as sneak previews before regular theatre audiences, and that the only distributor who had inquired to date was British Lion in London, where we would be screening the film sometime after leaving Venice. Erlanger hesitated only a moment before responding matter-of-factly,

"No, British Lion won't take it. Like most distributors, they require films that run from eighty to one hundred minutes. At sixty minutes, your film is too short. My suggestion is to take it to a good art film distributor – and I can arrange for you to meet some of those if you wish – or you should consider lengthening your film the extra twenty to thirty minutes to comply with standard feature film requirements for showing in regular movie houses. In this regard,

I believe your best approach would be for you to partner with an established film company here in Europe to shoot the extra scenes and then merely splice the whole together. It would be inexpensive to do and you could have a completed feature-length film in just a few months – perhaps even have it completed in time to show here at the Venice Film Festival in competition next year. You might give it some thought."

And think about it I did. Erlanger reminded me that the film was scheduled to be shown again that evening, and this time it would be at the Astra Theatre, a larger and more prestigious venue only a few blocks from the hotel.

"Once your screenings are over, I should wait and not make any decisions until all the inquiries have been received. And don't forget, the wolves will soon be at your door, so be careful whom you partner with."

Before departing, Erlanger volunteered to call the press office and have them bring as many of their people to the Astra showing as possible, adding,

"Press people can be very revealing – and very rewarding. You may even meet one you should know personally."

He smiled at his own remark, then handed me his business card with his contact information in Venice, Paris and Cannes, where he makes his home, concluding his remarks with the following friendly encouragement,

"I think you are a very talented young man and I would be pleased to help you in any way I can. Please do not hesitate to call me whenever the need arises."

He then added an unexpected zinger, and he did so flippantly, and with a roguish smile.

"You might be amazed to discover what I can arrange for you."

In parting, Erlanger asked whether I knew Jack Palance, mentioning the fact that he admired Palance as one of the greatest actors we have, then adding,

"I was told he would be in attendance at the festival, but I haven't seen him as yet."

After leaving the luncheon, I went back to my pensione, cleaned up and changed my clothes to prepare for the evening's activities. After all, I was here to sell the film, and this second screening in Venice would probably be my last chance to do so.

Fate, however, clearly decided otherwise. As things turned out, the picture was not meant to go down in flames so quickly. Word must have gotten out because attendance at the second showing was overwhelming and more enthusiastic than at the first one, all leading to more positive responses. This was especially obvious after the so-called "rape" scene, when some of the attendees actually cheered and applauded the action. Offers from a number of unknown parties for distribution rights in various parts of the world came in almost immediately, but none were accompanied by a realistic cash offer or an acceptable monetary element sufficient to affect a deal, so I reluctantly rejected all of them. I may have been the new kid on the block here in Venice, but at least I was dry behind the ears when it came to business. These kinds of rash offers are well-known in the business world as fishing expeditions by bottom feeders and bargain hunters who seek out the uninitiated and the uninformed. Offers like these almost always lack the financial backing or credibility of an ongoing concern, so they cannot be considered as being legitimate. Woe is me, I thought. The wolves that Erlanger mentioned had indeed arrived at my door, and all in record time.

After the screening that evening, there was enthusiastic applause throughout the theatre and enough hoopla and miscellaneous responses from the attendees while exiting to pique my hopes that something positive might actually result from it. Nevertheless, it wasn't until the following morning that I finally heard from someone I felt was legitimate enough to consider seriously. It was a gentleman representing himself as being with a French production company in Paris. He spoke English with a definite French accent but he was the first of all the callers who seemed genuinely knowledgeable and sincere, leading me to believe that this might actually be the call I had been waiting for. He gave his name as Jacques Serres, and as I understood it, he was acting as an assistant for his producer, who was at the festival with him to view worthy new properties for distribution throughout Europe and the Middle East. He explained that they had attended the showing at the Astra Theatre the previous evening, enjoyed it, and indicated they were interested in speaking with me about distribution rights. Nevertheless, remembering Erlanger's warning about whom to partner with, I explained that I needed to know more about his principal and the name of his company in Paris. Apparently, he anticipated my concern and quickly gave me all the information I requested. His principal, he explained, was a French/ Lebanese gentleman named Mario Araktingi, with headquarters in Beirut. The family was in the construction business in Lebanon and was quite successful, allowing Araktingi the ability to fund his production company in Paris. He then added that Araktingi asked that I please join him for cocktails and dinner at the Excelsior later in the afternoon, and I agreed. In the meanwhile, I called Philippe Erlanger to confirm the information Serres had just given me. To my surprise, Erlanger corroborated every word of it, adding that he had never met Araktingi personally but was aware that he had done films in Lebanon and knew there was nothing in the public record to indicate he was anything other than a legitimate business person with substantial financial backing. I thanked Erlanger for the confirmation, he wished me good luck with my new connection, and I was on my way.

Mario Araktingi was a large, robust gentleman in early middle age with a bushy head of wavy black hair and a pleasant, determined manner. He acted very businesslike but injected a sense of humor that was not unlike my own – somewhat wry and roguish. As a result, once he felt comfortable with me and the manner in which I responded to him, he seemed to open up and take me into his complete confidence. With business matters coming first, we spent the entire cocktail hour and most of our dinner time discussing the film. He, too, had read the review in the *Hollywood Reporter* and anticipated seeing the film himself in order to determine exactly what the reviewer had in mind when he said the rape scene was too explicit. His question to me then concerned the strict Hollywood production code and how I could have gained code approval had the rape really been that explicit. Needless to say, that question was answered for him in a moment upon viewing the film. In fact, when discussing it with me, he seemed completely enamored of the manner in which I depicted the rape, without reverting to any obvious genital contact, arguing that in his mind it wasn't a rape at all, merely a wonderfully depicted love scene "sans" the usual diversions. I had to admit that I had never actually thought of it in quite the same manner, but now that he did, I tended to agree with him. As I explained it to him, it was never my intent to depict a rape, but rather for the protagonist to merely experience orgasm through mental masturbation – the male figure simply being there as a prop. I summed it up by assuring him that in my mind that is exactly what she did and she did so successfully.

Thus, with the question of rape, orgasm and the explicit nature of whatever the reviewer thought he might have seen now having been settled, we went on to the overriding present situation of deciding what to do with the film and where I, as the film's creator, might go from here. Araktingi's immediate response was that he loved the film and was definitely interested in some sort of a co-production deal with me for release of the film throughout the international marketplace, or as he explained it, jokingly,

"From Austria to Australia and everywhere in between, including Malta, Gibraltar and all the ships at sea."

He hastened to add that they do not go into the U.S. for quite obvious reasons, suggesting that the U.S. distributors had that market all sewn up for themselves. But he then went on, seemingly compelled to get down to the dark and dirty side of the business by expressing his remorse with what he called the festival vultures that feed on innocent young filmmakers like me, and expressing his concern that I do not become involved with any of them. I thought to myself that this remark seemed rather compelling, considering the fact that I didn't know whether he was a vulture himself.

That concern, however, was quickly dispelled when Araktingi indicated he had already spoken about the film with his people in Paris, and since it was important for them to see it as well, thought it best that I bring the film to Paris for them to review before making an offer on it. He then added that they would pay for my airfare, the cost for shipping the film and my hotel accommodations while in Paris for as long as my presence was required. Vultures aside, I felt it was an offer I couldn't refuse, accepting it with but a single caveat – that I needed to accompany the film back to Rome, where Customs required the bond to be released before it could be shipped out of the country. Araktingi agreed, then pre-arranged to have the film shipped out of Rome for arrival in Paris as soon as possible.

At the time of my arrival, Orly was the principal airport in Paris, and when I landed there, Jacques Serres was on hand to greet me. I felt it was a good omen, because unlike Rome and Venice, where I didn't know a soul upon my arrival, at least I felt welcome in Paris by someone I had met previously. Serres then drove me through the heart of the city and across the Seine to my accommodations at the Hotel Belmont on Rue Du Bassano, which as he explained beforehand was only a block from the Champs-Élysées. He then went on to offer that it was also only one additional block to the Drug Store, a favorite English-speaking establishment in the heart of the French capital that was a blessing for all those Americans in Paris who were incapable of conversing in the French language – as I was. I took him at his word and before the day was out decided to take a stroll down to the Champs-Élysées myself just to prove he was right.

Paris, as most everyone is aware, is considered the most beautiful city in the world, and I made quick note of the fact that I should inspect every corner of this incredible place before I left it. But first things coming first, I had to sell the film or all the rest of my plans would be for naught. As I expected, the telephone began ringing early the following morning with a call from Serres, who advised that he would pick me up after breakfast for a meeting with Araktingi and the rest of his people at the company offices. I was told the point of the meeting was for all of them to become acquainted with me and to learn as much about the film as possible. Upon our arrival I was immediately brought in to see Araktingi, who introduced me to all of his associates. They were all clearly assistants or advisors to Araktingi, who for the rest of the day did all of the talking that I, at least, was privy to. After the introductions, Araktingi asked me to please recite whatever it was I wanted to tell them about the film.

"You know, things like how did you make it? How did you find your actors? Who financed it? What have you done before this? Remember, whatever you say here may be in the press tomorrow."

Actually, I felt Araktingi was very thoughtful in at least translating things for me that some of the others were saying and, conversely, translating what I was saying for them. But in reflecting back at the meeting and how it was conducted, I think I just started talking and simply let them take it all down in any way they could.

At one point a secretary came in to announce that the film had just arrived at the Customs office at Orly and would be available for pickup later in the day. Serres was then assigned the task of bringing the film in while another gentleman was asked to book a local projection theatre for the showing. The mood among all those present was remarkably jovial and upbeat, and I had the distinct feeling for the first time since coming to Europe that things finally appeared to be going my way.

Filmax was one of those projection theatres I would soon become familiar with in Europe. It catered almost exclusively to local production companies, the press and others in the French cinema who were intent on private screenings for publicity, sales or distribution purposes. Araktingi had invited a number of people to view the film, but much to my surprise, he decided to introduce me as "the new boy-genius from America." Unfortunately, it was an unsolicited and unwarranted remark I felt completely uncomfortable with, and I told him so. I explained that I never thought of myself as being a genius of any sort, just a new, young moviemaker intent on selling his first attempt at it. Araktingi finally agreed and apologized for his remark before going on.

After the screening there was enthusiastic applause, an elevated sign of acceptance and much positive chatter among the departing guests, but it wasn't until after lunch and another long meeting that I was finally given word that a deal would be in the offing before the end of the day. The deal I was offered, however, was not exactly the one I had anticipated.

The problem, as Araktingi explained it, was not that the film was bad in any way, because it was actually very good – exceptional, in fact, from their perspective. The only problem was that it was too short for distribution in many of the countries around the world that on the average require ninety-minute films for screening purposes. Philippe Erlanger, in fact, was the first to make note of this deficiency during our meeting in Venice, but as I soon explained to everyone, the film was done as an experiment and was never intended for distribution in regular theatres. My only thought was to achieve distribution in art theatres as a "new wave" type of production. In Araktingi's view, however, that would be a total waste of a truly exceptional piece of cinema that deserved more than mere new wave recognition. The answer in his mind was simply to lengthen the film another thirty minutes, but I was not so sure.

"Unfortunately, I think that is easier said than done."

I then tried to explain that any film – emphasizing that *A House of Sand* was no exception – is a complete story in itself. It begins at "A" and it ends at "Z," and if the story has been fully told at that point, then there is generally nothing that can be said thereafter to add anything to it. Araktingi disagreed, suggesting with a broad smile that we could simply shoot two or three more encounter episodes with Mary at a similar beach down on the French Riviera, splice them in and no one would be the wiser. Erlanger, in fact, suggested much the same, and I had to believe that he knew a hell of a lot more about film than the rest of us. But at this point in my budding moviemaking career, the mere idea of someone simply splicing some new footage into the middle of my little masterpiece was abhorrent to me – and the more I thought about it, the more I was convinced I was right.

Araktingi's suggestion just blew me away because it gave me my first clue that this gentleman really didn't know a thing about the fine points of telling a story on film. Not that I was a master at it as yet, but at least I knew just a little bit more about plot development, continuity of action and resolution, among other things – little gems of wisdom we should have all learned back in high school. But then, how could I expect this person to understand any of the artistic considerations and merits involved in filmmaking. He was, after all, a mere producer, and like most producers was interested only in the financial aspect of the project. I kept thinking back at Jack Warner and how he butchered *A Star is Born* to the complete dismay of its director, and my immediate conclusion was that I could not allow Araktingi to do the same with *A House of Sand*. My problem now was to cater to him and praise him for his suggestion, but to do everything in my power to ensure that he maintained his interest in the picture without destroying it. Nevertheless, I had to concede that he was certainly right in one important aspect. Yes, the picture was too short for general release, and the only way to change that was to lengthen it. The conundrum in my mind, however, was how to do that without destroying the original continuity and intent of it.

Then, suddenly, I had an epiphany, and it came to me out of the blue as though by a stroke of lightning. After that it took me only a moment or two to properly phrase my response before getting back to him.

"Well, yes, obviously, the film can be lengthened – any film can be lengthened – but the trick as I see it is to do so in a manner that maintains the integrity of the original footage, while merely adding a new element or dimension that broadens the overall scope of the story. If that doesn't make sense to you, please just give me another moment or two to consolidate my thoughts."

"Yes, yes, please take all the time you need."

Then, after a discreet pause, I gave it to him as slowly and deliberately as I could muster it.

"OK, let's look at it this way. The film depicts a complete story we both agree is fine the way it is, the only problem being that it is too short. As I see it, the difficulty in lengthening that story by splicing new footage into the middle of it is that it would be very difficult, if not totally impossible, to match the new footage with the original. What I mean is that the color, lighting, weather and location would all be different – none of them would match – not to mention the action, the flow and the continuity of the original performances with the new. No, a much better solution would be to leave the present film alone as it is and simply build a new story around it. The original film could then be used as a flashback or dream sequence in the new action and, in doing so, the resultant integration of the elements could be done flawlessly. And most important in my mind is the fact that in this way, the obvious physical differences in the two sequences could be emphasized for dramatic effect and be used as an asset instead of a liability in the development of the overriding new story."

I emphasized the word "overriding," stretching it out phonetically and forming my arms around it like an umbrella over our heads. Araktingi seemed pleased with the demonstration but was clearly unsure as to how it could all work for him. Maybe he simply felt he didn't have the manpower, or enough money, but I could tell he liked the idea of integrating the original story into a new, longer, more encompassing one. It was obvious that he maintained a production company of some size here in Paris, and I recognized the fact that the best way for him to utilize that asset was to put it to work and make it pay for itself. Suddenly I felt I simply had to keep explaining it to him just to keep him interested. Thus, in a final flurry of bravado, I continued to talk as long as I was able and let him have it until he capitulated – then, when all my shots had been fired, I delivered a coup de grâce I knew he could not resist.

"If you agree with this assessment of the matter, I will tell you what I will do. I will write the new story for you, and if you like it I will sell it to you. The story will then belong to you. I will write it so that it can all be filmed right here in Paris. No studio stuff or locations out of town – that's all very expensive – just local scenes where we can use all your own people and save you a lot of money, and to save you even more money, I will direct the film for you and you won't even need to pay me for that work until we finish shooting it. Finally, after this new footage has been edited, if we both like what we see and feel it is acceptable for release as a feature film, I will agree to contribute my original sixty-minute film to the project. You and I will then be co-producers of the resultant film and own it fifty-fifty."

Finally a glimmer of hope flashed through his eyes, then a smile followed by a nod of approval.

"Oh, and before I forget, I will need a full-time secretary – an assistant "Girl Friday" type to do all my bidding for me. She will need to be absolutely fluent in both English and French and accompany me on all my meetings, interviews, casting calls, the works – someone to really assist me with the language barrier. Unfortunately, I have come ill-equipped to do any of that on my own. So, if all this is acceptable to you, you can start looking for her first thing in the morning."

"Yes, yes, you are correct, let us get the girl first. I will have Jacques call around for interviews in the morning. In the meanwhile, I have to tell you I like the way you think – the way you presented your proposal. You are obviously a very astute businessman besides being a wonderful director, and I will be pleased to do business with you."

We shook hands on the deal, precipitating a response that almost choked him up with emotion. Then, suddenly, in an apparent attempt not to display any weakness – he placed a fatherly hand on my shoulder in a broad display of parental-like approval.

"I have only one request."

"Yes?"

"May I call you Bob?"

"But of course."

"Please call me Mario."

"Hello, Mario."

"Hello, Bob, welcome to Paris."

CHAPTER 31:

Paris and Dorothy Marchini

Sometime during our lifetimes a few of the more lucky ones among us will meet one or more people who are destined to carve a positive niche in our psyches and remain there forever. I say forever because the whole idea of what I am hoping to explain here transcends the limits of time that we as individuals will be given on earth. Dorothy Marchini was one of those people for me.

Dorothy was an English-born lady from Saltdean, Sussex, near Brighton, who was fathered by an Italian immigrant. She felt cloistered by the restrained Victorian attitudes persisting in England during her formative years, preferring the more unbridled French lifestyle when she reached maturity and moved to France soon thereafter. When I met Dorothy in 1962, my best guess was that she was in her mid- to late thirties. She was thin and wiry and possessed the energy and endurance of an ox. She was not a raving beauty and she knew it, but like Golda Meir, Margaret Thatcher, Eleanor Roosevelt and a plethora of other extremely successful women – all of whom carried a similar burden – it did not restrain her from becoming the most important, outspoken, forcefully driven asset in her domain. In Dorothy's case, that domain was the province of the French cinema establishment in Paris. Dorothy made up for whatever she lacked in the beauty department with the most interesting personality I ever encountered. And if that wasn't enough, she also possessed an incredibly wry sense of humor and utilized it – unrestrained if necessary – whenever she thought well enough to employ it. She was forceful but not dominating; she was sweet but not saccharine; and she recognized exactly how far she could go with whomever she was engaged – and she never exceeded that boundary of propriety or proper decorum unless, of course, there was an overriding reason for her to do so. She could suggest and even demand when required and was almost never wrong with the result. Most important for

271

me was the fact that she knew literally everyone connected with the film business in Paris and, apparently, everyone knew her. She was a powerhouse of information on things to do to produce a film in France, and she knew all the right people to contact in order to get those things done. She was exactly the type of person I needed to get me through this project, and I didn't waste a minute of my time to get her.

Jacques Serres called me the day after my meeting with Araktingi to advise he had spoken with this woman he described as being "the most sought-after person in Paris." He explained that she had just been released by 20th Century Fox from a picture she had been working on in Paris for more than a year. The film was Fox's epic World War II D-Day drama, *The Longest Day*, and she had been hired on as the personal secretary to the film's producer, Darryl Zanuck. The problem, as Serres explained it, was that in his conversation with her that morning, she indicated she had two interviews for work scheduled later in the day, so the only time I could see her was immediately – meaning now, around nine in the morning – adding,

"This woman is extremely popular. Everyone wants her. But she told me she doesn't want to get involved in another huge project like *The Longest Day*, just something small right now. So if she likes you and likes the project, you may have a chance."

In response, I told Serres,

"Just give me ten minutes to shower and shave and I'll be ready for her."

Ten minutes later, just as I was stepping out of the bath, there was a knock at the door. Thinking it was probably just the room maid, I wrapped a towel around my middle and headed out to answer it. Opening the door, I found this woman standing there stoically, and she was obviously not the room maid.

"Dorothy Marchini to see Mr. Darwin."

"Oh, excuse me. Please come in. I didn't expect you so soon. Just give me a moment to put a robe on."

"Yes, please do."

Her response seemed quite brusque and snippy but understandable,

I thought, under the circumstances. Then, as I emerged in my robe, I welcomed her in.

"I'm Mr. Darwin, please sit down."

"No, I'm here to see Mr. Darwin, the director. You must be a different Darwin."

"No, I'm Robert Darwin, the director."

"No, you're too young to be a director."

"Oh, why do you say that?"

"Well, at your age, you might find I know more about directing than you do."

Suddenly the whole tenure of our conversation became very humorous for me and I began to laugh. Not that I loved what she said, but it was the mere fact that she said it. It gave me my first glimpse and insight into the very spirit and essence of this woman – and I loved it.

"Well, what's so funny?"

"I assume you're here to be interviewed for the secretarial position?"

She nodded affirmatively.

"Well, I'm laughing because I'm the one who's supposed to be interviewing you, and from the sound of it so far, it appears that you are interviewing me."

"Oh well, yes, I'm sorry, I see what you mean. Obviously I don't want to spoil things so early on, but you see I'm just a woman and I have to be careful with whom I become involved. But the more I look at you, the more I think you might be pretty harmless. Nevertheless, I do have one important question for you before we go on. Since you do seem to have a propensity, or at least an inclination, for conducting your interviews in your bathrobe – which does not seem to fit in with your overall persona at all – I must ask you a very pertinent question."

"Yes, please do."

"You aren't a flasher, are you?"

"A flasher? No, of course not. Why do you ask?"

"Well, my last employer was and I just don't want to repeat

anything like that."

"Your last employer? You mean Zanuck? Darryl Zanuck? He actually flashed you?"

"Yes, at the very beginning – the very first day in fact. Just like now, with you. I walked into the room, like this, and he stood there in his bathrobe, like you are. He asked me my name and before I could even answer him he flashed me."

"Flashed you, are you sure?"

"Oh yes, he flashed me alright. He even fluffed it up a bit for me, gave it a few pats like this just to see if he could get any interest out of me. Not that I cared about it one way or the other or how big or small it was."

"So what was it, big or small?"

"Oh, it was big alright. Huge, in fact."

"So what did you do?"

"Well I told him immediately, 'No, no, there'll be none of that. If you want me to work for you, you'll have to behave. Just cover it up. Go ahead, cover it up.' And much to my relief, that was what he did. He covered himself and never did it again. I think maybe he just did it to see how I would react. But he gave me the job anyway and we got along just fine after that."

"And so then you worked with him throughout the picture and you had no more problems with him?"

"Absolutely. It was an extremely difficult project for both of us, but in the end it was extremely satisfying, as well."

"Well, then, since I'm still in my bathrobe, maybe I should just flash you like he did. You can react, and then I can give you the job like he did, and if we are lucky it should all just work out fine for us like it did with Zanuck. What do you think?"

"Well, if I thought you were serious and would still give me the job, I'd let you do it. But no, you're too nice of a gentleman to take advantage of an innocent demoiselle like me."

We both roared with laughter.

"You *are* a nice gentleman, aren't you?"

"Yes, I am, and you're getting the job even without the flash. But

I'm holding off all bets for what I might do in the future."

I then added, jokingly,

"So don't hold me to a promise I might not be inclined to keep."

That was it. The interview was over and I hired Dorothy on the spot. There was no question in my mind that she was satisfied with me and I certainly liked her. The question of proper decorum and salutations came next and we quickly settled on Dorothy and Bob, but when I told her my good friends only called me Bobby, she retorted quite authoritatively,

"Only privately, Bobby, and only between us, but never on the outside or when we are working."

And, of course, she was right. I then told Dorothy she could babysit me and try to teach me everything she thought I needed to know about directing, and every other little nuance of my character she felt I might be delinquent in – but only if she really thought it was that necessary. We laughed again and I suddenly became aware that this laughter between us had become our bond – our private symbol of approval. It was like a shake of the hands or a verbal indication in the affirmative. I liked it and I instantly told her so.

I then admitted to Dorothy that I had heard the story about Darryl Zanuck and the way he flashed people way back when I first came to Hollywood in 1952, and the fact that it also happened to her just confirmed the story in my mind. I then told her,

"The fact that you admitted such a horrible indiscretion to me just proves your honesty, and if it makes you feel any better, I can tell you that I'm honest too, and I am truly not a flasher. So I think we are going to get along just fine."

At the time, I didn't know Dorothy to be very demonstrative, but she agreed with my assessment and then gave me a nice ladylike hug.

The following morning Dorothy signed on as my secretary and production assistant with Araktingi's company, and from that day forward, Dorothy was my sidekick until the picture was "in the can." First things coming first, however, she arranged with the hotel to exchange my single room and bath for a two-bedroom suite in order for her to set up her office in the second bedroom. Interviews, readings, script meetings and all the rest would be handled in the sitting room. The three-room setup worked out well for us because, as an example, when we were casting the picture, Dorothy would come in early, wake me and have breakfast with me in the sitting room, then go over the day's appointments before I even went back to take my shower. Of course, I always appeared in my bathrobe and Dorothy always responded with a degrading comic smirk and a remark or two like "Oh, it's too small," or "It's much too big," or simply, "Disgusting!" It was a running joke between us and it helped cement our relationship by keeping everything on an even keel. It even helped to do so when overwhelming problems on the outside threatened to derail the whole project.

Later that day I decided to call Ralph Jarvis in Honolulu to inform him that I had made a co-production deal to lengthen and finish the film in Paris and would be staying on in Europe indefinitely. Since I had no idea when I would be back in Los Angeles, if ever, I asked him whether he would be interested in purchasing the Mulholland house from me, including all of the furniture. I explained that I needed money to live on while working in Europe, so I would be willing to give him first choice on a lease/option deal to buy it. As I expected, Ralph immediately said yes, we settled on a price and the terms and in a few minutes the deal was done. Most important for me, however, was the fact that Ralph agreed to have the lease payments begin immediately and be retroactive back to August 15, the day I left for Venice. Once the papers were signed, Ralph credited my bank account for the back payments and then had all my personal belongings packed and placed in storage at Bekins. The Mulholland house now belonged to him.

Paris, I soon discovered, was divided into twenty different divisions or wards called arrondissements, and as Dorothy explained it, she lived over on the Left Bank in the 14th. Her apartment was in an old 19th-century fifth-floor walkup that the city controlled as a "prix fixe" living accommodation, and although the building boasted only minimal facilities, she was proud of the fact that the building's owner could never evict her or raise her rent. Thus, I quickly learned of Dorothy's penchant for frugality. She shared this apartment with her longtime French boyfriend, Jean, and over the course of the next few weeks, we dined out together almost every evening. My only problem with Jean was that he was an inveterate smoker, and if that alone wasn't bad enough, he smoked only the strongest, most vile-smelling cigarettes in the world, the French Gitanes and Gauloise brands. Luckily for me, Dorothy wasn't a smoker either, so whenever the three of us went out, Jean was forbidden from smoking in our presence. Needless to say, the odor of smoke on his breath and clothing was almost as bad. It was just the smoke in our faces that was missing.

An important aspect of my relationship with Dorothy was my overriding interest in learning more about French food and wine – a passionate pursuit of the gastronomic senses I pursue to this day. I have always fancied myself as a "gourmand" of sorts – the kind of person who really enjoys fine dining and the highest quality in food, drink and service. In fact, it was one of my first attempts at being that specific with Dorothy that got us going on this very subject. I asked her whether she would allow me to take her out to Maxim's for dinner. She declined, stating it was overrated and too expensive, and then she took us to one of her favorite establishments – a move that rewarded me with one of the most revealing and delightful dining experiences of my life.

The place was up in Montmartre, on a narrow, dimly lit back street just a short distance behind the Sacré Cœur. There was no obvious sign or writing out front that might have identified the place. It was quite small inside, with only eight or nine tables, but it had a wonderful French country charm about it that I soon grew to recognize and love as the symbol and mark of the most satisfying dining experiences I had ever encountered. Dorothy explained this gem as being a typical French country-style establishment that was small enough to succeed as a simple mom-and-pop operation. Those that were slightly larger generally utilized other family members to fill out the required wait positions, but other than that, most of them operated in much the same manner as this one. The primary difference from one establishment to the next was not in the quality of the food and service – since most were excellent – but in the type, genre and variety of the chef's creations.

Luckily for me, I had learned how to read a French menu long before I ever thought of coming to Paris, so once I arrived, I promised myself I would make good use of that knowledge at every occasion. Unfortunately, the limited nature of that knowledge became excruciatingly apparent this very first evening when I attempted to utilize it.

"Dorothy, I thought I was quite well-informed about most of the things I might encounter on a menu in this country. I know what légumes are, poulet, bœuf, veau, poisson and the rest, but what on earth is oursin?"

"Oh, Bobby, oursin is the most delicious thing you will ever have the pleasure of eating. It is one of those wonderful fruits of the sea that French chefs have a particularly interesting time in preparing – and all in their own inimitable way."

Dorothy then ordered oursin for two along with a nice bottle of Pouilly Fuisse and the rest of that meal is what I refer to as part of my "culinary history," since it became one of those gastronomic experiences I was destined to remember for the rest of my life. Oursin, it turned out, was nothing other than plain, ordinary, everyday sea urchin, a spiny, unappetizing-appearing creature that can be found in oceans all over the world, but it is revered for its delicate substance only in places like France, where thoughts of cooking ungodly creatures like this are dwelt upon. The roe of these animals is harvested as corals and is prepared in every possible way according to the whims and proclivities of the chef who, in the instant case, was one of the best.

Over the course of the next several months, Dorothy and I went out to other wonderful little cafés where we could partake in more pleasurable evenings that might compare favorably with that first one, but more important things came first. It seemed we were obliged to make a movie that I was slated to write and direct, and I hadn't given the project a single thought as yet. I told Dorothy and Araktingi that I needed to go into seclusion somewhere for a week or two and, hopefully, come up with at least the modicum of a script. Obviously Paris and all the attendant hoopla would become too distracting. Besides, in the short week or two since I arrived in Paris, the seasons had subtly changed from late summer to a chilly fall with evening temperatures plummeting down into the twenties, and I longed for a much warmer clime. Dorothy suggested a nice little place she knew of down on the Riviera between Cannes and Monaco where I could just kick back and relax. She said it would still be warm there, and with the tourists long gone, she believed it would be the perfect atmosphere for me in which to get some work done, and I agreed. The next morning Dorothy packed my meager bag and I was gone.

The place Dorothy suggested was perfect for my needs and, naturally, she was right on all accounts. It was a nice little pied-à-terre in a small rooming house that was right on the beach, where I could take a quick obligatory dip every morning. Most importantly, however, with no tourists around as distractions, the place was quiet, the weather was ideal and the whole package presented the perfect atmosphere in which I could get the job done that had been laid out for me. Luckily, there was one of those small French country-style restaurants I had recently acquired an affinity for just up the street, and that is where I took most of my meals. The nearest village was Saint-Michel with Beaulieu-sur-Mer a little farther on, so the overall arrangement appeared perfect for what I was there to do.

Getting down to the job at hand, I was able to complete the outline for our new script in record time. The dialogue, locations, camera angles and all the rest would come later, but I was confident I could accomplish all of that back in Paris. My time on the Riviera, therefore, was a total success. I had accomplished what I went down there to do, and the mere fact I had succeeded in that effort gave me the positive rush I felt I needed to bring back to Paris and help propel me on to the next level.

Before arriving back in Paris, I called Dorothy to arrange for a full-scale production meeting with the entire staff. As I told her, I needed to explain the story line to all those who would be working on the picture, to give them a rough idea of the locations they would need to scout for and generally outline the myriad tasks that lay ahead for them. At the meeting, Dorothy did all the translating for me, then added her own brand of forceful delivery for full effect. Araktingi was in attendance, but respectfully allowed Dorothy and me to do all the talking.

The story I came up with was simple and to the point and I felt it would blend in perfectly with the original footage that could be inserted in its entirety in the middle of the new footage as a dream sequence. The ending would be bittersweet, but endearing – the kind of conclusion, I explained, that leaves audiences with a good feeling in their hearts upon leaving the theatre.

When I was through, Araktingi came over to assure me of his approval.

"Very good, Bob. I like the story and the way you explained it. I'm sure it will be a very good film."

I thanked him for his support and then reminded him that I still needed a vehicle to get Dorothy and me around Paris on our own.

"Yes, Bob, I have Jacques working on a car for you now."

In the end I felt Araktingi was genuinely pleased that I had taken charge of the project in such an overt, positive manner. It was all stuff about making movies I felt he really didn't have any knowledge of, and if that was the case, then perhaps he had even less experience in making a movie than I did. On the other hand, maybe he was just another rich guy who simply wanted to make a name for himself as a movie producer. There were certainly many others that came along before him – Howard Hughes, perhaps, being the most prominent one that comes to mind.

Later that evening, when I walked into the hotel and approached the front desk for my key, I couldn't help but notice the well-proportioned young woman standing next to me. Never one to ignore such an opportune moment when a promising chance for a discreet encounter was at hand, I glanced over nonchalantly for a quick look only to discover that she was dressed in the uniform of an Air France stewardess and, much to my surprise, found that she was also absolutely gorgeous. A moment later, she looked over at me, we both smiled and, in an instant, I knew I was in for another tumultuous liaison. All that I can tell the reader is that the second we were inside the door of her room we tore our clothes off and went at it like two crazed cats in a back alley – and that is the way we continued our scandalous union until we were spent.

After that wildly tempestuous encounter was over, we just rolled around on the floor laughing hysterically at what we had just done. I don't recall much of what was said after that, except to say that we decided to retire to my room for the rest of the evening, called room service for a late dinner in bed and then continued on with our exuberant sexual escapade until morning. It was a most delightful happenstance.

My new roommate's name was Theresa and she wasn't scheduled to report for her next flight until later the following day. As a result, I decided to allow Dorothy to wake us with the usual coffee and croissants around eight. Naturally, I was thrilled to see that she was pleased with the new situation I had arranged for myself. Not surprisingly, however, the moment Theresa was off for the airport, Dorothy began to grill me as to exactly how I was able to land such a delicious dish in just the few short hours since she dropped me off. From the manner in which she was questioning me it was clear she expected a lurid tale of sexual intrigue akin to the scandalous contents of a 25 cent paperback. Dorothy, I decided, was a "salacious story queen," one of the millions of women out there – most of whom are middle-aged spinsters, unfulfilled housewives, and the like – that dote on the lurid details of sexual liaisons, and I told her so.

"Dorothy, you shouldn't think of the fundamental nature of human sexuality so negatively. Actually, it is all rather beautiful. Our meeting happened quite innocently downstairs at the reception desk, and if it will make you feel any better about it, my first thought was that, perhaps, with you being the perfect secretary you might have actually set it all up for me in advance."

"Oh, how sweet of you, Bobby, but no, it wasn't me. How could it have been? I've never been a match maker; I wouldn't know how to go about doing it."

The next morning, Dorothy answered a knock at the door. It was the bellboy with the keys and paperwork for my new car. He described it as a silver-gray Simca Mille parked right out in front of the hotel. Dorothy was thrilled and delighted. Now, she explained, we wouldn't need to use her old beater for my biddings any longer – and that pleased both of us very much.

CHAPTER 32:

The Via Veneto and Jack Palance

By November 1, cold and dreary winter weather had descended upon Paris with a vengeance. Fog shrouded the city on a daily basis and the mean temperature was down in the teens. Worst of all, many of the hotels, shops and other public buildings held on to their World War II austerity measures and refused to turn the heat on until November 15, regardless of how cold it actually became outside. The thinking, obviously, was purely plebeian. I concluded that since the French managed to get themselves through the war without any heat, they decided they sure as hell didn't need any heat now. As I soon learned, the French were thrifty and frugal to a fault. Besides, there were few tourists in town during this time of year, and since the French were obviously good at punishing themselves, what the hell, why not. It was a stupid choice in my mind, but the only thing we visitors could do was to leave Paris to the French during such cold spells and head for warmer climes.

A quick call to my agents in Rome was all it took, and within the hour I was on my way. They arranged for a small pensione for me just behind the Excelsior Hotel and a mere two-minute walk to the Via Veneto. It was quiet and secluded and the ideal environment for me to complete the work I had at hand. As I told Araktingi earlier, I was hopeful to do the screenplay in three or four months, but in truth it all depended on the number of quality hours I could put in on my trusty old Royal portable typewriter every day.

The first week in November was still short-sleeve-shirt weather in Rome. It was warm and balmy, and I loved it. This opportune weather allowed me the luxury of rapidly establishing a daily routine in which I could enjoy an early morning breakfast at the Excelsior, catch up on all the latest news and then return to the seclusion of my little pensione for two to three hours of work before taking my first break. Noon was really when the day began for most Romans, and it wasn't much different for the rest of us immigrants who made this beautiful ancient city our temporary home. Thus, if my morning session was fruitful and yielded satisfying results, I'd clean up and head down to one of the little cafés on the Via Veneto for a leisurely lunch. Glamorized in such films as Federico Fellini's ode to decadence, *La Dolce Vita*, as "the" place in Rome to "see and be seen," the Via Veneto quickly became the informal meeting hub for all those who needed, wanted or craved the madness created by the myriad of paparazzi, pulp-fiction writers and unsavory journalists who inhabited the place on a twenty-four-hour basis. There was also the totally unsavory side of the place akin to a souk for slaves – a near-pornographic meat market of semiclothed bodies, where the sheep came willingly and without reservation, and all with no more expectation than the stars they could conjure up in their eyes. It was where respectable agents paraded their most promising young starlets for instant recognition to be gazed at, photographed and, hopefully, published in tomorrow's newspapers for all to see. The Via Veneto was vital to the pulse of Rome, and it was also the best place for a promising young American director like me to be seen, as well.

My favorite haunt was the Café de Paris, where I was able to reserve a small three-seater out front on a daily basis. It was all arranged through the agency as an extension of my account at the Excelsior, thus allowing me to sign all my tabs and avoid the need for carrying large amounts of local currency, which at the prevailing exchange rate of approximately 1,600 Italian lire to one U.S. dollar would otherwise have been a cumbersome necessity. Operating overseas with a single credit card and as little cash as possible was a precautionary measure I learned from other well-travelled friends who had preceded me, and it also worked very nicely for me.

My table was just inside the pedestrian walkway and next to the front entrance of the café, allowing for easy access and viewing in all directions. Interestingly, it took only an hour or so on my first day at the café to reel in my first acquaintance, an actor friend from Los Angeles named Burt Nelson who happened to be in town to answer a casting call at Cinecitta Studios, then the largest and busiest film studio in Italy. The studios were bombed and largely destroyed by Allied forces during the war, but they were rebuilt ten years later and now hosted more large film projects than any other facility on the continent. Cinecitta was where *Ben Hur*, *La Dolce Vita*, *Satyricon* and *Helen of Troy* were all filmed, and it was now the magnet that drew unemployed actors from Hollywood and around the globe for their shot at immortality. The "spaghetti western" era was still a few years off, but the chance for work at Cinecitta was real and they were all here to claim a part of it.

Some days later I had just settled down at my table when I was summarily interrupted by a tall, grizzly gentleman who leaned over me and whispered an unimaginable provocation in my ear, but it was delivered by a voice instantly recognizable to anyone with even a modicum of interest in film.

"Doctor Darwin, I presume?"

Obviously it was a play on words, but when I looked up at the craggy face and the wily smile, I knew my suspicions were confirmed. My interloper was none other than Hollywood megastar Jack Palance. Without hesitation, I decided to present my response back to him in the same spirit in which his opening line was delivered to me, and I did so in my very best proper English impersonation for emphasis.

"Aw, Sir Henry is it? Sir Henry Morton Stanley?

He nodded affirmatively.

"Well, you old sot, I didn't recognize you in your dark glasses."

We both laughed.

"I see you have an excellent sense of humor, Doctor Darwin. Thank you for accepting my dismal impersonation."

I shook his hand and then motioned for him to sit down and join me, and before long we were into a deep conversation gleaning all kinds of notable minutiae out of each other. As it turned out, Palance was in Rome for the same reason as Burt Nelson and all the rest of the displaced Hollywood actors who frequented the place. His reasoning was simple and directly to the point.

"There's a lot more work being handed out here than in Hollywood, so we all want a part of it."

I then asked him how he located me.

"How did you know my name and where to find me? I've been here only a few days…"

Palance then retorted, matter-of-factly,

"We know more about you than you can imagine, Mr. Darwin."

Palance explained that it was normal for the local agencies to place "info" inserts or "blurbs" into the local trade papers whenever someone in the business came to town. Then he pulled a crumpled copy of a trade publication named *Cinema Nuovo* from a rear pocket and pointed out where my arrival was posted. It was all in Italian, but according to him all he needed was the name, the rest all came through – as he called it – the "Ravioli Radio."

"In Hawaii it's known as the Coconut Wireless. You know, just plain old word of mouth. One tongue tattles to another and before long the whole town knows about it."

Next, Palance began asking about my heritage. He wanted to know where I was born, my parents, where they were from – all the usual stuff – and when we came to my father and I mentioned the fact that he was from the Ukraine, I thought he would fall off his chair.

"Ukraine? Where in Ukraine? I'm from Ukraine, too."

"From Odessa, on the Black Sea," I responded.

"Oh, my father was from a little town you could have never heard of, Ivan Zolote, but it was not that far from Odessa."

Palance just bubbled with excitement, exclaiming how wonderful it was that a lowly rag like the *Cinema Nuovo* could bring the two of us Ukrainians together and in such an unlikely place as the Via Veneto. Then, standing momentarily, he thrust his arms out and waved them from one end of the street to the other, then proclaiming as though from a script,

"It's just like Fellini pictured it, isn't it?"

I had to agree, but we quickly went on to other things. A couple of paparazzi soon caught wind of us, but Palance just waved them off, exclaiming we had more important matters to discuss. Eventually, the question of our true names came about, whereupon he suggested that a name like Darwin could simply not have sprouted from the loins of a Ukrainian father. Again, I agreed, but when we got around to our true first names he almost fell off his chair a second time. His true first name was Volodymyr and mine was Waldemar and in an instant we both came to the same incredible conclusion.

"They're both the same name! Waldemar is simply Volodymyr in German, or Vladimir in Russian. They are all the same name."

Palance was simply ecstatic at the revelation, likening the disclosure to some sort of a miraculous phenomenon.

What a strange turn of events, I thought, that none other than a megapersonality like Jack Palance should ferret me out on the Via Veneto, and all of a sudden, we discover we have a common heritage. Like blood brothers out of a distant childhood, we were destined to form a common ground – or perhaps, if on a less dramatic basis, to simply share a meal. Evidently, Palance wasn't about to give up the ghost for anything less, so I simply invited him to join me for lunch and he graciously accepted.

Finally – as I anticipated he would – Palance maneuvered the conversation around to the script I was working on. He asked what the story was all about and finally as to whether there might be some small morsel in it for him. I told him I hadn't gotten that far into it as yet but would keep him in mind as I went along. I then asked for his contact information and assured him I would keep him apprised of any potential role as soon as the casting phase came up.

"Darwin, you know we Ukrainians must stick together. If we don't, the Russians will just come in and kill us all off."

How prophetic, I thought, because that is exactly what happened to my father's family. Then, as he stood up to leave, Palance looked me dead in the eye, grabbed the sides of my head in both hands, drew me closer to him and kissed me squarely on the lips. He murmured something in Ukrainian that I obviously did not understand, then withdrew himself rearward in an exaggerated version of a stage exit and was gone.

For a moment, I think I must have just stood there motionless. I didn't know how to react to such a dramatic departure. As far as the kiss was concerned, the act itself did not upset me at all. Men kissing one another on the lips is common practice in Russia, Ukraine and many other Middle Eastern cultures. It is a sign of love, honor and respect between men, but in my particular case the last time I was kissed in this manner was by my loving father when I left the family home in 1952. It was in his culture and I found nothing improper about it. What upset me just a little about being kissed by Jack Palance in this manner was the fact that I felt he expected an extra-special effort on my part to write something into the script specifically for him and to do so primarily because of our common Ukrainian heritage. Naturally I knew I couldn't do that for him or for anyone else unless I honestly felt it would contribute materially to the story.

I saw Jack Palance only one more time during my stay in Rome. This time it was a couple of weeks later and down the street at Harry's Bar, another favorite hangout for displaced Americans of all persuasions. I was actually having a drink with one of the associates from my agency when Palance wandered by. He was friendly and pleasantly affable as before but somewhat subdued. He explained that he had found nothing of interest coming up for him at Cinecitta, had received an invitation to spend the weekend with friends at Cannes and was therefore leaving in the morning. Suddenly, with the mention of the name Cannes, a thought hit me. It was an epiphany I immediately decided I was obliged to relay to him.

"Jack, Cannes may become a very auspicious destination for you, but it all depends on whether a certain party I know is in residence. His name is Philippe Erlanger. He is an official with the French Ministry of Foreign Affairs. He knows everyone connected with the French cinema business in Paris, and if there is a part in any film coming up for production in France that you could play, Erlanger is the one person who would know it."

In conclusion, I dug through my wallet for the business card

Erlanger had given me in Venice, wrote the numbers down on a paper napkin and handed it over to him with the extra encouraging words I knew he could have never anticipated.

"By the way, Erlanger is a great fan of yours. He thinks you're one of the greatest actors we have."

Palance obviously ate up my words; it was the kind of appreciation I feel every true thespian lived for. Nevertheless, he thanked me profusely for the lead, gave me a standard man-to-man hug, and departed. Unfortunately for Palance, when I returned to Paris a few weeks later and checked with Erlanger, he confirmed that Palance had called his Cannes number but since he was not in residence at the time, a meeting between them never occurred. I told Erlanger I thought that was unfortunate, because I really felt the two of them could have fostered a mutually beneficial relationship whereby the Palance talent he so admired might have been utilized in some French production through the auspices and direct involvement of his office. Erlanger agreed, but obviously the question was now moot. Palance was probably back in the U.S. by now and might never return.

This missed chance by Jack Palance was another example of the various negative vagaries of the film business; success being all about location and timing. If you hit them both correctly and directly on the mark, you might at least have a chance of being considered for a particular job, but if you don't, you most emphatically will have missed out.

CHAPTER 33:

Paris Pre-Production

S uddenly the weather in Rome turned rainy and quite cool and I decided it was time for me to seek warmer environs once again. Unfortunately, a quick call from Dorothy drew all such thoughts from my mind. She confirmed that the heat was back on in all the buildings throughout Paris, negating any reason for me to stay away any longer.

"Besides, we need to begin the interviews, schedule auditions, cast the parts, scout for locations and set up a production meeting to get the crew going. I've done all I can without you, now you have to come back and do the rest."

Obviously, I had to agree. Later that day I locked up my little pensione, paid all my tabs and was back on the next plane for Paris. Once in the air I took out a pencil and pad and laid out a schedule of exactly what I had accomplished on the script to date and what I felt was left for me to do to complete it. It was a surprising turn of events, because it was clear that I had accomplished much more while in Rome than I had expected. The story line, schedule of locations and a good third of the dialogue were all complete, and I decided I could easily attend to the rest of it as we went along. Certainly, I would have many more distractions and social activities to contend with in Paris, but I had no doubt in my mind concerning my ability to complete the remaining script long before it was needed.

As I advised Jacques Serres and the location crew before leaving for Rome, the opening shot in our story is of an airliner landing at Orly. During my absence, Serres had approached Air France seeking permission to film that shot at their facility, but the request was denied. Other airlines were then approached but, in the end, they also denied our request. Undaunted, I told Serres that I would see what I could do on my own. The following day, I walked into the TWA ticket office on the Champs-Élysées and asked whether I could speak with someone in their public relations department. Luckily, the airline's local corporate offices were located on the upper floors of the same building. Thus, I was directed to the company's public relations manager, who advised that TWA had already taken stock footage of one of their new Boeing 707 jetliners landing at Orly and, after a short discussion, agreed to allow us to use this film in our picture.

What a stroke of luck! Not only would this save us two or three days on our shooting schedule, but the cost to us would be nil. Araktingi, of course, was ecstatic, even going a step further by praising me in front of his crew as an example of what all of them should be doing to save money. As I suspected they might, pre-production salaries and expenses were eating Araktingi up, and we hadn't even shot a foot of film as yet. Even so, I was pleased that my small contribution helped ease his concern, at least for the time being.

The Olympia Music Hall Fiasco

One day I was introduced to Michel Babouhot, a very successful young gentleman who owned Pierre Fauvret, the most exclusive men's shop in all of Paris. The meeting was arranged to set up the wardrobe schedules for all of the male characters in the film, but since we quickly realized we both harbored similar interests in the pop music field and otherwise, we soon became good friends. Like Dorothy, Michel knew everyone who was anyone in Paris, thus, I was not surprised when he invited me to attend the Olympia Music Hall, the most prestigious pop music emporium in Paris, for an opening night occasion. As Michel explained it, one of his closest friends was Johnny Hallyday, the French rock-and-roll star, who was grooming a young French-Bulgarian singer named Sylvie Vartan for stardom. Apparently, Hallyday had arranged for Vartan to do an opening set at a concert at the Olympia starring British rocker Vince Taylor and had set aside two tickets for Michel and me to attend. Michel's comment then told me all I needed to know.

"I told Johnny all about you, the new young American director in town, and he is anxious to meet you. Besides, it's the kind of social event you should attend, just to be seen if nothing else."

Naturally, I accepted Michel's invitation in spite of the fact that I had never heard of Hallyday or Vartan, but it was Dorothy who set the record straight for me by confirming that Johnny Hallyday was indeed the hottest French pop star of the decade, having made a name for himself by singing all of his rock-and-roll songs in French. Apparently, he was the first French rock-and-roller to do so. It was a breakout move on his part that earned him the dubious, if not exalted, title of the "French Elvis." Evidently, the epithet suited him well and he rapidly forged a career out of it. Although virtually unknown outside of the French-speaking world, he was a true superstar in France, and he maintained that aura of celestial invincibility few rock-and-roll performers in other countries could ever dream of achieving.

As I soon learned, a first-nighter at the Olympia was not unlike similar events at other major cities such as New York, London or Los Angeles. The crowd at the Olympia that evening was in major pandemonium mode. I likened it to the crowd of unruly Judy Garland fans at the *A Star is Born* preview I attended in Panorama City back in 1954. The chaos and mayhem at both occasions was much the same. Nevertheless, no one could have predicted the incredible bedlam that would occur inside the Olympia only a few moments later.

The seats Johnny Hallyday had arranged for Michel and me were in the second row, center, directly in front of the stage, and at the time we were led to our seats, the row of seats directly in front of us was still vacant. It wasn't until the house lights were dimmed and the opening strains from the orchestra came drifting through the hall that a group of five or six latecomers were led down the aisle, with a contingency of paparazzi bringing up the rear. Screams accompanied by selective applause and epithets in French I could not understand added to the confusion as the group was led in to be seated directly in front of us, and it wasn't until that moment that I recognized the most prominent persona in the group. It was the diva of all divas, Marlene Dietrich, who I was later told had played the Olympia herself on occasion and was extremely popular in Paris as well. A moment later, Marlene turned around directly in front of me to face the audience and take an impromptu bow. The uproar and applause that followed drowned out the orchestra, bringing the entire proceeding to a halt. After much confusion as to what to do next, Johnny Hallyday himself came out onstage to beg the audience to be seated and to calm down in respect for the young singer he was about to introduce. It was just an opening set for another performer who was actually headlining the show, but it was important for Hallyday because he was banking his reputation on her ultimate success, which at least in the present sense was not to occur. The crowd was simply not in the mood for it. Nevertheless, Sylvie Vartan was introduced to mild applause, taking up her position at the microphone directly in front of and facing the venerable Marlene Dietrich. It was her moment in the spotlight, and for the first twenty or thirty seconds of her performance was accompanied by nothing more than deathly silence. Unfortunately for Vartan, the silence would not last long. First, only a catcall or two from the rear of the hall, some negative remarks, an epithet or two and finally it was simply too much for Marlene to bear. Throwing her arms up in an ultimate sign of disrespect, she urged the young hopeful to step down, but when she did not, all it took for Dietrich to put an end to the agony in her own inimitable way was to simply raise her skirt as high as propriety would allow, cross her legs in a sexually provocative manner and display the famous Dietrich gams in all their glory for the entire world to see.

Total pandemonium followed as one paparazzi after another rushed forward to get their treasured shots of the action taking place not onstage but directly in front of it. The Dietrich strategy worked. Poor Sylvie was drowned out by all the commotion and finally ran offstage in despair. Clearly, this was not her day – it just took her a little too long to realize it, allowing a contemptuous Dietrich the opportunity to torpedo her performance before it could go any further. What a way for an aging diva like Dietrich to wreck a promising young career. Like a flash in the proverbial frying pan, it was over and gone in an instant, and I actually felt sorry for Sylvie and the fact that this event had occurred.

In spite of this debacle, Sylvia Vartan's career was not derailed for long. Johnny Hallyday put his reputation on the line when he backed Vartan, and he was not about to give it up so quickly. Within a couple of years, and with Hallyday's continued backing, Vartan finally made a name for herself with a couple of hit records, becoming the new darling of the French pop music scene. Edith Piaf was old, set in her ways and revered, but Sylvie Vartan was young, vibrant and current, and when she finally hit her stride, Hallyday even married her as a reward. At long last recognized as the "golden couple" of French rock-and-roll, it was a match made in heaven that the French rock hounds ate up in droves.

Other important social events followed, and one of the most memorable ones occurred for me at the annual opening of the prestigious Paris Opera. Sadly, it was not the performances onstage or the absurdly overdecorated Paris Opera House itself that I remember so vividly, but rather the extravagant cultural phenomenon of the incredibly coiffed, draped and dollopped French women who attended the event. Most were dripping in diamonds and adorned in the latest Paris fashions, but it was not the visual manifestation of their beings that drew my attention to them. Rather it was the unfortunate lack of attention these women gave to their personal hygiene that piqued and finally overwhelmed my olfactory senses. They exuded the most ungodly combination of overperfumed underarm body odors that anyone passing nearby should ever be compelled to endure. Now I knew why the French invented perfume. Sadly, however, the sickening sweet fragrance of the essences they used only exacerbated the problem, thereby drawing more attention to the underlying predicament – sadly, a cultural phenomenon only the French can truly lay claim to.

By the middle of December I told Araktingi I thought it was time to bring Mary Staton over from Los Angeles to prepare for her role. He agreed and had Serres book a ticket for her to arrive in Paris on January 3. Meanwhile, I had Dorothy arrange for a room at the Belmont for her in order to keep her in the middle of things when auditions began. At the same time, I began interviewing a number of young male actors from throughout Europe for the part of Willy, the male lead in the picture that runs throughout the story. It was a part, I thought, that if done well could propel the actor playing it to stardom. As I wrote the part, Willy was a twenty-one-year-old student from Switzerland, the middle European country that boasts a multilingual society where almost everyone speaks French, German and English, and most of them do so fluently. Therefore, I wrote the part to be multilingual on purpose, since I felt the multiple language choice would create a larger pool of actors with French or German accents from which we could draw.

Dorothy, however, had her own fixed opinion about the role. Foremost in her mind was a well-known German actor named Helmut Griem, who in my opinion would have been perfect for the part had he been somewhat younger, but at thirty I considered him too old. Other German actors in the correct age group were all too inexperienced, the wrong physical type or just too rough around the edges. One of them actually came on as an effeminate Deutsche Brando and another as a rough-hewn, uncultured Belmondo, replete with a willowy German-cum-French lisp. Neither of these impersonations worked for me and I summarily rejected them. Dorothy maintained that I was too severe, but I ignored her protestations and stood my ground. As I explained it to her, it was simply a matter of type.

"Willy has to be good-looking, clean-cut, charming, sweet, kind and endearing."

A cheap imitation of Brando, Belmondo or some other present-day heartthrob was simply not what I was looking for, and I told

Dorothy I would accept nothing less.

Mary Staton arrived at Orly as scheduled and was immediately whisked into the moviemaking fray by Araktingi himself, who suddenly decided it was his duty to take his "new star" under his wing. The requisite welcoming parties, interviews and blurbs in the various trade papers were all in-line with the customs of the day and, of course, Dorothy and I were obliged to tag along whenever our participation was called for. Even so, I felt my time could be put to better use by interviewing and auditioning actors for the various other parts that had yet to be cast, so I tended to shy away from all the frivolity as much as possible.

It was sometime during this process that I asked Dorothy to call Famous Artists, the same agency that Dick Clayton worked for in Los Angeles. This agency had corresponding offices in major cities throughout the world, and I thought they might just have someone on their roster locally who might be our Willy. A couple of days later, one of their associates came by to show us some publicity shots of young actors under contract to the agency, but again, none of them fit our bill and I was obliged to tell them so.

"You have to understand that Willy has to be exceptional. Attractive? Absolutely – he has to look like a fashion model – but he also has to be charming, sweet and endearing like the kid next door. In addition, he has to have a good speaking voice – one that goes with the personality – and, finally, he must speak English fluently and preferably with a Swiss-German or French accent."

I explained that I was well aware it was a tall order, but that in my mind I couldn't believe there wasn't a single young man in all of Europe who could fit the bill.

Not surprisingly, I was right. A callback a couple of days later informed us that they indeed had a young actor in their file that fit the bill physically, but he was very inexperienced and, perhaps, was incapable of producing the kind of skilled performance we envisioned.

My response was swift, emphatic and to the point.

"Let me worry about all that. Just send him over so we can get a look at him."

CHAPTER 34:

Philippe Forquet

The following morning, I was shaving in the adjoining bathroom when I heard Dorothy answer a knock at the door. In response, all I heard was a short, six-word introduction, but it was delivered by the most refined, young male voice I had ever had the privilege of hearing.

"Philippe Forquet to see Robert Darwin."

Oh my god, I thought, is this our boy? Naturally, Dorothy immediately engaged our visitor and within the two to three minutes it took me to dress and present myself, she had already gleaned the most important statistical information out of him.

"This is the young actor Famous Artists called about. His name is Philippe Forquet. He is French, twenty-one years of age and just has a couple of minor roles to his credit, but he speaks English fluently and..."

"Yes, Dorothy, thank you, thank you. But I'd rather hear Philippe tell me all this himself."

I shook Philippe's hand and immediately noticed that this was not just another ordinary, twenty-one-year-old, run-of-the-mill French actor. This guy was amazingly handsome and cultured for his age, yet he exuded a childlike quality of innocence and vulnerability I found to be incredibly engaging. He was tall and lean and possessed all the physical attributes requisite of a movie star – and if all that wasn't enough, there was that amazing voice, and in a moment I decided I needed to hear more if it.

"Philippe, please sit down here. I would like you to tell me all about yourself. Dorothy will be present to take down notes for our file, otherwise the floor is yours. Please, you can begin anytime you'd like."

My words were followed by a long pause of nothing more than deathly silence. Philippe just sat there, his mouth quivering slightly as though on the brink of speech but incapable of doing so. He was obviously mulling the words around in his head, but none appeared ready to come to his lips. In that brief moment I realized Philippe's first vulnerability – he was extremely bashful and shy. Nevertheless, I was determined not to allow such a minor obstacle to derail this interview, so I decided a little push might actually be necessary to get him going.

"Why don't you just start with when you were born and then you can just take it from there."

Luckily, that was all the prodding it took, and after a few moments of diminishing hesitation he began speaking like a magpie.

"Oh, thank you. Yes, that would be a good place to start. Well, I was born here in Paris. It was on September 27, 1940, during the Nazi occupation. However, my family home is in Saint-Quentin, in the Picardy region of northern France, and that is where I grew up."

I just let Philippe talk, and keep talking he did. Although he began slowly, he continued speaking freely. Once he reached his stride, he exuded much enthusiasm, which, finally, helped him keep up the pace without any hesitation whatsoever. The bashful streak I had detected earlier seemed to dissipate in the excitement of the moment, and he simply continued on as the myriad of remembrances from his earlier years came to mind. Frankly, at this point in our interview I wasn't really interested in the content of what he was talking about. My only interest was in hearing more of his incredible speaking voice.

"Tell me, Philippe, where did you learn to speak English so well? Your accent is beautiful and practically flawless."

"I did a film earlier this year. It was only a small part, but it was an American film, *In the French Style*, with Jean Seberg."

"Who was the director?"

"Robert Parrish."

"Did you know any English when he gave you the part?"

"Yes, a little, but he insisted I do better, so I just made up my mind to learn it and I did."

"That's very admirable, Philippe, I wish I had the determination to do the same with my French."

"Oh, it isn't that difficult. I could teach you. You would find I am a very good teacher."

I was overwhelmed by Philippe's offer and I expressed my gratitude to him. But we had other more important matters to consider at that moment. I liked the positive manner in which Philippe was presenting himself, and considering the fact that his offer might have been in jest, I decided he also had a great sense of humor – the end result being that I was totally smitten by his engaging personality. One look at Dorothy and I knew she was as sold on Philippe as well, so I decided there was no reason to delay the agony any longer and I told Philippe exactly where he stood.

"Philippe, we have a part in our picture I would like you to read for. It's the part of Willy, a Swiss-German university student on holiday here in Paris. It's the male lead and it runs throughout the picture, so there is a lot of dialogue. I think you are right for the part physically, and you certainly have the right voice for it, so it's just a matter of determining whether you can get into the part emotionally. I could hand you some lines right now and have you read them cold, but since you have little experience in that department, I don't think that would do us much good. What I would like to do instead is to excerpt a few pages of dialogue from the script, let you take them home to study for a couple of days and then come back and show us what you can do with them. What do you think? Would you like to do that?"

Needless to say, Philippe was overjoyed at the prospect and thanked me profusely for the offer. A couple of days later, when he came in for his reading, I had Mary Staton come in to read with him. Since this was also Mary's first starring role in a feature-length picture, she didn't have much more experience than Philippe did. However, Mary had done the first part of the picture at Point Dume and was certainly used to my directing, so I concluded she would be less nervous about the reading than Philippe and, hopefully, exude a calming effect that might help him get through it as well.

Unfortunately, my concerns were well placed, but Mary's calming influence had no effect on Philippe's performance and the reading went very poorly. Oh, Philippe learned his lines alright and he enunciated all the words quite well, but his performance was wooden, insensitive and totally lacking of any feeling or emotion. There was one line that came out particularly egregiously, "Mary, I think I love you." He delivered it in such an impassive and detached manner that I thought he was speaking to an inanimate object. Even Dorothy glanced over at me in disbelief. Obviously, his agency was right. He had little acting experience and now we knew the extent of what would be required to get him up to speed.

Clearly, my work would be cut out for me – but I was not deterred. He was still the best prospect we had and I was not about to forget that. Besides, I had Mary to help me with his readings and hopefully, between the two of us, I was confident we could get Philippe to loosen up and, eventually, give us the performance we could all be proud of. It was a chance I was willing to take in spite of the fact that the success of the entire picture rested upon it.

By the first day of March, the interviews and auditions were over, all of the major roles had been cast and we were deep into rehearsals. I scheduled an hour or two with Philippe every day just to loosen him up and to help get him through some of the lines he was having a particularly rough time with. Then, one day, we got to a word he seemed completely incapable of enunciating. Mary asks, "Where are you from?" In response, Willy says, "I'm from Switzerland." The problem, however, was that Philippe seemed incapable of pronouncing the syllable "Switz." It simply kept coming out as "Swizz," and try as he might he couldn't correct it. Dorothy suggested that we just change the line to make it easier for him, but Philippe would have none of that.

"No, no…it's OK. I will just practice at home and I will get it. I promise you, I will get it."

And eventually, he did. Several weeks later when we actually shot that scene, I could see a great sigh of relief come over Philippe's face when I called out "Cut and print!" He looked over at me with a broad smile on his face and when our eyes met, I gave him a big "thumbs up." It was the kind of positive moment we could both cherish for the rest of the shoot. It certainly made my day and there is no doubt in my mind that it also made his.

By April 1, the weather finally cleared sufficiently for the camera crew to begin shooting some of our background scenes. Rehearsals continued on a daily basis with Philippe and Mary consuming most of my time. In my mind I wanted those two to be as close to perfection as possible, and I did everything in my power to help them achieve that goal. Finally, on April 5, the first warmth of the season descended upon Paris and the decision was made to begin principal photography on the following Monday. April 8, therefore, was our "D-Day," and after the long arduous winter we endured to get to this point, we were all chomping at the bit to get on with it.

The first scene to be shot was an interior in an upper-floor apartment at 4, rue Boutreillis that commanded a stunning view of Notre Dame. The shot was used as a backdrop behind Willy and Mary after they consummated their relationship. It created exactly the right atmosphere I visualized for the shot, and in my mind it was perfect. A couple of extra takes for protection was all it took, allowing us to go on to the next location. By Thursday we were at the St. Hilaire, a large nightclub where singer Anton Valery would sing the lyrics to the theme melody "A House of Sand," which Les Baxter had composed for the original footage back in Los Angeles a year earlier. Needless to say, Dorothy had arranged for all the location shots to be set up in logical order, allowing us to breeze through our shooting schedule in record time. We shot our final scenes at the base of the Eiffel Tower on the morning of May 18 and then returned to the St. Hilaire for some background shots. When I called out "Cut and print" for the last time on that day, the film, as they say, was "in the can!"

Suddenly I realized that I had completed the directing of my first full-length, feature motion picture, and I felt as confident and comfortable with what I had accomplished as the proverbial rooster in a henhouse. What a relief, I thought. I had finally accomplished what I had set out to do when I arrived in Hollywood some ten years earlier. A great inner satisfaction instantly permeated my being. I experienced an emotional high unlike any I had undergone in a long while. Nothing, I thought, could change my destiny now. I was a full-blown movie director, and a good one, and soon the whole world would know it. But again, things don't always turn out exactly as first expected.

CHAPTER 35:

Post-Production Woes

With principal photography completed and all of our work accomplished in record time, I was naturally very ebullient – as were Dorothy, Philippe and Mary – but grumbles and miscellaneous negative protestations from certain members of the crew during our final shooting days left me reeling with the impression that all was not well at the production office. Consequently, when I finally questioned Dorothy about it, she gave me the bad news I hoped I would never hear.

"Well, I hadn't planned on telling you this until after you got your last shot, but the truth is we are having severe money problems. The company missed a couple of payrolls last month, finally paid everyone late, and now they are late again. A number of the crew members have had enough and are threatening to file a complaint with the labor board."

Of course, I had no idea, and I told Dorothy so.

"How could you have? From what Jacques told me, Araktingi's brother, who runs the family business in Beirut, put his foot down because of all the money that had been siphoned off for this picture. So as far as Jacques knows, Araktingi has been flying all over Europe trying to raise funds from other sources. Worst of all, according to Jacques, is that there isn't even enough money in the till to cut and edit the film. The result being, this production has come to a halt, and that's where it will stay until more money comes in to finish it."

Clearly, money problems were the bane of almost all motion picture projects, whether they are large studio productions or small independent films such as ours. I was just too busy directing the film to have given it any thought. Now that I was aware of it, however, I told Dorothy not to panic or go off half-cocked thinking that the day of doom has arrived. My thought was that we should give Araktingi a week or two to come through and then, if he doesn't, I would call

Philippe Erlanger for advice on how to proceed.

Until this time, Dorothy and I had been conducting our business from this large, expensive, duplex suite at the Belmont Hotel, and now that our need for all this room no longer existed, I suggested we simply relocate to something more appropriate. Dorothy agreed, adding that she would check around in the morning to see what was available. That said, it did not take her long to act, and within a couple of days she had located the perfect place for us. It was a nicely furnished, five-room apartment on the top floor of a modern apartment complex on Avenue D'iena just a half block from the Arc de Triomphe de L'Etoile. The living room was appropriately outfitted with a large writing desk and suitable cabinets that Dorothy immediately commandeered for use as her office, and under the circumstances I decided I had no standing in the matter to deny her of her wish.

One quick look with the requisite nod of approval from Dorothy and that is all it took to acquire the place. I signed the lease on the spot, went back to the Belmont to pack my meager belongings and moved into our new facility before the end of the day. Naturally, Dorothy was thrilled, as was I. It was an excellent move on our part at a time when budget constraints were definitely required, and I was pleased that we were able to contribute to that end in a very timely manner.

By the end of May, a couple of weeks had passed since the last roll of film had gone through our cameras. Nevertheless, as a result of Araktingi's absence and the lack of available funds with which to proceed, not a single person had been paid and nothing positive had been accomplished in post-production to finish the project. Thus, with Dorothy prodding me to call Erlanger for official guidance, I finally relented and did so, but I couldn't have been more surprised to learn that he had already been fully apprised of our unfortunate situation.

"You should know that when it comes to the labor unions and

any complaints they may harbor, it does not take long for the entire industry to become aware when a dismal financial situation such as this comes to pass. Despite that fact, the law protects not only the poor workers who are owed their hard-earned pay, but also the unfortunate debtor, who in this case is a foreign subject with more incontrovertible rights than he would have if he were a Frenchman."

Erlanger went on to explain that the appropriate agencies had been in touch with Jacques Serres, who in Araktingi's absence was the highest-ranking officer in the company. Serres had assured them that Araktingi would be returning over the June 1 weekend with the funds with which to pay all of the company's debts. Naturally, I was ecstatic with the news, but when I spoke with Serres the following morning, I requested an immediate meeting with Araktingi in order to confirm it, explaining that any excuses or postponements would not be acceptable. Serres understood and arranged for the meeting as requested, but the results of that meeting were significantly less than what I had anticipated.

The site for the meeting was at a restaurant in Porte Maillot in the northwestern section of Paris; it was only a short fifteen-minute drive from the Champs-Élysées, but I considered it odd that the meeting could not have been held at any of our usual nearby haunts. Araktingi was friendly enough when I entered, even stood up to shake my hand, but he was subdued and avoided looking me directly in the eye. My first impression was that he had probably been in hiding and possibly living in Paris all along, just too embarrassed perhaps to face all the people he was indebted to. Nevertheless, he confirmed the fact that his brother had denied him the right to use any additional family funds to finish the picture, and therefore he was obliged to seek the necessary funds elsewhere – a task he assured me he had successfully completed. He exclaimed that he had enough money committed to him to satisfy his entire obligation concerning the film but, unfortunately, had to commit to a payout that could be funded only in phases. The first of these would be available to him within the coming week, but those funds would be sufficient only to satisfy his payroll obligation; the second phase would pay me for my work, with enough left over for the initial post-production costs, including the editing, but unfortunately that portion would not be available for another four to five weeks. All of the final costs, therefore, would be funded later, as required.

Naturally, this delay in completing the film was a severe disappointment for me. Not only would it postpone the sale and distribution of the film, but it caused a serious scheduling problem for me, since my original plans were to finish the project in its entirety before going on an extended vacation throughout the Middle Eastern and North African regions – a journey I considered would take at least three to four months to complete. Dorothy, however, was more judicious about the matter than I was, suggesting I merely do my tour in segments, taking a portion of it at that time and the rest of it later after the film was sold. Naturally, I balked at the idea at first, but finally relented. It was a good idea and, under the circumstances, I had no option other than to agree. Thus, I decided to do portions of the Middle East and Egypt first, then the rest of it later on. Araktingi even offered to have a friend of his in Beirut act as my tour guide, interpreter and travelling companion during my stay in Lebanon, adding with emphasis that it would all be at his expense. Needless to say, it was an offer I was loath to refuse and, in the spirit of the moment, accepted it without hesitation. Thus, I left Paris with the satisfaction of knowing I was not leaving the project in a state of disarray. I was confident that the picture would be completed in due time, perhaps only a few weeks later than first anticipated.

Vasso Gabriel was a nineteen-year-old college student and aspiring actor when he welcomed me to Lebanon at the Beirut Airport. This was the friend that Araktingi promised as my tour guide while in this country. Vasso was a well-mannered, good-looking young kid and the kind of teenage heartthrob that any impressionable young female would wet her undies over. He had a great outgoing personality and was charming, friendly and eager to please me. After all, I was an American film director and Vasso, like Yvette Duguay,

Jack Palance, Vivien Leigh, Burt Nelson and so many others I had met over the years, was just another actor "between pictures," and as a consequence was out looking for work just like the rest of them. Vasso, however, was not without credits. He starred in the title role of *Le Petite Etranger* (*The Little Stranger*), a film Araktingi had produced in Lebanon a few years earlier. Although the film was not yet in release, the publicity from its preview at the Cannes Film Festival a year earlier followed him wherever he went. Vasso was only sixteen years of age when he made that film; he was now three years older and still waiting patiently for the next offer. His family, however, was not about to allow Vasso the luxury of wasting any more of his precious school years on such a vaporous possibility, thus they were insisting he return to school in September – only two months hence – in the event that no firm new acting offers materialized for him.

Beirut was a beautiful city – heralded as "The Paris of the Middle East" – and for the next several days Vasso treated me to a personal tour of the place. French was the predominant foreign language spoken in Lebanon, but with the presence of the American University in Beirut, most young people, at least, spoke fluent English, as well. With my hotel set as our home base, Vasso organized a schedule of attractions he decided I should see and then directed us on short trips to neighboring sites around the country to fill out each day. He was a most knowledgeable guide and a perfect companion for my stay, and I thanked him profusely for all he did for me. To his credit, however, Vasso quickly took advantage of the many hours he was spending with me by making his pitch and openly soliciting help from me for his own career, which was clearly going nowhere. Much like Jack Palance's unsolicited onslaught of me in Rome, Vasso was playing the only card he had – his ability to sell himself with all the charisma and personal magnetism generally required of the act, and to do so with anyone in the business who might possibly be of help to him. Naturally, I did not discourage him, and although I had no idea as to the extent of his acting abilities, I considered that he was certainly eager, willing and good-looking enough to make it in films, so I agreed to help by introducing him to my agents in Rome. Obviously, the requisite meeting with his parents came next, and after much soul-searching, they gave their approval. I then suggested I take Vasso to Rome with me upon my return from North Africa. Thus, before leaving Beirut, I called the agency and pre-arranged an interview for Vasso a few weeks hence. It was obviously a last ditch effort on his part – a final glimmer of hope for his future in film – and, understandably, he was eager to get on with it.

As previously planned, the next stop on my trip would take me to Iran and Syria, then Israel and finally Egypt – if time allowed – with calls back to Dorothy every week for any news concerning *A House of Sand*. My visit to Iran, however, was short but not sweet. My guide was no Vasso and Tehran was no Beirut. To make matters worse, I found the rest of the country to be banal, primitive and filthy, so I went on to Syria as soon as possible. Damascus, at least, was a vibrant and exciting city with marginally better hotel accommodations, but the single overriding fact regarding Syria was its people, many of whom were uncommonly friendly and eager to help a lone foreigner like me. It gave me a sense of security and belonging even though it was impossible for us to converse with each other in any way. Israel, however, was another matter altogether. Although everyone I encountered spoke perfect English, no one was helpful, obliging or friendly. On the contrary, they all seemed suspicious of my presence and I quickly acquired the impression that they couldn't wait for me to leave, so I was pleased to accommodate them as soon as possible.

Unfortunately, without a prior reservation in my pocket and no direct flights to Cairo, I found the only available transportation out of Israel was on an ancient 1930s-vintage Douglas DC-2 aircraft being operated as a quasi-commercial local that eventually got me to Cairo, but with five or more intermediate stops along the way. The cabin of this aircraft had no interior side panels and no head liner. The wicker seats were barely functional, but at least they were bolted to the floor. My fellow passengers included chickens, ducks and geese, all thankfully caged, but their racket and stench within the close confines of that ungodly cabin were barely tolerable. The only other memorable aspects of the flight were the widely scattered bullet holes visible throughout the exposed outer skin of the aircraft and the incessant sputtering and coughing of the engines. It was a trip to remember, but at least we landed in Cairo in one piece, if not exactly on time. Thus, with my Iran and Israel visits purposely cut short, I arrived in Cairo long before schedule, giving me plenty of time to visit all of the historic sites. I then capped my adventure with a leisurely cruise back down the Nile on an old 19th-century, steam-powered paddle wheeler, reminiscent of Agatha Christie's epic adventure in *Death on the Nile*.

A quick call to Dorothy told me it was now time to get back to work. She confirmed that Araktingi had indeed obtained the necessary funds with which to finish the picture, and in my absence had directed Serres to hire a couple of editors to get the work started. I then told Dorothy to make an appointment for me to meet with the editors bright and early the following Monday morning. I then flew back to Beirut to pick up Vasso, accompanied him to Rome, introduced him to my agents, arranged for his accommodations and then continued on to Paris to finish *A House of Sand*.

Vasso was now on his own and alone in the big city of Rome for the first time, but as I promised his parents beforehand, in the event that nothing worthwhile materialized for him during those few weeks that were available to him, I would have my agents arrange for his return to Beirut before the beginning of his next school semester in September.

Unfortunately, the whims and quirks of the film business were clearly not in tune with Vasso's needs at this particular moment in time, and like Jack Palance and his aborted meeting with Philippe Erlanger and the unresolved hopes and prayers of so many others before Vasso and since, it became clear that the timing, location and confluence of the stars above were simply not in alignment for him. Time was of the essence and there was simply not enough of it available for the agency to promote anything positive for Vasso.

The only definite aspect of the matter was the fact that by returning to Beirut before September, Vasso would at least be continuing on with his education and thus would probably have a future available for him that would be marginally better than the one he might have made for himself had he spent the rest of his life pursuing his acting aspirations in vain.

Vasso's case proved to me that a young hopeful has no better chance at gaining success in the film business in Rome than in Paris, London or Hollywood – the vagaries of the system are the same worldwide, with the correct timing and location being the principal factors.

CHAPTER 36:

Sale of *A House of Sand*

Having been away from the project for several weeks, I was really concerned about what might have been accomplished during my absence. But once I returned and viewed the work that had been done, I was shocked – the editing had been totally botched. It seems the editors hired by Serres had been cutting the film without any thought, concern or direction for pace, mood or continuity. Worst of all, they did not understand English, so there was no way for me to even inform them of what they had done wrong. A call to Serres was just kicked up to Araktingi, which made things even worse because talking to Araktingi about artistic matters was like barking at the moon. He knew even less about the subtle art of film editing or the fact that the editors Serres hired had made a mess of it. Finally, however, I did convince him that the film needed to be taken to a professional lab where it could be edited correctly. CTM Labs in Paris was where each clip of the film was then taken to be laboriously restored and the film re-edited properly, with me looking over the shoulders of the newly appointed editors to give final approval. It was a long, arduous, time-consuming process requiring my constant attention, but with the professional staff at CTM at my disposal, the editing was finally completed correctly. The tracks were then added and a final release print produced in a few weeks.

The James Bond Era

All, however, did not go well for us when we arrived in Piccadilly with the first copy of our completed film in hand. On October 5, 1962, the world was treated to the premiere of a totally new genre of action films. James Bond as Secret Agent 007 was born and within weeks *Dr. No*, the first film of the series, became the hit attraction of the year. *Dr. No* offered sex, unbridled action, witty dialogue, and an overabundance of violence, half-naked women and a great new action hero as 007, Sean Connery. All we had with *A House of Sand* was Philippe Forquet and a very little bit of sex, which apparently was not enough. When we took our film to British Lion for screening, they felt it was not strong enough to stand up to the new 007 genre of action films that the world was now "salivating over" (their description, not mine) and Rank, United Artists and Janus International – all next in line – felt much the same. On the other hand, Golden Era, a small but well-respected British distributor, liked it and offered to take it on as a feature-length film for the international market, and after some extensive wrangling, we agreed to sell the film to them.

Obviously, once the film was sold, I was out of the project completely and it was now in the hands of others. My input was no longer required and the production company in Paris was disbanded. Dorothy immediately accepted a job with another company and Araktingi apparently left Paris to conjure up another project elsewhere. Before we parted, however, we did speak about co-producing another film in some warmer clime, but because of his demonstrated money problems and total lack of artistic understanding, my heart told me not to get involved – so I declined. In fact, my primary interest at that time was to get back to the states to see my parents. They were getting older and I simply did not feel comfortable staying away from them much longer.

My arrival back in the United States greeted me with a mixed bag of news, most of which was bad. To my dismay, my dad was not feeling well. He had aged considerably during my absence, complained constantly of chest pains and respiratory congestion and, as a result, I had him hospitalized for a complete physical. After several days, however, no definitive cause was determined; he seemed to improve and asked to go home. The doctor and I concurred because there really wasn't much the hospital could do for him. He was in his nineties, was comfortable at home and that was all he really wanted. Finally, having spent as much time with him as I was able to, I headed back to Los Angeles to pick up the pieces of the life I had left behind so many years before.

Sadly, I found that three of the best friends I made during my pre-Paris Hollywood days had passed away, and that all of their deaths were related or attributed to drugs. Just the thought of such an incredible waste was mind-boggling to me since I had never allowed myself the distraction of indulging in drugs or any of the associated "pleasurable" activities. Luckily for me I always considered that I had a "built-in" high; therefore, I didn't need any sort of dope to surreptitiously manufacture a phony high for me. These were all intelligent and attractive young men who, much like me, had great futures in store for them. All three were now gone and I just couldn't get the thought of that loss out of my head.

At the same time, I found the city I returned to was not the place it was when I left it. The atmosphere was startlingly oppressive and stifling; it was airless and overwhelmingly dreary. Smog had become the new enemy in the City of the Angels, and apparently no angels had come forth to enlighten the populous as to what to do about it. Drugs and crime had become its other major concerns. I took an apartment at Dale Sherwood's Hollywood complex, but quickly found that my old "piss-and-vinegar" attitude about the Los Angeles lifestyle simply didn't hold water for me anymore. The city encompassed an entirely different environment from the one I was used to and I couldn't embrace any facet of it.

The charm that Los Angeles once held for me had been irrevocably eroded, as was my interest in the film business. Obviously, I hadn't counted on the interminable money problems one encounters when making a film, the production delays and the undeniable fact that no one man can control the entire project. Worst of all, and the most unacceptable aspect of the business for me, was the terrible, irreplaceable loss of time between takes and inevitably, between each individual job. It was the one incontrovertible fact about the moviemaking business I could not accept. My mind was simply too active to accept such inactivity. In spite of it all, however, I did achieve my primary goal of writing and directing my own film and I sold it – a minor miracle in itself – nevertheless, I was not sold on the film business, per se, and I finally determined it to be contrary to everything I basically believed in.

A quick review of the last ten years of my life left me with an inescapable conclusion I really didn't wish to ponder – but I wisely realized I had no choice other than to accept it. Yes, I had made a fine living as an actor in Hollywood, even though I honestly never wanted to be one. I also sold a number of my writings – albeit mostly only short stories, magazine articles, treatments and the like – but I did so primarily in the foreign market, thus never achieving the recognition in Hollywood as the screenwriter I strove to be. And yes, I succeeded in producing and directing a wonderful short, experimental motion picture that I masterfully transformed into a full-length feature film in Paris and then sold it for distribution on the world market. The only undeniable truth of the matter, however, is the sad and indisputable fact that all I really created was another insignificant motion picture that, without any stars involved to propel it to immortality, would be gone and forgotten before anyone even knew it existed.

On the positive side, my agent, John Darrow, was ecstatic over my success in selling the picture, but, obviously, he knew nothing of all the problems I encountered with the financing and the terribly botched editing. It was not a walk in the park for me and I told him so. Even so, he insisted I go back and do another picture as soon as possible, emphasizing the fact that I was hot now, then suggesting that a year from now I might just be another "out-of-work" director if I didn't make an immediate attempt for a second shot at it.

Some days later I had a call from George Cukor with an invitation for dinner. Darrow, apparently, told him I was back, leading him to voice comic disappointment that his name was not on my call list. Obviously, Cukor had not lost his sense of humor and, needless to say, I made my excuses for not calling and he graciously accepted them. As we sat down for our pre-dinner Dubonnets, he also expressed his satisfaction with the way *A House of Sand* turned out for me, but when I told him of the many difficulties I encountered along the way, he immediately launched into a tirade of his own about how difficult it was even for someone with his stature to get anything done in Hollywood anymore. It seemed a strange confluence of complaints with both Cukor, the highly acclaimed, established Hollywood director, and me, the neophyte first-timer, both bitching about the same basic problems, but I listened to him dutifully because I could not disagree. In Cukor's case, he had just completed the biggest blockbuster film of the year, *My Fair Lady*, but with the studio bugging him to cut corners every day, he complained bitterly that he still couldn't get things done the way he wanted. And he was bugged about another matter that kept dogging him, that being the inordinate amount of time he was forced to waste between pictures after Marilyn Monroe's untimely death during the filming of *Something's Got to Give*, but he could only comment about it sarcastically.

"Since I was her director on her last picture, it was almost as though everyone was blaming me for allowing her to take all those pills – like I was the one who prescribed them for her or thrust them into her mouth. The fact is she couldn't have gone on and finished the picture anyway, regardless of whether she took any more pills, because she was that far out of it already."

Cukor went on, as though transfixed by the memory of it.

"That beautiful, innocent childlike face was gone. You could see it in her eyes, her mental anguish and in her demeanor the moment she walked on the set, and it was chillingly obvious in all of the dailies. She had lost that wonderful youthful spark and spontaneity she once possessed and was clearly on the fast track to oblivion, and there was nothing any of us could have done to stop her."

I never told Cukor about my own sad encounter with Marilyn years earlier because there was simply no need to. He was obviously much more aware of her demons than I was and was forced to deal with them on a daily basis.

Cukor was now sixty-five years of age. He had slowed down considerably since the last time I saw him, but at least he got through *My Fair Lady* in spite of all his complaints, and he was going on with his life with a positive outlook on things. His Oscar win the following spring for directing that film obviously made the whole effort worthwhile for him.

Patrick Curtis and Jo Raquel Tejada

It was sometime during this period that I ran into an old friend from my pre-Paris days. His name was Patrick Curtis and he was another one of those former "actors turned entrepreneurs" when the aura of stardom no longer appeared to be working for him. His days as Melanie's baby in *Gone With The Wind* were far behind him and he was now in the process of making a new name for himself as a talent agent and fledgling producer. We ran into each other quite by accident on the street one day and immediately took up where we had left off. He remembered that I wanted to shoot a little film out in Malibu the last time we saw one another, and when I told him the entire story of how I actually shot the film and wound up completing it in Paris, he was all ears and devoured every word I could tell him about it.

Pat, it seemed, had a problem. He had this girlfriend who he felt had all the attributes of a movie star, and although she had little training and no experience, she had a "knockout" body he felt could propel her all the way to stardom. Her name was Jo Raquel Tejada and she was twenty-three years old, had little acting experience and was burdened with two young children from a previous marriage. But in Pat's eye she had it all. Pat took on the duties as her manager and agent, but he acknowledged that all his efforts to promote her in Hollywood had failed. Nevertheless, he refused to give up on her because he knew that she had that indescribable star quality every agent, manager and promoter looks for and lives by.

"You can call it an obsession if you'd like, but yes, Bob, I do feel that positive about Jo Raquel and I simply can't give up on her."

My first impression was that, at the age of twenty-three and with two small kids to care for, she carried too much baggage to make it, but Pat was resolute and begged me to at least come see her just so that I could critique her for him. Naturally, I was intrigued enough to take the time to see her, so I agreed.

At the time of our visit Jo Raquel lived with her two young children in a very small cottage in Burbank just across Barham Boulevard from the Warner Brothers Studios. The place was small with few amenities, but for Jo Raquel and her kids, it was home. When we arrived, Pat simply walked in through the front door with me in tow.

"Hi honey, it's Pat, come on out. I've got someone I'd like you to meet."

There was a curt but friendly response from the kitchen – probably something akin to "be out in a minute" or the like – when a few moments later this young woman appeared in the kitchen doorway. She held one small child in her arm who was breastfeeding from her fully exposed left breast and a second somewhat older child hanging onto her slip from the side. My first thought was that Pat was 100 percent correct. Her body, which was in full view through her flimsy dress, was absolutely perfect. Her breasts were magnificent. Even the face – which harbored no makeup – was strikingly beautiful. The only physical problem I noticed was her teeth; they were quite unacceptable for a movie queen and would require extensive dental work to correct. Otherwise I felt it was simply a matter of giving her adequate exposure at the right time and place to stir up enough interest with which to pull something off.

I spoke with Jo Raquel only briefly, asking her a few questions just to gauge the quality and timbre of her voice, and although I found it to be rather nasal and a little forced for a mature woman, I felt that a little training with a good voice coach would probably be all she really needed to correct it.

On our way back to town, it didn't take Pat long to blurt out the sixty-four-dollar question.

"Well, what do you think?"

I gave one long last pause, then told Pat exactly what he wanted to hear.

"Pat, I think you have a winner, and I know exactly how you should promote her."

For the next several minutes it seemed I did nothing more than bolster Pat's ego, confirming what he thought about Raquel and her chances for making it big on the silver screen, but in the end it all boiled down to the "how" and the "where" of it.

"For starters, Pat, you have to have her teeth fixed."

Pat concurred, confirming that he had already made an appointment for her with one of the best orthopedic dentists in town.

"Second, since you've already attempted to sell her in Hollywood and acknowledge that it didn't work, I suggest you forget about Hollywood and take her directly to Rome, because Rome is where all the action is today."

Suddenly, I had Pat's attention, and I knew it was the time to give it to him with both barrels.

"Pat, I can tell you this. If you dress Jo Raquel in the slinkiest, sexiest outfit you can find and park her beautiful body on the Via Veneto for all the passersby to gawk at, I guarantee that in ten minutes every paparazzo in Rome will be there to photograph her, and by morning those photos will be plastered all over the daily tabloids. Then, if all goes well, some hungry producer will take her on and "discover" her before the week is out. That's the way they do it over there; the Via Veneto is famous for it. It's a way of life for budding starlets, and it's amazing how many of them are picked up that way, given a screen test or a small part in some movie."

And as history has recorded it, Pat did listen to me and he did take Jo Raquel to Rome as I suggested. Although the scenario for her breakthrough might not have gone exactly as I described it above, it was still basically the way it happened for her. She emerged as Raquel Welsh, the newest and most beautiful sex symbol in the world, and I can only add that I was pleased to have played that miniscule small part in bringing it all about for her.

A month or two later, I was back on a plane for Europe myself. Golden Era advised that they lacked the publicity materials on the original footage we shot at Point Dume. These were the photos I left behind when I took off for the Venice Film Festival and that they now required to promote the final "feature" version of the film. Obviously, I could have simply mailed the photos off to London in an envelope and been done with it, but I thought otherwise and decided to use the opportunity to deliver the materials personally and then go on to complete my trip through North Africa that I had promised myself a year earlier, adding Turkey, the Balkans and the rest of southern Europe for good measure.

I arrived back at my apartment in Paris on October 11, 1963. It was the same day I heard the fateful news that Edith Piaf had passed away, and I found the entire city frozen in grief. Every shop was closed, and when I walked down the Champs-Élysées that evening I could have fired a cannon down that broad boulevard and not struck a single soul. It appeared as though all of France was in mourning for their lost love. Her funeral was akin to that of our martyred president, John F. Kennedy, who was assassinated a few short weeks later. Suddenly it seemed as though the entire world was in mourning, first for a revered singer, then for a beloved president. The glory that once was Camelot really had ended, and one had to wonder where all the negative vibes were coming from and what this new era of gloom was all about.

A House of Sand finally premiered in London on June 15, 1964, and after the requisite first-run, it was released to markets throughout the world. The film generally garnered good reviews, including one in the *London Daily Cinema* that, in my mind, said it all. A few excerpts follow:

"Rating: Strange, imaginative variation on the true-love-conquers-all-in-Paris theme: treatment over-fanciful, but emotionally affecting and romantically winning. An appealing off-beat attraction.

"Critic's View: Once again an unsure American girl finds love in the French style and, once again, that old-bogey – fear of sex based on past experience – is vanquished in the arms of an understanding lover.

"But the film has a definite approach of its own, which is sometimes slow, sometimes precious, but never to me, at any rate, uninteresting. The impression of beatnik Paris is surely established and a colored dream sequence shows, erotically but not sensationally, the girl's obsession with sex which she both invites and repels, half scared, half fascinated with it.

"The budding affair between Mary and Willy is quite movingly handled, though Philippe Forquet's astonishing good looks and boyish mannerisms get in the way of complete conviction. As Mary, though, Mary Staton gives a remarkably impressive performance, encompassing a wide range of emotion that might have floored a more experienced actress.

"The Film's style is modern, but not obtrusively so, the pop music backing is apt and, all in all, it is the kind of movie that could very well create a small stir, particularly among the younger critical set."

As I recall, I was traveling somewhere through Northern Africa when the film premiered, but by the time I returned to London, it was long gone on its world release. My old friend David Korda, however, who had moved back to London by that time, did see the film during its initial run, but told me how disappointed he was over the fact that Golden Era had spent only a minimal amount of money on promotion and advertising. Thus, he felt the reception was cool and much less than it could have been. I finally caught up with the film a good year or two after the fact at a small neighborhood theatre in Malaga, Spain. To merely say I was disappointed in what I saw would diminish the gravity of my reaction, because the quality of the particular print that was playing in this theatre was appalling. Obviously, it must have played at dozens of different movie houses in God only knows how many cities, towns and theatres throughout the region, and it had clearly suffered all of the usual scrapes, tears and totally incongruous splices that most theatrically released prints are heir to. But in the process, this print had been cut down to something around eighty minutes, with most of one episode nefariously missing from the dream sequence and three or four smaller but indiscriminate cuts in the Paris footage. In short, the film as shown in this theatre was no longer the one I had spent four long years to create.

Naturally, I realized I had no way of knowing who the primary butcher was. It could have been the new owners, the Spanish distributor or – more likely – any one or more of the many projectionists in the dozens of theatres where the picture had been shown, since prints are routinely damaged and then carelessly spliced back together. Obviously, other prints elsewhere throughout the world might have been in better or worse condition than this one. Thus, I was stuck with the undeniable knowledge that this was the way of the business and the end result of a project with my name on it.

Films, however, are haphazardly cut all the time, and I was well aware of that. Once again, I thought back at how George Cukor felt when Jack Warner cut a half hour of immortal Judy Garland footage out of *A Star is Born*; nevertheless, I felt that the devastation for me was far more sweeping than anything he might have endured because directing, after all, was Cukor's life, and he knew how to take his lumps and simply go on to the next project. Although he was between pictures just as often as all those he directed, he made the most of it because he recognized that directing was all he knew how to do. It was, is, and most likely always will be the way of life in Hollywood that the vast majority of actors, writers and directors are saddled with.

What price Hollywood? Just ask anyone who's been involved with it for any length of time and they will tell you, unequivocally:

"It's a bitch, but there isn't a thing we can do about it."

I don't mention all of this negativity just to be "hard on" Hollywood and the film business in general – because I loved and cherished every minute that I was a part of it – it is merely the nature of the beast that I condemn. I have cited the Jack Palance, Vivien Leigh, George Cukor and Vasso Gabriel cases, among others, as prime examples simply because I was so personally familiar with them. But thousands of others were, are and continue to be in the same boat as they were, and that is the saddest fact about Hollywood that no one can ignore. Cukor, however, was near the end of his career in 1964; I was just at the beginning of mine. My umbilical, therefore, was never irrevocably connected to Hollywood; I had untapped talents in other fields I hadn't even thought about using as yet. The incessant waiting and unimaginable waste of time one experiences while trying to acquire a name for oneself in the film business were facts of life that simply were not compatible with my psyche, and in the end that simple truth overwhelmingly convinced me to abandon my allegiance to it. It wasn't that I was burned out. On the contrary, I was merely disillusioned with the way the business operated, and I realized I did not have the requisite fire in my belly to continue on in a business that offered little encouragement along the way.

I started forth with a burst of energy and a dedication to an endeavor I soon learned was contrary to everything I believed in, yet I dove into it with little knowledge of the business and no control over the outcome. Luckily for me, however, I had an easy way out. I merely abandoned my commitment to the process, turned the key in my mind and walked away from it. It was a supreme mental maneuver on my part that awakened my spirit and, in retrospect, proved I had done the right thing. In the end, I had no trouble in being hard on Hollywood and abandoning the entire motion picture scene, because when I did I went on with my life and felt a great weight had been lifted from my soul.

CHAPTER 37:

Après Hollywood

In December 1966, my brother called to tell me our dad was very ill and that I needed to come home. Obviously, I was on the first plane back to Newark, where he picked me up and gave me the bad news. A tumor had been discovered in his throat that was diagnosed as being malignant. In speaking with his doctor the following day, he confirmed that the tumor was cancerous and inoperable because of its location, and that with my dad's age, it would probably take him in his sleep within a few weeks. Nevertheless, when I sat down with him later in the day, it was clear that he was aware of his condition and had resigned himself to his fate.

"Sunny boy, my only wish is to be left with my family and to celebrate the holy day. Then I can make peace with my maker and leave you to care for your mother."

A few days later, my dad initiated a conversation with me that I was destined to remember for the rest of my life. He sensed that even though I had achieved my goal of becoming a film director, I was not at all content with the business and the countless pitfalls encountered along the way, so he was extra careful to phrase his words for maximum effect.

"You are now at a crossroad in your life where you can continue on with what you were doing or go on to bigger and better things by finally benefiting from all the knowledge, wisdom and good sense you have accumulated to this time. You have a clear, bright mind that is capable of accomplishing anything you set it to. You are still so young. Please promise me to avail yourself of your potential and to do so now before you waste any more precious time on lesser endeavors. Because when you do, I can assure you that you will be well rewarded with ultimate happiness and success, not only in the immediate future but for the rest of your life."

My dad was very passionate when he spoke, and when it was

about important things like these, he did so with the strength of Samson and the wisdom of Methuselah. It was like a sermon from the mount or an edict from God and not something I could easily ignore or forget. Of course, I knew my dad was right, but little did he know that I had already decided to abandon the Hollywood scene and go on to other endeavors. Nevertheless, I didn't think the time was appropriate for me to go into all the sordid details, so I merely took his hand and assured him I would abide by his wishes.

The rest of the holidays then went well for him, his sickness was rarely mentioned, he seemed comfortable and he received countless visits from all of his best friends. Only one small problem remained. According to the Julian calendar, the holy day in the Ukraine falls two weeks after the Roman Christian holiday, namely, on January 6-7, and that was the date my dad wanted to meet. Unfortunately, it was not to be; he passed away on January 2, in his sleep, exactly as the doctors had predicted.

Needless to say, I was heartbroken and overwhelmed with grief, as was my mom. I'm sure my brother felt some sort of a loss but he didn't show it. I spent the next month in Linden just taking care of all my dad's business matters, paying his bills and closing out all of his accounts. Luckily, he left a very respectable estate for my mom, so at least I didn't need to worry about that. He had also left a sizable trust for each of his two sons, and although I had never withdrawn any funds from mine until that time, my brother's marriage soon took care of his. My only remaining problem was to prepare my mom for a new path through life, alone and without the husband she had married forty-four years earlier. Thankfully, she adapted quickly, taking on the role of the grieving widow with grace, style and much aplomb, and I was proud of her for the grand manner in which she chose to handle it.

I was still in a deep funk over my dad's passing when I returned to Los Angeles in mid-March. Even my best girlfriend, Dale Sherwood, suggested I occupy my mind with other things, but try as I might, I just couldn't knock it. Oh, I did get back to my flying, (an earlier interest of mine) became current with all my ratings, even leased a new airplane, then took off on an extended trip visiting friends throughout the West, but it really wasn't until sometime in May when I returned to Los Angeles that a life-changing event occurred that finally snapped me out of it.

I was introduced to a gentleman named John Hernstadt, who was staying at the Beverly Hills Hotel. The introduction came through Dale who, knowing of my background in business and finance, suggested I was probably the best if not only person in the world who could help him. She explained that John came from a prominent, highly respected family in New York, was recommended by a very influential banking friend from Wall Street, and was here to buy investment-grade properties and a ranch on which to raise Thoroughbred horses. She then emphasized that the person he was seeking needed to be honest, possess valid credentials and be one he could absolutely trust and rely on.

"Oh, and by the way – if you read me correctly – that person will also need to be someone who can take over and manage all of his business affairs. It is a situation I would consider very seriously, it being the kind of opportunity that occurs perhaps only once in a lifetime."

Obviously, I did read Dale correctly, because I called John back the following morning, and determined that she was 100 percent correct. I was precisely the type of person he needed to handle his affairs, but most important for me, it was also the kind of opportunity I needed to quickly segue into the business and financial end of the spectrum as my dad had always begged me to do. In very short order, we formed an investment partnership, pooled all of our assets and embarked on a real estate buying bonanza of trophy properties unlike anything either one of us had ever imagined. Over the ensuing years our partnership did in fact develop into a sizable financial empire, replete with the acquisition of crowning real estate assets not only in California, Texas and Idaho, but in rich oil and natural gas properties in Texas, Oklahoma and throughout the South. Clearly, my dad was right. All the time I had squandered while between pictures in the film business was now being utilized fruitfully and with an end result that was infinitely more rewarding than anything I could have done for myself in Hollywood.

Was I being hard on Hollywood? You bet! Was I pleased with the new course my life had taken? Absolutely! Even so, I fully realized that it was simply a matter of my being in the right place at the right time, and doing so for one more time – my only contribution being that I was wholly prepared for the event when it occurred and thus knew exactly what to do about it.

Again, all I could say to myself was,

"How lucky could I have ever been?"

CHAPTER 38:

Fin

Life after the end of a decade-long effort in the motion picture field would be inherently more difficult for most survivors to endure, but it was infinitely less challenging for me because I refused to dwell on the negative aspects of it. My new business partnership had clearly blossomed into a financial juggernaut that soon became self-sustaining, allowing me more time to devote to myself, my love life and my many other interests. Thus, I decided to take my future in hand and forge ahead with yet another innovative phase in my life, and I was hell-bent on spending it all in a positive and overtly constructive fashion.

In 1976, after an unforgettable once-in-a-lifetime introduction at the Honolulu airport to one of the most recognizable and beloved Hawaiian beauties of all time, I embarked upon the signature romance of my life, which after a mere eighteen months of unimpeded bliss and happiness was cut short by her unexpected illness and premature death. Clearly this story of Mae Beimes and me would be better told at another time and in a different writing. It is mentioned here only in passing to illustrate the fact that the event occurred at a time when all other aspects of my personal and business life were successful and at the peak of their fruition, thus exemplifying the reality that the mettle and resolve of my demeanor and the unrelenting positive attitude in my psyche confirmed once again that they were the overriding factors that got me through a very tragic experience.

By 1990, however, most of the friends, associates and lovers I had acquired during my Hollywood days had also passed away, including the half dozen or so who had the greatest influence on me during the brief period I allowed myself to be captivated by the aura and vaporous mystique of the place. Gone were my darling Vivien Leigh, my agent and surrogate father John Darrow, my first love Yvette

Duguay, my photography guru George Huene, my mentor and chief booster George Cukor, and the man who really started it all for me, Jack Benny. I often wondered where my journey through life would have taken me had that master comedian not heard me tell that raunchy joke outside the Television City studios that sweltering afternoon and taken me under his wing. It was a fortuitous encounter with a megastar who recognized a unique talent in me and, in the process, changed my life forever.

Twenty-five years later, however, I had become successful in my own right – no, not on the silver screen or even in spite of it, but in the often unforgiving, but immensely satisfying worlds of business, investment and finance, as my dad had so shrewdly predicted for me so many years before. It was a path through life that was infinitely more rewarding than anything I might have achieved in Hollywood, and all because I wouldn't allow myself to waste one more day of my life while lounging around "between pictures" or sitting disconsolately on the sidelines while waiting for others to "set up the shot."

So, whatever happened to *A House of Sand* in its afterlife along with its two stars, Philippe Forquet and Mary Staton? As I expected it would, after the film's premiere in London in 1964, it was released on the international market and eventually earned back its cost. Philippe Forquet went on to garner a relatively unique niche in the French cinema market when he went to Hollywood and starred alongside Sandra Dee in *Take Her, She's Mine*. In 1969 he was given a featured role in *Camille 2000* – now a cult classic – and in *The Young Rebels* in 1971, finally retiring from films a few years later. Unfortunately, Mary Staton did not receive the accolades I expected for her nor any additional offers after *A House of Sand* was released. As a result, she decided not to waste any more of her precious time on acting, was soon married, and retired from the business shortly thereafter.

Clearly, the greatest tragedy in any of our lives is the thoughtless waste or frivolous consumption of the finite amount of time we have been given on this wonderful planet of ours. How lucky could any of us be to have even been conceived and born, considering the incredibly minute chance of the necessary confluence of events ever having the probability of occurring? Just the thought of this minuscule happenstance is mind-boggling. Thus, to waste even a moment of the time that has been given us is not only a sin, but a tragedy – and Hollywood be damned for fostering it. It is the frivolous undercurrent of the film business that levels the playing field for all those who become enmeshed in it.

I was keenly aware that I had been granted so much more of what it takes to get ahead in life than my average contemporary could ever hope for, but to my credit, I knew exactly what to do with it once I decided on the most efficient manner in which to use it. It was the spark that propelled me from Hollywood to ultimate success, with the whole world as my playing field. Sadly, many others possess that spark, but most simply don't realize it, or worse, they know it and squander it on drugs, miserable marriages or questionable life-altering decisions.

Interestingly, I arrived in Hollywood directly out of college and, as such, was completely unprepared for what I was seeking. I came without a single lead, reference or introduction to get me started, yet I ultimately achieved exactly what I went there to do. The capricious requirements of the Hollywood system, however, are what spoiled it all for me.

Nevertheless, and in spite of all the negativity that one can spew forth about the place, I must admit that my overall attitude toward Hollywood in general has never faltered, because the greatest lasting irony about the place – and its only unquestionable redeeming factor – is its undeniable ability to attract the multitudes of hopefuls who still come to Los Angeles every year on the slightest of outside chances that they might make something out of their lives in the movie business. It is of little concern to most of them that they possess only a modicum of talent or no training and are imbued with nothing more than an indestructible, irreversible inner drive with which to accomplish it. The examples of total success, of course, are endless, with names like Hudson and Monroe, perhaps, being among the most memorable. As inspirational fodder, the mere thought of achieving a similar success is all that these aspirants require as fuel to satisfy their hunger, and it is a credit to Hollywood and its ongoing history that it has succeeded in bringing at least a handful of these new hopefuls to fame and fortune every year – regardless of the incredibly overriding chances against it. Sadly, however, for every successful candidate, thousands of other equally talented and creative individuals all fall by the wayside or go on with little or nothing to show for their labors. The possibility of success in Hollywood is the fuel that keeps them all going and the single factor in their lives that drives them on, year after year, until age inevitably diminishes and then extinguishes the flame and whatever hopes and dreams that remain. Yes, that is the spark that drives people to Hollywood, and in the end it is the only compensating aspect about the place that makes it all worthwhile.

The multiple negative aspects of Hollywood, however, outdo any positive characteristics one can ever cite or come up with. The time one wastes just attempting to get ahead in Hollywood is futile; it is also totally unfathomable and unrecoverable. And this is just as true for the independent new filmmaker who merely requires financing for a pet project as it is for the seasoned actor, writer or director who needs a current credit to add to his or her "not so burgeoning" current résumé. And then there are the sexual predators among us who rob the most beautiful of each year's new crop of hopefuls of their innocence and sense of well-being. One can only be thankful that so many formerly abused women, and men, have finally abandoned their closets to come forward and tell the world that "enough is enough!" Even so, one can only imagine how long the present state of empowerment brought about by the #MeToo movement will exist. One has to believe that new sexual perpetrators are born every minute, and there can be no doubt that the present spate of outing each and every one of them cannot continue unabated for very long. After all, Hollywood will still be the sex capital of the world, and sexual predators will certainly be just as present in the future as they are today – the only difference perhaps being that they might just be a little more restrained.

Needless to say, my business partnership with John Hernstadt was the catalyst that finally set me off in the right direction. Although he passed away more than ten years ago, the time since has treated me excessively well. I have engendered an entire cadre of new friends – all, obviously, much younger than me – allowing my days to continue to evolve and be just as busy today as they were before. I still maintain the various business interests I developed since leaving Hollywood, and I continue to wheel and deal for the daily bread. My psyche has always been fueled by my insatiable appetite for the positive aspects of life – my cup always being half full rather than half empty, the wonders of happiness over sorrow, the good over the evil, a great propensity and appreciation for humor and, above all, the maintenance of extreme optimism over uncertainty and despair. Sadness and gloom be damned! Unfortunately, many people just seem to exist from day to day in a negative stupor, wasting the hours of one day just to get to the next. I approach each day with an abundance of confidence and as a chance for a new experience, utilizing each hour as the opportunity for an exciting new adventure, thus making the most of what life has in store for me. I simply do not dwell on the negative or on the inevitable end of all this; unquestionably, it is that attitude that has always made the difference for me.

Life has now come around full circle for me. I no longer concern myself with the past nor mourn for what has been or could have been. Those are all diversions of the soul that at my age, at least, do not seem to bother me anymore. The process of living, inevitably, takes its toll on our flesh, but the will to live and enjoy the life that was so miraculously given to us incredibly goes on. It is all part of the grand equation that all living creatures are heir to. Nevertheless, I can be content with the fact that I led a most charmed existence during the time when the hormones ran rampant and, in the end, I believe it all helped give me an incredible ride. Best of all, however, is the fact that I still enjoy my life and am still imbued with incredibly excellent health in both mind and body, and there are no greater gifts that one can expect out of our lives than those.

Again, all that I can truly ask myself is, "How lucky could I have ever been?" And the answer to that question sums it up for me just perfectly.

"Luckier than any person should ever be allowed to be. But I can only thank my genes, the will to succeed and an overwhelming resolve for making it so."